INTRODUCTION TO THE STUDY OF THE HINDU DOCTRINES

By
RENE GUENON

Translated By
MARCO PALLIS

GYAN

Published by

Gyan Publishing House
5, Ansari Road
Daryaganj, New Delhi-110002
Phone: 011-47034999, 9811692060
E-mail: books@gyanbooks.com

Distribution Network
gyanbooks.com
India, USA, Canada, UK, Australia, France

ISBN : 978-81-212-2688-2 (HB)
First Published, 1945

2nd Impression 2021

Printed at: Gyan Press, Delhi.

Introduction to the
Study of the Hindu Doctrines
Author: Rene Guenon

INTRODUCTION TO THE STUDY OF THE HINDU DOCTRINES

By

RENÉ GUÉNON

TRANSLATED BY

MARCO PALLIS

LONDON
LUZAC & CO.
46 GREAT RUSSELL STREET, W.C. 1
1945

CONTENTS

PART III

THE HINDU DOCTRINES

PART IV

WESTERN INTERPRETATIONS

TRANSLATOR'S FOREWORD

Of M. René Guénon's longer works, *Introduction Générale à l'Étude des Doctrines Hindoues* was the first to be published, and in a sense it can serve as an introduction to all the others, but more especially to those which, like *Man and his Becoming according to the Vedānta*, set out to expound metaphysical doctrines under their more profound aspects and in greater detail. To anyone not already acquainted with the comprehensive nature of the author's point of view, the title of the present book can only afford a comparatively restricted idea of its scope, so that prospective readers, hitherto familiar with the usual works of erudition that pass under the general heading of "orientalism," might expect to find the Hindu doctrines treated here also as a "special field of research," with a view to results that could be of no practical value to the ordinary run of men—for such is the spirit in which the majority of Western scholars, amongst whose ranks must also be numbered Westernised Orientals, approach the study of all the traditional doctrines, irrespective of whether they belong to the East or to Europe itself. In contrast to the orientalists, the author starts out with quite other ends in view, requiring an entirely different method for their realization, as well as an entirely different angle of approach. There is therefore no question of a "special subject," and this book might just as well serve as a key to the understanding of any of the traditional doctrines, or of them all. As for the Hindu doctrines themselves, which only occupy Part III, they have simply been selected to exemplify the principles and workings of a traditional civilization, this particular traditional form having been chosen because it was the most suitable for the purpose, as the author himself has explained.

The order in which the subject-matter is presented has been well calculated to carry the reader on from stage to stage, without ever calling upon him to take any sudden leap in the dark ; particular attention has been given to the nice choice of terms, such as lend themselves to unequivocal definitions, but this has been accomplished without having recourse to the clumsy and pedantic jargon that habitually congests modern scientific literature and which, while serving to impress more gullible minds, rather tends to put off many otherwise well-qualified inquirers.

Part I is mainly taken up with the task of clearing away certain ingrained prejudices that are part of the common inheritance from the " Renaissance," with its adulation of the Græco-Roman culture and its compensating depreciation, both deliberate and instinctive, of other civilizations. All kinds of subsidiary questions are sorted out, largely historical in character, before passing on to Part II, which is in many ways the most important section of the book where, by establishing the fundamental distinctions between various modes of thought, the real nature of metaphysical or universal knowledge is made to stand out. This it is which forms the life-blood of all tradition ; an understanding of its nature is the first condition for any genuine intellectual exchange, whether between individuals or groups, and still more so for that personal realization which alone is deserving of the name of "Knowledge" unqualified, the name which it still bears throughout the East. Thus words like "religion," "philosophy," "symbolism," "mysticism," "superstition," etc. which people have come to use in a vague and often most misleading way, are here given a precise meaning, through an investigation both of what they are and of what they are not, until finally metaphysic itself, together with the tradition which is its appropriate vehicle of communication "in all the worlds," is allowed to emerge in its universality as knowledge of the Principle which is also the goal, *alpha* and *omega*.

The reader is now sufficiently well equipped for Part III with its more detailed examination of the particular tradition chosen to illustrate the theme, namely the Hindu doctrine and its applications at various levels, eventually leading up to the *Vedānta*, which constitutes its metaphysical essence.

Lastly, Part IV resumes the task of clearing away current misconceptions, but this time it is concerned not with the West itself, but with distortions of the Hindu doctrines that have arisen as a result of attempts to read into them, or to graft onto them, modern Western conceptions, from a variety of motives. This prepares the way for the author's concluding chapter, in which he lays down the essential conditions for any genuine understanding between East and West, an understanding that can only come through the work of those who have attained to the realization of that "wisdom uncreate" which is not specifically ancient or modern, Eastern or Western, but universal, even though at the present moment it is in fact hardly to be met with, apart from possible individual exceptions, outside the Eastern traditions.

In view of the fact that the author's message is addressed in the first place to the Western reader, whose need is in some senses the most pressing since the dwindling away of his normal tradition has left him well-nigh without guidance in his quest for knowledge, it is imperative that he should be warned against taking the author's strictures on various features of Western civilization as evidence of some missionary activity or other on behalf of a particular traditional form. Such a warning might seem superfluous, for the author himself is repeatedly at pains to repudiate any such suggestion ; but past experience has shown that some people refuse to be disarmed by any denial, because their own predilection for controversy and proselytism leads them to attribute a similar attitude to others ; and it will not be surprising, even after this caution, if some would-be critic asserts that M. Guénon wishes to discredit Christianity and to convert the Europeans into Hindus—as if Europe were not already sufficiently un-Christian through its own efforts.

In the East misconceptions of this type are practically unknown, for it has not yet been forgotten there that if Ultimate Truth is one and only, the language of truth necessarily consists of many dialects, adapted to the needs of different races and individuals ; with the recognition of the distinction between principial knowledge and the differing forms through which it must express itself if it is to become intelligible to minds as yet unperfected, the wish to carry on any kind of propaganda can scarcely arise. But it is quite otherwise with people who are almost completely possessed by the demons of sentimentality, and it is therefore necessary to repeat again and again that, for the Westerner, the first-fruit of assimilating that metaphysical knowledge which has "accidentally" been preserved in the East while being forgotten in Europe would be the reconstitution of a traditional civilization in the West complete in all its orders, whether intellectual, social, artistic or otherwise ; but such a civilization, in its outward form, would necessarily be adapted to the special requirements of the European temperament. The present situation of the West is rather to be compared to that of the foolish virgins who, through the wandering of their attention in other directions, had allowed their lamps to go out ; in order to rekindle the sacred fire, which in its essence is always the same wherever it may be burning, they must have recourse to the lamps still kept alight by their wiser companions ; but once relighted, it will still be their own lamps that they will be lighted by, and all they will then have to do is to keep them properly fed with the kind of oil at their own disposal, refined and perfumed as befits their immediate purposes. A Hindu somewhere has written that the inability of Westerners to interpret the East is bound up with their failure to penetrate the deeper meaning of their own sages and even of the Gospels. Reciprocally, it may be said that by a genuine assimilation of the essential content of the Eastern traditions, they might be helped to recapture the spirit that dwells at the heart of Christianity itself, instead of restricting themselves, as generally happens, to a humanistic transcription of the doctrine many of them still profess, that relies for its authority almost exclusively on "historical facts" that can be placed and dated, thus relegating to the background the universal character of its fundamental truth.

Such are the benefits that Westerners might hope to derive from the serious pursuit of that knowledge to which this and kindred volumes are able to introduce them ; yet it is questionable whether the practical value of a book such as this would be any the less for present day Indians and other Orientals ; since so many of them, through being made to suffer the elaborately organised ignorance that passes under the name of a "modern education"—often dearly purchased for them by still pious but unsuspecting or complacent parents—have had their powers of discernment so disastrously upset that they seem no longer capable of receiving ideas through the medium of their own language ; and their readiness to swallow quite uncritically the most hazardous hypotheses, even those relating to their own traditional doctrines, provided they have been put forward by some European sociologist or philosopher, is evidence of a state of mind that can only be described as defeatist ; and among these people are to be found men of supposedly high standing and illustrious lineage, occupying responsible positions as rulers, leaders or instructors, but whose professed leadership is of the very essence of dependence and servility.

To minds and wills in such a state, it may prove a

salutary tonic to come upon the work of a European by birth, though an Oriental by spiritual affiliation, who is able to reinterpret their own tradition for them and to remind them that the highest conceivable knowledge is there for the asking at their own doorstep, while at the same time enlightening them as to the true nature of Western civilization both by giving it credit for some genuine achievements as well as by exposing its many deficiencies. Part II in particular, by explaining the precise shades of meaning of many terms that English-speaking Orientals frequently make use of but only half-understand because their fluency in the foreign language is superficial and does not extend to the background, can be of the greatest service in helping these people to restore order to their bewildered thoughts. Besides, it is not only those who have gone so far in surrender who can derive profit from the reading of this book ; for it is comparatively rare to find anyone in the East who has become possessed even of a smattering of Western languages or literature or science and who has not at the same time unconsciously fallen a victim to some confusion ; though in many cases the damage is still superficial and if once it were repaired the experience might help to render the patient immune to possible reinfection.

For instances of this sort of thing one has only to glance through many of the newer Hindu publications in English, even some that sincerely believe that they are expounding the orthodox teachings, in order to discover passages where quite unjustifiable concessions have been made to the modern outlook, especially under its pseudo-intellectual form of "science," in an attempt to show that the ancient Hindu texts agree with certain fashionable theories of the present day, as if this were bound somehow to enhance the authority of the texts in question ; besides, these comparisons usually rest on the basis of some quite misleading assimilation of Sanskrit and English terms. Again and again one comes across remarks that imply an acceptance of the modern Western scale of values, as if that were an unquestionable criterion of validity. To mention one case, in an exposition of the theory of caste, we have seen the *Shudras* actually assimilated to the " proletariat," which is quite preposterous since the Western " proletariat " and " bourgeoisie " alike, by their plainly recognizable characteristics, clearly fall under the heading of *Chandalas* or men deprived of vocation. So also, in another passage of the same work, in describing the four *ashramas* or stages of life, it was suggested that attendance at school conceived after the Western fashion might be accepted as an equivalent alternative to the period traditionally due to be spent under the tuition of the *guru !* Another particularly common form of error, which crops up continually, is bound up with the use of such terms as " evolution " and " progress," with all the loose thinking to which they give rise ; and these examples could be multiplied almost indefinitely.

As for those who are not Hindus by tradition, such as Moslems, Buddhists, Chinese and others, they will find this work hardly less useful, for its first two sections will serve their needs equally well, and all they will have to do is to supply Part III for themselves, by substituting the doctrines of their own traditional form in place of the Hindu doctrine within the general framework as here laid down. So also in the last part, they will soon perceive that Hinduism is not alone in having been travestied by those who dabble in the interpretation of the Eastern teachings, and that the other traditions have all at some time suffered in like manner.

In conclusion a word should be said about those Orientals—and they are still a majority though an unvocal one—who have not departed from their traditional norms and many of whom might in a sense be compared to children, innocent indeed but as yet untried in the crucible of temptation. Clearly those among them who have actually attained a high degree of metaphysical realization stand in no personal danger, for they come under the Gospel denomination of the "chosen" whom henceforth no satanic assault can by any means cause to fall away. But for all those who are of lesser degree, the danger is real in view of the continual pressure around them, and it is good policy to be forearmed.

Thus, if for the Westerner a true knowledge of the traditional doctrines offers the only effective means of escaping the impending disaster that so many dread but feel powerless to prevent, through a process of inward reintegration and of reform in the literal sense of the word, so also for the Easterner it remains the indispensable means of consolidation, self-renewal, independence and recollection ; and for the two jointly it spells the bridging of the existing rift.

For all these reasons it is much to be desired that this book, and others by the same author, should eventually be translated not only into European languages—as is being done at this moment into Spanish as well as into English—but also into the principal Eastern ones, so that each man may be able to read it in that language which most closely harmonises with his own mental constitution ; however, this must for the present remain a more distant hope, and meanwhile Eastern readers will have to be content to read it in a European tongue. It should be added that during the course of the present translation the author has revised certain portions of the text ; the present version therefore will be found to differ slightly from previous French editions.

PREFACE

In the West a great many difficulties stand in the way of any attempt at a close and serious study of Oriental doctrines in general or of the Hindu doctrines in particular, and the greatest obstacles are perhaps not those which originate from the Orientals themselves. Clearly the first condition for such a study, and the most necessary of all, is to possess the mental qualifications for understanding the doctrines in question, and by this we mean for understanding them truly and thoroughly; it is this aptitude which, with very few exceptions, is lacking among Westerners. On the other hand, the fulfilment of this one vital condition can be considered a sufficient qualification, because once it is recognized by Orientals they show no reluctance whatever in communicating their thoughts without reserve.

But if there is really no other serious obstacle to the study of the Eastern doctrines except the one we have just mentioned, how is it that orientalists, that is to say Westerners who devote themselves to the study of Eastern things, have never managed to overcome the difficulty? One could hardly be accused of exaggeration in maintaining that they never actually have overcome it, seeing that so far they have only succeeded in producing works of erudition, valuable perhaps from a certain point of view, but nevertheless of no interest at all when it comes to the question of understanding even the most simple of true ideas. The fact is that a knowledge of grammar and an ability to make a word for word translation are not in themselves sufficient to enable a person to enter into the spirit of a language or to assimilate the thoughts of the people who read and write it. One might even go further and say that the more a translation is scrupulously literal the less likely it is to be faithful or to reveal the true nature of the original thought, because the correspondence between terms of expression belonging to two different languages is far from exact. Especially is this the case when those languages are widely separated, not merely from a philological standpoint, but also by reason of great diversity in the conceptions characteristic of the peoples speaking them; no amount of book-learning will be of any avail in bridging differences of this nature. For that purpose something more is wanted than a mere "textual criticism," going to lose itself in an endless maze of detail, something more than the methods of grammarians and scholars, more even than the so-called "historical method," indiscriminately applied, as it is apt to be, everywhere and to everything. No doubt dictionaries and similar compilations have their relative uses which no one wishes to dispute, nor can it be said that all such work is entirely thrown away, especially when one remembers that those who devote themselves to it are, as often as not, unsuited to other branches of study; unfortunately, however, as soon as erudition becomes a "speciality" it tends to be regarded as an end in itself, instead of a means to an end, as it normally should be. It is this invasion of the intellectual field by erudition with its special methods which constitutes a genuine danger, because it threatens to absorb the attention even of people who otherwise might perhaps have been capable of devoting themselves to work of another kind, and also because the habits which grow with the use of such methods narrow the intellectual horizon and cause irremediable harm to those who submit to them.

But this is not all, for we have not yet touched on the most serious side of the question. Among the many productions of the orientalists, works of pure erudition, although admittedly the most cumbrous, are not the most harmful ; when we said that their studies amounted to no more than this, we meant nothing more of any value, even in a restricted sense. Certain people, however, have wished to go further by embarking upon the task of interpretation, while still continuing to employ their usual methods, which have nothing at all to contribute in this sphere ; at the same time they introduce all the preconceived notions which go to make up their own particular mentality, with the manifest intention of forcing the theories they are studying into the habitual framework of European thought. In short, questions of method apart, the cardinal error of these orientalists is to look at everything from their own Western standpoint and through their own mental prism, whereas the first condition for the correct interpretation of any doctrine is to make an effort to assimilate it by placing oneself as far as possible at the viewpoint of those who conceived it. We have said "as far as possible" because everyone cannot be equally successful, though everyone can at least make the attempt; on the contrary, the exclusiveness of the orientalists we are referring to, and their predilection for "systems," have the effect of making them believe, owing to some extraordinary aberration, that they are able to understand Eastern doctrines better than the Orientals themselves: a presumption which would be merely ridiculous, were it not also allied to a fixed determination to establish a kind of "monopoly" of the studies in question. Actually, except for these specialists, there is hardly anybody in Europe who takes an interest in such matters, unless one includes a certain class of extravagant dreamers and enterprising charlatans who could be treated as a negligible quantity if they did not also exercise a deplorable influence in more respects than one: we will go into this side of the subject in greater detail when its turn comes.

Confining our criticism for the moment to those among the orientalists who might be described as "official," we wish by way of a preliminary observation to draw attention to one of the abuses that arises most frequently from the application of the "historical method" already alluded to: this is the error which consists in studying the Eastern civilizations as one might study some civilization long since extinct. In the latter case it is clear that, for want of a better alternative, one is obliged to be content with approximate reconstructions of the past, without ever being sure of establishing an exact correspondence with what formerly existed, there being no way of obtaining direct proof. It is forgotten, however, that the Eastern civilizations, or those at least with which we are at present concerned, have continued to exist without interruption to the present day, and that they still possess their authorized representatives whose advice is of incomparably greater value for the understanding of those civilizations than all the academic learning in the world ; only, if the intention be to consult these people, one should not start out from the curious principle that one is oneself better informed as to the real meaning of their ideas than they are themselves.

On the other hand, it must also be stated that Orientals, having formed a rather unfortunate though quite understandable opinion of European intellectuality, care very little for what Westerners in general may or may not think about them ; therefore, they make no attempt to enlighten them, but on the contrary, taking up an attitude of somewhat disdainful politeness, they shut themselves up in a silence which Western vanity is never at a loss to interpret as a sign of approbation. The fact is that "proselytism" is practically unknown in the East, where in any case it could serve no purpose and would be regarded purely and simply as a sign of ignorance and lack of comprehension : a statement which will be explained in due course. Its silence, for which the East is often reproached, but which is really so justifiable, can only be broken on rare occasions in favour of isolated individuals endowed with the requisite qualifications and showing a proper intellectual aptitude. As for those who give up this attitude of reserve on other than the last-mentioned grounds, there is only one thing to be said : that as a rule they represent elements of no great interest, being persons who, for one reason or another, have taken it upon themselves to purvey doctrines which they have corrupted under the plea of adapting them to the Western mentality ; we shall have something to say about them also later on. The point we wish to emphasize at the moment and to which we drew attention from the outset, is that the Western mentality is alone responsible for the present situation, which places the greatest difficulties in the way of anyone who, through exceptional circumstances, has succeeded in assimilating certain ideas and wishes to express them as intelligibly as possible, though without distorting them ; such a man must be content, within the limits of what is possible, to expound the ideas he has understood, while carefully abstaining from any thought of popularization and without worrying in the slightest about trying to compel the convictions of other people.

Enough has been said to make our intentions quite clear : we have no wish here to produce a work of erudition, for the point of view we have adopted takes us much further than that. As truth is not for us a question of mere historical fact, it would really seem a matter of small importance to determine the exact source of this or that idea—an idea indeed can interest us only because, having understood it, we know it to be true ; a few remarks, however, on the nature of Eastern thought may set some persons thinking, and this simple result would in itself be of greater importance than might at first be apparent. Moreover, even short of attaining this end there would still be a good reason for undertaking a treatise such as the present one : Orientals might see in it an acknowledgment for all that we owe them intellectually, for no Westerner has ever introduced us to anything of the kind, not even in a partial and incomplete way.

Firstly then, after disposing of a few preliminary but indispensable questions, we will outline, as clearly as possible, the essential and fundamental differences existing between the general modes of Eastern and Western thought. After that we shall concentrate more particularly on questions connected with the Hindu doctrines in so far as they contain special characteristics that distinguish them from the other Oriental doctrines, though all these doctrines possess enough features in common to justify the opposition between East and West in a general way. Finally, with regard to the Hindu doctrines, we will draw attention to the inadequacy of the interpretations current in the West ; in the case of some, we might even say their absurdity. As a conclusion to our survey, we will outline, with all necessary precautions, the conditions for an intellectual adjustment between East and West, conditions which are far from being fulfilled on the part of the West, as is only too apparent ; but it is merely to a possibility that we wish to draw attention, without going so far as to consider it capable of immediate or even of early fulfilment.

PART I

PRELIMINARY QUESTIONS

CHAPTER I

East and West

The first thing to be done in the study which we have undertaken is to determine the exact nature of the opposition which divides East and West and, with this object in view, to define the meaning which we think should be attached to the two terms of this opposition. It may be said as a first rough and ready approximation that for us the East is essentially Asia and the West is essentially Europe ; but this in itself requires some further explanation.

When for example we speak of the Western or European mentality, using either of these two terms indifferently, we mean the mentality proper to the European race taken as a whole. We will describe therefore as European anything bound up with this race and we will affix this common denomination to all the individuals issued from it, whatever part of the world they may happen to inhabit : thus Americans and Australians, to mention two cases only, are Europeans from our point of view and come under exactly the same heading as men of the same race who have continued to live in Europe. It is of course quite plain that the fact of removing oneself to another region or even of having been born there, cannot of itself alter the race nor consequently the mentality belonging to it ; and even if a change of environment is liable sooner or later to produce certain modifications, these will only be modifications of quite a secondary kind, not really altering the fundamental characteristics of the race but on the contrary liable even to accentuate some of them. Thus it can easily be seen that certain tendencies which form part of the modern European mentality have in the case of the Americans been pushed to their extreme limit.

Nevertheless at this point a question arises which we cannot afford to overlook entirely : we have spoken of a European race and of its own special mentality ; but does a European race really exist ? If by this is meant a primitive race, possessing its original unity and a perfect homogeneity, then the answer is in the negative, because nobody can question the fact that the present population of Europe is made up of a mixture of strains drawn from very different races and that there exist fairly well-marked ethnical differences not only as between one country and another, but even inside each of the national groups themselves. However it is none the less true that the European peoples possess enough features in common for it to be possible to distinguish them quite easily from all other peoples ; this unity, even though acquired rather than primitive, is enough to allow one to speak, as we are doing, of a European race—only this race is naturally less fixed and less stable than a pure one ; the European elements, when mingling with other races, will be more easily absorbed, and their ethnical characteristics will disappear rapidly. But this applies solely in the case of intermarriage ; when there is only juxtaposition, the mental characteristics, which are those which interest us most, appear on the contrary in sharper relief. Moreover, it is these mental qualities which best characterize European unity such as it is : whatever the original differences may have been in this respect as in others, a mentality common to all the peoples of Europe has been formed little by little in the course of history. This does not mean that a special mentality does not exist for each of these peoples, but the peculiarities which distinguish them are only of secondary importance when compared with the common foundation on which they appear to rest ; they are, in short, as the species of a common genus. Nobody, even among those who doubt whether it is permissible to speak of a European race, will hesitate to admit that there exists a European civilization ; and a civilization is nothing else than the product and expression of a certain mentality.

We will not attempt straightaway to define the distinctive features of the European mentality, because they will reveal themselves clearly enough during the course of this work ; we will simply remark that a number of influences have contributed to its formation, the proponderant one being undoubtedly the Greek, or, if preferred, the Græco-Roman influence. As far as the philosophic and scientific points of view are concerned, Greek influence is practically supreme, in spite of the appearance of certain special tendencies which are entirely modern and of which we will speak later. As for Roman influence, it is more social than intellectual, and it asserts itself especially in the concepts of the State, of law and of institutions ; besides, intellectually, the Romans borrowed nearly everything from the Greeks, so that it is largely Greek influence which has made itself felt indirectly through the

Romans. One must also note the importance, from the religious point of view especially, of the Judaic influence, which moreover is found similarly present in a section of the Orient ; we have here to do with an element which is extra-European in its origin, though part of it is a constituent of the present European mentality.

If we turn now to the East, it is not possible to speak in the same way of an Oriental or of an Asiatic race, not even with all the reservations which we admitted when considering the European race. We are dealing here with a more extended whole, containing much larger populations and presenting far greater ethnical differences ; in this whole, several more or less pure races can be distinguished, presenting well-defined features of their own and each possessing a civilization markedly different from that of all the others : an Eastern civilization cannot be said to exist in the same sense as a Western civilization ; there are in reality several Eastern ones. There will therefore be room for special remarks about each of these civilizations, and in due course we shall point out the broad general divisions which can be established ; but in spite of everything, if one is less bound by form than by meaning, sufficient common elements, or rather principles, can be found to make it possible to speak of an Oriental mentality as opposed to a Western mentality.

When we say that each of the Eastern races has its own particular civilization, that is not absolutely accurate ; it is only strictly true of the Chinese race, whose civilization has its real foundation in ethnical unity. In the case of the other Asiatic civilizations, the principles of unity on which they repose are of an entirely different nature, as will be explained later, and this it is which allows them to embrace in this unity elements belonging to widely differing races. We speak of Asiatic civilizations because those we have in mind are such by their origin, even though they may have spread to other regions, as has happened chiefly in the case of the Islamic civilization. But we must make it clear that, apart from Moslem elements, we do not in any way regard as Orientals the people who inhabit the east of Europe, or even certain districts adjoining Europe : one must not confuse an Oriental with a Levantine, who is rather quite the opposite, and who, at least as far as his mentality is concerned, displays most of the characteristics of a typical Westerner.

At a first glance one is bound to be impressed by the disproportion between the two entities which constitute respectively what we have called East and West ; though they may stand opposed to one another, there is in reality neither equivalence nor even symmetry between the two terms of the opposition. The difference is comparable to that existing, in the geographical sense, between Asia and Europe, the second appearing only as a simple prolongation of the first ; in the same way, fundamentally, the position of the West in relation to the East is that of a branch growing out of the trunk, and it will now be our task to explain this point more fully.

CHAPTER II

The Divergence

If we compare what is usually referred to as Classical Antiquity with the Oriental civilizations, it will readily be seen that, in some respects at least, it has more in common with those civilizations than modern Europe has. The differences between East and West seem to have been continually on the increase, but this divergence can be said to have been one-sided, in the sense that it is only the West which has changed, whereas the East, broadly speaking, has remained much the same as it was in times which we are accustomed to call ancient, but which nevertheless are comparatively recent. Stability—one might even say immutability—is a quality which is quite commonly conceded to the Oriental civilizations, notably to the Chinese, but it is perhaps not quite so easy to agree over the assessing of this quality. Europeans, since the days when they began to believe in "progress" and in "evolution," that is to say since a little more than a century ago, profess to see a sign of inferiority in this absence of change, whereas, for our part, we look upon it as a balanced condition which Western civilization has failed to achieve. Moreover, this stability shows itself in small things as well as in great ; a striking example of this is to be found in the fact that "fashion," with its continual changes, is only to be met with in the West. In short, Occidentals and especially modern Occidentals, appear to be endowed with changeable and inconstant natures, hankering after movement and excitement, whereas the Oriental nature shows quite the opposite characteristics.

Therefore, if one wished to represent diagrammatically the divergence we are discussing, it would be wrong to draw two lines moving in contrary directions away from an axis. The East would have to be shown as the axis itself and the West as a line starting from the axis and moving further and further away from it, after the fashion of a branch growing out of a trunk, as mentioned before. We are all the more justified in using this symbolism since the West, at least from the outset of the period called historical, in so far as it has had an intellectual life at all, has lived primarily by borrowing from the East, directly or indirectly. The Greek civilization itself is far from possessing the originality ascribed to it by people of restricted vision, who would willingly go to the length of declaring that the Greeks libelled themselves whenever they happened to acknowledge their debt to Egypt, to Phœnicia, to Chaldæa, to Persia and even to India. All these civilizations may well be incomparably more ancient than the Greek, but this does not prevent some people, blinded by what may be termed the "classical prejudice," from persistently maintaining the theory, in the face of all the evidence, that it is those other civilizations which are indebted to the Greek and have felt its influence : it is extremely hard to carry on a discussion with such people because their opinion rests on rooted preconceptions ; but we will return to this subject later in order to treat of it at greater length. It is nevertheless true that the Greeks did possess a certain measure of originality, though not of the kind usually supposed; it was largely confined to the form under which they presented and displayed borrowed ideas, which they altered more or less happily in the process of adapting them to suit their own mentality, so unlike the mentality of the Orientals, and in many respects directly opposed to it.

Before going any further, it should be explained that we have no wish to dispute the originality of the Hellenic civilization in respect of what appear to us as certain secondary points of view, that of art for example; we only contest its originality from the purely intellectual standpoint, which was moreover much more restricted among the Greeks than among Orientals. This curtailment, one might even say this cramping of intellectuality, is strikingly confirmed if we compare the Hellenic with the surviving Eastern civilizations of which we possess direct knowledge; and the same will presumably be true also of a comparison with the vanished civilizations of the East, according to all that is known of them and judging, above all, from features they clearly possessed in common with the other Oriental civilizations both past and present. Indeed the study of the East as we know it to-day, if undertaken in a really direct way, would be of great assistance towards the understanding of all Antiquity, on account of that very quality of fixity and stability to which we have referred; it would even facilitate the understanding of Greek antiquity, for which purpose we cannot rely upon any direct evidence, because here again we are dealing with a civilization which is quite definitely extinct; the contemporary Greeks can hardly lay claim to be the representatives of the ancient Hellenes, of whom they are probably not even lineal descendants.

It should be remembered nevertheless that Greek thought was, in spite of everything, Western in its essence and that it already contained among its other characteristics, the origin and, as it were, the germ of most of those tendencies which developed much later among the modern Westerners. We must not therefore push this analogy between Greek and Oriental civilizations too far ; if kept however in proper proportion, it can be of considerable service to those who feel a genuine desire to understand Antiquity and to interpret it with a minimum of conjecture. In any case there can be no danger if we are careful to take into account all that is known for certain about the character of the Greek mentality. Any new tendencies met with in the Græco-Roman world are really almost entirely of a restricting and limiting nature, so that the reservations called for when making a comparison with the East must derive almost entirely from a fear of ascribing to the ancient peoples of the West a quality of thought which they did not really possess : whenever they are found to have taken something from the East, it must not be imagined that they completely assimilated it, nor is one justified in concluding that this borrowing denotes identity of thought. Many interesting points of likeness can be established for which there is no parallel in the modern West, but it is none the less true that the essential modes of Oriental thought are markedly different ; therefore unless one's mind has shaken itself free of the Western outlook, even in its ancient form, one will inevitably neglect and misjudge just those aspects of Oriental thought that are the most important and characteristic. Since it is plain that the "greater" cannot issue from the "less," this one distinction, in the absence of any other consideration, ought to be enough to show to which category a civilization belongs that has borrowed from others.

To return to the simile we used a short while back, it must be pointed out that its main defect—natural to all schematic representations—is that it rather over-simplifies matters by representing the divergence as widening continually from the days of antiquity to the present time. In reality there have been respites in the divergence, there have even been less remote times when the West again received the direct influence of the East: we allude mainly to the Alexandrine period and to the contributions to European thought during the Middle Ages made by the Arabs, some of which were entirely their own, the rest being derived from India; their influence in the development of mathematics is well known, but it was far from being limited to this particular field. The divergence continued once more with the Renaissance, at which time the rift with the preceding period became very marked; the truth is that this so-called "rebirth" proved to be the death of many things, even in the arts, but above all in an intellectual sense; it is difficult for a modern man to grasp the whole extent and range of what was lost during that period. The attempted return to Classical antiquity had for its result the diminution of intellectuality, a phenomenon comparable to that which had already occurred at an earlier time in the case of the Greeks themselves, but with this cardinal difference that now it was manifesting itself in the course of the existence of one and the same race and not during the passage of ideas from one people to another. It is almost as if the Greeks, at a moment when they were about to disappear from history, wished to avenge themselves for their own incomprehension by imposing on a whole section of mankind the limitations of their own mental horizon. When the Reformation also came to add its influence to that of the Renaissance, with which it was perhaps not altogether unconnected, then the fundamental tendencies of the modern world took definite shape ; the French Revolution—which was equivalent to a rejection of all tradition —with all its repercussions in various fields, was bound to follow as a logical consequence of the development of these tendencies. But now is not the moment to discuss these questions in detail, with a consequent risk of being drawn too far afield ; it is not our present intention to write a history of the Western mentality, but only to say as much as is necessary to show how greatly it differs from Oriental intellectuality. Before completing what has to be said about the moderns in regard to this question, we must again return to the Greeks and set forth in greater detail things we have so far only hinted at ; these further explanations will help to clear the ground and to cut short various objections which it is only too easy to foresee.

We have only one more word to add with regard to the divergence of East and West : will this divergence go on increasing indefinitely ? Appearances might lead one to think so, and in the present state of the world, the question is one which is undoubtedly open to discussion ; nevertheless, for our part, we do not think such a thing possible and we will give our reasons for this opinion at the finish.

CHAPTER III

The Classical Prejudice

We have already indicated what we mean by the "classical prejudice" : it consists essentially in a predisposition to attribute the origin of all civilization to the Greeks and Romans. It seems scarcely possible to account for this attitude except by means of the following explanation : because their own civilization hardly goes any further back than the Græco-Roman period and derives for the most part from it, Westerners are led to believe that it must have been the same in every other case and they have difficulty in conceiving of the existence of entirely different and far more ancient civilizations ; it might be said that they are mentally incapable of crossing the Mediterranean. Furthermore, the habit of speaking of "civilization" in the absolute, also contributes largely towards maintaining this prejudice. "Civilization," understood in this way and regarded as one entity, is something that has never existed ; in actual practice there have always been and there still are "civilizations." Western civilization, with its special features, is simply one civilization among others, and what is so pompously called "the evolution of civilization " is nothing more than the development of that particular civilization from its comparatively recent origins, a development which is, moreover, far from having always proceeded by a regular and all-round " progress " : the remarks we have just made about the so-called Renaissance and its consequences could serve as a striking illustration of an intellectual retrogression which, furthermore, has gone on increasing down to the present time.

To the impartial observer it is plain that the Greeks, from the intellectual point of view at least, really borrowed very largely from the Orientals, as they themselves frequently admitted ; however unveracious they may have been at times, on this point at least they cannot have lied, for they had no possible interest in doing so, indeed quite the contrary. As we said before, their originality principally lay in their manner of expressing things, by means of a faculty for adaptation one cannot deny them, but which was necessarily limited by the extent of their comprehension ; briefly, their originality was of a purely dialectical order. Actually, since Greeks and Orientals differed in their characteristic ways of thinking, there were necessarily corresponding differences in the modes of reasoning which they employed ; this must always be borne in mind when pointing out certain analogies, real though they be, such as for instance the analogy between the Greek syllogism and what has fairly correctly been called the Hindu syllogism. It cannot even be said that Greek reasoning is distinguished by an exceptional strictness ; it only appears stricter than other methods of reasoning to people who are themselves in the habit of employing it exclusively, and this illusion is due solely to the fact that it is restricted to a narrower and more limited field and is therefore more easily defined. On the contrary, the faculty most truly characteristic of the Greeks, but which is little to their advantage, is a certain dialectical subtlety, of which the dialogues of Plato provide numerous examples ; there is an apparent desire to examine each question interminably, under all its aspects and in minutest detail, in order to arrive finally at a rather insignificant conclusion; it would appear that in the West the moderns are not the first people to have been afflicted with "intellectual myopia."

Perhaps, after all, the Greeks should not be blamed too severely for restricting the field of human thought as they have done ; on the one hand this was an inevitable result of their mental constitution, for which they cannot be held responsible, and on the other hand they did at least in this way bring within reach of a large part of humanity certain kinds of knowledge which were otherwise in danger of remaining completely foreign to it. It is easy to realise the truth of this if one considers what Westerners are capable of to-day, when they happen to come into direct contact with certain Oriental conceptions and set about interpreting them in a manner conforming to their own particular mentality : anything which they cannot connect with the "classical" idiom escapes them completely and whatever can be made to tally with it, by hook or by crook, is so disfigured in the process that it becomes almost unrecognizable.

In short, the "Greek miracle" as it is called by

its enthusiastic admirers, is reduced to something of comparatively small importance, or at least, whenever it implies a fundamentally new departure, this departure is usually in the nature of a degeneration ; it stands for the individualization of conceptions, the substitution of the rational for the truly intellectual, and of the scientific or philosophical for the metaphysical point of view. It matters little, moreover, whether the Greeks were or were not more successful than others in turning certain forms of knowledge to practical use, or whether they deduced consequences of this particular kind, whereas those who preceded them did not do so ; it might even be said that, in this respect, they assigned a less pure and disinterested purpose to knowledge, because their turn of mind only allowed them to remain within the domain of principles with some difficulty and as though by exception. This inclination towards the "practical" in the most ordinary sense of the word is one of those factors that were fated to become increasingly marked during the course of Western civilization, until in modern times the tendency became frankly predominant. Only the Middle Ages, being much more given to pure speculation, can be said to have escaped it.

As a general rule, Westerners have very little natural aptitude for metaphysic ; a comparison of their languages with those of the Orientals would alone be sufficient to prove this point, provided of course that philologists were really capable of understanding the spirit of the languages they studied. On the other hand, Orientals show a strongly marked tendency to disregard applications. This is quite understandable, because anyone who above everything else cultivates the knowledge of universal principles can only take a lukewarm interest in special sciences, bestowing upon them at the most a passing curiosity, which would anyway be unlikely to call forth a large number of discoveries in this order of ideas. When one knows as a mathematical certainty, or one might even say as a more-than-mathematical certainty, that things cannot be otherwise than what they are, one becomes as a matter of course disdainful of experiment, because the verifying of a particular fact, whatever its nature, never proves anything more or anything different from the mere existence of that particular fact ; at most, the observation of facts can occasionally provide an example to illustrate, but in nowise to prove, a theory, and any belief to the contrary is to labour under a grave delusion. This being so, there is clearly no object in pursuing experimental sciences for their own sake, and from the metaphysical point of view they only possess an incidental and contingent value, like the objects they are applied to ; quite often in fact, the need is not even felt to deduce particular laws which could, however, be extracted from the principles themselves as applications to a given and specialized domain, if this appeared worth the trouble. Thus the magnitude of the gap separating Oriental "knowledge" from Western "research" becomes strikingly apparent ; all the same, it remains an astonishing thing that research can have come to be regarded by Westerners as an end in itself, quite independently of any possible results.

Another point that should not be overlooked and

which appears as a corollary of what has gone before, is that no one in the world has ever shown less inclination than the Orientals to follow the cult of Nature, as it was followed in Græco-Roman times, since for them Nature has always meant the world of appearances ; appearances no doubt possess a reality of their own, but it is only transitory and impermanent, contingent and not universal. Therefore, to men who are metaphysicians by temperament, "naturalism," in the many guises it is capable of assuming, only appears as an aberration, or even as a positive intellectual monstrosity.

It must however be admitted that the Greeks, in spite of their tendency towards naturalism, never went so far as to attach to experimentation the excessive importance that the moderns have given to it ; one finds throughout antiquity, even in the West, a certain attitude of contempt towards experiment, which would be difficult to explain unless it be taken as revealing a trace of Oriental influence ; it would otherwise be rather difficult to account for this attitude on the part of the Greeks, whose pre-occupations were hardly metaphysical in character and for whom æsthetic considerations very often took the place of the deeper reasons which escaped them. It is therefore these æsthetic considerations which are usually invoked in order to explain their lack of interest in experiment, though we ourselves believe that there were other operative causes, at least in earlier times. In any case this does not alter the fact that, in a certain sense, one can already observe among the Greeks the point of departure of the experimental sciences as understood by the moderns, wherein the "practical" tendency is linked to the "naturalistic" tendency, neither of them being able to reach full development except at the expense of pure thought and disinterested knowledge. Thus the fact that Orientals never devoted themselves to certain special branches of science is in no wise a sign of inferiority; from the intellectual point of view indeed it is quite the reverse, for it is nothing but the normal consequence of the fact that, in their case, their main activity was turned in another direction and towards totally different ends. It is precisely the different ways in which the mental activity of man can be exercised that stamp each civilization with its own particular character, by determining the basic direction of its development; here also lies the explanation of the illusion of progress among those who, being acquainted with one kind of civilization only, can conceive of no other line of development than their own, believing it to be the only way possible, so that they take no account of the fact that a development in one sense may be largely counterbalanced by retrogression in another.

If we turn to the intellectual order, which alone is essential to the Eastern civilizations, it will be seen that there are at least two reasons for thinking that the Greeks must have borrowed almost everything pertaining to that order from those civilizations, that is to say, whatever is of real value in their conceptions: one of these reasons, the one we have hitherto stressed, follows from the rather limited aptitude of the Greek mentality in this respect; the other is that Hellenic civilization is of a much more recent date than the principal

Oriental civilizations. This is particularly true of India, although whenever any connection between the two civilizations can be authenticated, some persons push the "classical prejudice" to the point of declaring *a priori* that this connection must be due to Greek influence. However, if an influence of this sort was ever in fact felt by Hindu civilization, this could only have occurred very late, and the effects must necessarily have remained quite superficial. For instance, it is possible to admit the existence of an occasional artistic influence, though even from this special point of view Hindu conceptions always remained very different from those of the Greeks; but in any case, unmistakable traces of such an influence are only to be found in a certain period of the Buddhist civilization, extremely restricted both in space and in time; moreover, this civilization is not to be confused with Hindu civilization proper. However, this obliges us to say something on the subject of the relationship that may have existed in ancient times between different peoples dwelling more or less far apart, and we will also add a few words about the difficulties which, in a general way, are raised by chronological questions, so important in the eyes of the partisans of the notorious "historical method."

CHAPTER IV

Relations between the Peoples of Antiquity

There exists a fairly widespread belief that relations between Greece and India did not begin, or rather did not assume appreciable importance, until the time of Alexander's conquests; whatever can unmistakably be assigned to an earlier date is therefore simply put down to casual resemblances between the two civilizations, while anything which arose or is supposed to have arisen later, is naturally said to be the result of Greek influence, to meet the requirements of the peculiar logic inherent in the "classical prejudice." Here again we encounter an opinion which, like so many others, is devoid of serious foundation, because intercourse between the peoples of antiquity, even when they lived great distances apart, was much more general than is usually supposed. On the whole, communications were then not much more difficult than they were no more than a century or two ago, or, to be exact, until the invention of railways and steamships; travel in earlier times, no doubt, was less frequent and above all less speedy than in our time, but people travelled more profitably, because they gave themselves time to study the countries they visited; often journeys were undertaken with the sole purpose of carrying out such studies and for the intellectual benefits to be derived from them. This being the case, there are no plausible reasons for treating the accounts of the travels of Greek philosophers as "legends," the less so as these travels explain many things which would otherwise remain incomprehensible. The truth is that long before the early days of Greek philosophy, means of communication must have reached a stage of development of which the moderns are far from forming a correct picture, and this state of things was normal and regular, quite apart from migrations of peoples, which doubtless only took place intermittently and under exceptional circumstances.

Among other proofs which could be brought forward in support of what has just been said, we will only mention one that specially concerns the relations of the Mediterranean peoples, and we will do so because it refers to a little-known, or at least little-noticed fact, which never seems to have received the attention it deserves and which, in any case, has always been quite incorrectly interpreted. The fact we are referring to is the adoption around the whole of the Mediterranean basin of a common basic type of coinage, with variations of a secondary nature, serving as local distinguishing marks ; although it is not possible to fix its exact date, the adoption of this uniform monetary system must go back to very early times, at least if one is only taking into account the period most commonly regarded as antique. People have tried to interpret this fact as a simple imitation of Greek coinage which accidentally found its way into distant countries ; this is another example of the exaggerated importance which they are always inclined to attribute to the Greeks, and it is also an example of the unfortunate tendency to treat as an accident everything which cannot be explained, as if "accident" were anything but a word used in order to disguise our ignorance of real causes. What appears certain is that the common monetary type in question, of which the essential characteristic is that it bears a human head on one side and a horse or a chariot on the other, is not more specifically Greek than it is Italic or Carthaginian, or even Gallic or Iberian ; its adoption must surely have demanded a more or less explicit agreement between the several Mediterranean peoples, even though the modalities of that agreement must needs escape us. What is true of this monetary type is also true of certain symbols and traditions which are found again and again, unaltered and spread throughout still wider areas; moreover, if no one denies that continuous relations were maintained between the Greek colonies and their parent cities, why should such doubt be felt about relations carried on between the Greeks and other peoples ? Besides, even if a convention such as the one mentioned actually never did exist, for reasons that may be of several kinds and which need not be gone into here being moreover difficult to ascertain definitely, this does not in any way prove that the establishment of more or less regular exchanges was therefore prevented ; the means must simply have been different owing to the necessity for adaptation to different circumstances.

In order to gauge the significance of the facts we have indicated, though we have used them only by way of illustration, it must be added that commercial exchanges could never have been carried on continuously without being accompanied sooner or later by exchanges of quite another order, and more especially by intellectual exchanges ; in certain instances it may even have happened that economic relations, far from taking first place, as they do with the modern peoples, occupied a position of more or less secondary importance. The tendency to refer everything to the economic standpoint, whether it concerns the internal life of a country or its international relations, is actually quite a modern one ; the ancient peoples, even in the West, with the possible exception of the Phœnicians, did not look on things in this light, neither do Orientals even to-day. Here we will take the opportunity of pointing out again how dangerous it always is to try, by the light of one's own personal point of view, to arrive at an appreciation of human beings whose circumstances and mentality are different; being otherwise situated in time and space, and who therefore certainly never did adopt that point of view and could not have had any possible reason for doing so ; nevertheless this is an error only too frequently committed by the students of Antiquity and it is also one, as we said at the beginning, which orientalists never fail to commit.

To return to our starting point : the fact that the earliest of the Greek philosophers lived several centuries before the period of Alexander does not in any way authorize us to conclude that they knew nothing about the Hindu doctrines. To quote one example, atomism, long before it appeared in Greece, was upheld in India by the school of Kanāda and later by Jains and Buddhists ; it is possible that it was brought to the West by the Phœnicians, as certain traditions seem to suggest, but on the other hand various authors declare that Democritus, who was one of the first of the Greeks to adopt this doctrine, or at least to formulate it clearly, had travelled in Egypt, Persia and India. The early Greek philosophers may even have been acquainted not only with the Hindu but also with the Buddhist doctrines, for they certainly did not live earlier than Buddhism. Furthermore, Buddhism soon spread outside India into Asiatic regions lying nearer to Greece, which were therefore more accessible; this circumstance would appear to strengthen the argument, which is quite a tenable one, that borrowings were made chiefly, though not exclusively, from the Buddhist civilization. What is curious, in any case, is that the points of resemblance which can be established with the doctrines of India are much more striking and numerous in the pre-Socratic age than in subsequent periods ; what then becomes of the part played by the conquests of Alexander in the intellectual relations of the two peoples ? They do not in fact appear to have introduced any Hindu influences, except that contained in the logic of Aristotle—to which we have already alluded in connection with his syllogism—and also in the metaphysical part of the same philosopher's work, in which it is possible to point to intellectual affinities with India far too close to be purely accidental.

If, with the object of safeguarding the originality of the Greek philosophers at all costs, the objection is put forward that there exists an intellectual fund common to all humanity, it is none the less true that the existence of this fund is something too general and vague to provide a satisfactory explanation for likenesses that are both close and clearly defined : besides, differences of mentality in many cases go much further than is supposed by those who have only known one human type ; between Greeks and Hindus especially, these differences were considerable. Such an explanation only holds good when it is a question of two comparable civilizations that have developed in the same direction, though independently of one another, producing conceptions that are fundamentally the same, however unlike they may appear in form ; this is the case with the metaphysical doctrines of China and India. But even within these limits, it would perhaps be more convincing to recognize in this concordance the results of an identity of primordial traditions, as one is obliged to do for example in cases where a common use of the same symbols is observable, implying a relationship that may, however, go back to ages far more remote than the beginning of the so-called "historical" period ; but to discuss this question would lead us too far afield.

After Aristotle the signs of Hindu influence on Greek philosophy become more and more rare, even to the point of disappearing, because that philosophy shut itself up in an increasingly limited and contingent sphere, ever further removed from any real intellectuality, and this sphere was for the most part that of ethics, which is concerned with questions that have always been quite foreign to the Orientals. It was only among the Neo-Platonists that Eastern influences were again to make their appearance, and it is there indeed that certain metaphysical ideas, such as that of the Infinite, are to be met with for the first time among the Greeks. Until then, in fact, the Greeks had only possessed the notion of the indefinite, and "finished" and "perfect" were synonymous terms for them—a particularly characteristic trait of their mentality ; for the Orientals on the contrary it is the Infinite which is identical with

Perfection. Such is the gulf that separates a philosophic conception, in the European sense of the word, from a metaphysical idea; but we will have occasion to revert to this matter in greater detail later on, and these few remarks must suffice for the moment, since it is not our present intention to make a detailed comparison between the conceptions of India and Greece respectively, a comparison which would moreover encounter many difficulties little dreamed of by those who only view the question superficially.

CHAPTER V

Questions of Chronology

Questions of chronology are among those which perplex orientalists most, and their embarrassment is usually not without justification; but they are mistaken on the one hand in attaching such enormous importance to these questions, and on the other hand in believing that they can solve them for certain by resorting to their usual methods, whereas in actual fact the conclusions they arrive at amount to so many more or less fanciful hypotheses, over which they are far from reaching any agreement even among themselves. There are some cases however which present no real difficulty, if only people would abstain from complicating them deliberately by the introduction of "critical" and "hyper-critical" arguments and quibbles of a useless kind. Such a case, for instance, is that of documents like the old Chinese annals, which contain an accurate description of the state of the heavens at the time to which they refer ; the calculations for determining their exact date, based as they are on indisputable astronomical data, leave no room for any doubt. Unfortunately this case is not general, in fact it can almost be called exceptional, and other documents, Hindu documents in particular, provide nothing of the kind as a guide to research, which merely goes to show, however, that their authors were not in the least interested in "dating themselves" for the purpose of establishing a priority of one kind or another.

The claim to intellectual originality, which has played a considerable part in calling the schools of philosophy into being, is, even among Westerners, quite a modern tendency, which in the Middle Ages was still unknown ; pure ideas and traditional doctrines have at no time been the property of this or that individual, and the biographical particulars of those who expounded or interpreted them are of minimal importance. Besides, even in the case of China, our earlier remark hardly applies to any but historical documents, and these after all are the only ones where the determining of chronological details offers any real interest, since this verifying of dates has meaning and importance from the point of view of history alone. Moreover, to add to the difficulty, it must be pointed out that there exists in India, as also no doubt in some of the vanished civilizations, a system of chronology or, to be more exact, something having the appearance of chronology, that is based on symbolical numbers, which must not be taken as literally representing numbers of years ; and is not something analogous to be met with even in Biblical chronology ? This so-called chronology however is really meant to apply to cosmic and not to historical periods ; a confusion of the two should be impossible, unless it be as a result of astonishing ignorance ; nevertheless it must be recognized that orientalists have only too frequently fallen into errors of this kind.

Among these same orientalists there is noticeable a common tendency to try and discount the antiquity of the civilizations they are dealing with as far as they possibly can, often beyond all reason, as if they feel embarrassed by the fact that these civilizations had been able to exist and were already in a full state of development in such remote ages, long before the earliest origins that can be claimed for our present civilization or rather for those civilizations from which it is directly derived ; this seems to be the only excuse for their preconceived ideas on the subject—a lame excuse indeed. Moreover, this same bias has been allowed to affect things much closer to the West in every respect than the civilizations of China and India, or even Egypt, Persia and Chaldæa : thus for instance, an attempt was made to advance the date of the Hebraic *Kabbala* in such a manner as to suggest that Alexandrine and Neo-Platonist influences had been at work there, whereas it is most certainly the opposite that took place. The reason for this confusion resides, as usual, in the fact that it is agreed *a priori* that everything must have come from the Greeks, that it is the Greeks who held the monopoly of knowledge in antiquity, just as the Europeans imagine themselves to possess it to-day, and that they were the appointed educators of humanity—just as these same Europeans claim to be at the present moment—and the fountain of its inspiration. Nevertheless Plato, whose evidence ought not to be doubted in this connection, was not afraid of recording in his *Timaeus* that the Egyptians looked on the Greeks as "children" ; Orientals to-day could still find ample reasons for saying as much about the Westerners, were it not that an almost excessive politeness has often prevented them from going to such lengths. However we can recall an occasion when just this same opinion was expressed by a Hindu who, on hearing the ideas of certain Western philosophers expounded for the first time, was so far from being impressed that he declared them fit, at best, for a child of eight years.

Anyone who feels that we unduly belittle the part played by the Greeks, by presenting them entirely in the part of "adapters," might object that we are not acquainted with all their ideas and that there are many things that have not come down to us. In certain respects, no doubt, this is true, particularly as regards the oral teachings of the philosophers ; but is not what we do know of their ideas amply sufficient to enable us to judge of the remainder ? Analogy, which is our only available means of proceeding to a certain extent from the known to the unknown, cannot but bear us out ; moreover, according to the written teachings we possess, there are at least strong reasons for supposing that the corresponding oral teaching, precisely in so far as it contained something special and "esoteric," that is to say something of a more inward nature, was even more strongly inspired by the Orient, to which it must in many ways have been related. Indeed the very inwardness of that teaching cannot but provide a confirmation of the fact that it had remained nearer to its sources and was less deformed than the other teachings of the time, because it had been less adapted to the general mentality of the Greek people ; otherwise its comprehension would clearly not have demanded a special training, above all a training so long and arduous as that, for example, in force in the Pythagorean schools.

Besides, archæologists and orientalists would hardly be in a position to contradict us by invoking an oral teaching, or even lost works, since the "historical method" of which they are so enamoured has, as its essential characteristic, the consideration only of monuments that can be seen and of documents that can be handled ; and it is here precisely that we see the "historical method" revealed in all its insufficiency. In this connection we would draw attention to a point that is too often lost sight of and which is the following: if the manuscript of a certain work is discovered, the date of which is ascertainable by one means or another, then this undoubtedly proves that the work in question is not of a later date; but that is all, and the possibility of the work having originally been composed much earlier is in no wise excluded. It may quite easily happen that older manuscripts of the same work are found later, and moreover, even if none such are discovered, it is not right to conclude that none are extant, nor, with all the more reason, that none have ever existed. Furthermore, in a civilization that has lasted down to our own time, it is hardly likely that such books as still remain will be abandoned to the chances of an archæological discovery, as might have occurred in the case of an extinct civilization ; nor on the other hand, is there any reason to believe that their custodians would one day feel themselves compelled to part with them for the benefit of learned Occidentals, all the less so as there may be a special interest, on which we will not dwell at present, attaching to their preservation compared with which curiosity, even when garnished with the epithet of "scientific," is of very little account. On the other hand, in the case of civilizations which have vanished, one is bound to admit that, in spite of unremitting research and many discoveries, there must be a great number of documents that will never come to light for the simple reason that they have been destroyed accidentally. As accidents of this kind often took place contemporaneously with the civilizations themselves and not necessarily after their disappearance, and as similar accidents can be observed taking place quite frequently around us to-day, it is extremely probable that much the same thing must have occured in the case of the other civilizations which have continued down to our time ; there is even all the more likelihood of this having happened in that a longer succession of centuries has elapsed since the origin of these civilizations. But there is yet a further point to note : even without accidents, old manuscripts can disappear in quite a natural and so-to-speak normal fashion, simply as the result of wear and tear ; in that case they are replaced by others which necessarily bear a more recent date and which become in course of time the only ones the existence of which can be confirmed. A particularly good idea of this process can be obtained by observing what takes place constantly in the Moslem world; a manuscript circulates and is transferred according to requirements from one centre of learning to another, often in very remote localities, until it is so badly damaged by use that it becomes practically unserviceable; a copy is then made, as accurately as possible, and this copy will henceforth take the place of the older manuscript and will be used in the same way, itself to be replaced by another when it has deteriorated in its turn, and so on indefinitely. These successive replacements may certainly prove a great hindrance to the special researches of the orientalists; but those engaged on this kind of work give no thought to any such considerations, and even if they were conscious of them, they would certainly not consent to alter their habits for so unimportant a reason. All these remarks are so obvious that it might seem hardly worth while making them, were it not that the prejudice which we have pointed out as affecting orientalists blinds them so completely as to conceal this evidence from their eyes.

There is yet another fact which the partisans of the "historical method" could hardly take into account without finding themselves in disagreement with their own tenets; it is that oral teaching almost everywhere preceded written teaching and that it has been the only method of teaching in use for periods of possibly very long duration, though it may be difficult to determine their exact length. In a general way and in most instances a traditional text is no more than a recording, at a relatively recent date, of a teaching which was originally transmitted by word of mouth and to which an author can rarely be assigned; thus even were one entirely certain of being in possession of the original manuscript—though there is perhaps actually no recorded case of this having happened—it would still be necessary to know for how long the previous oral transmission had continued, and this question is likely, far oftener than not, to remain unanswered.

This rooted preference for oral teaching may have been due to various causes and it does not necessarily imply the absence of writing, the origin of which is certainly extremely remote, at any rate in its ideographic form, of which the phonetic form is but a degeneration brought about by the wish for simplification. It is known, for instance, that the teaching of the Druids always remained entirely oral, even at a time when the Gauls were certainly acquainted with writing, since they made free use of a Greek alphabet in their commercial relations ; moreover the Druidical teaching left no authentic traces, and the most one can do perhaps is to piece together, as best one can, a few very sparse fragments. It would however be a mistake to suppose that oral transmission was bound, in the long run, to alter the teaching : given the importance attaching to its integral preservation, there is, on the contrary, every reason for thinking that all necessary precautions were taken in order that it might be maintained uncorrupted, not only in its essence but even in its form ; one may also realize how this preservation is perfectly possible by observing what occurs even to-day among all the Eastern peoples, for whom the written record has by no means entailed the suppression of oral tradition, for they have never considered it an entirely adequate substitute. Curiously enough, it is commonly recognised that certain works were not written down at the moment of their composition ; for example this is admitted in the case of the Homeric epics in classical antiquity and of the heroic poems of the Middle Ages ; why then are people unwilling to admit this when it is no longer a question of works referring merely to the literary order but to the purely intellectual order, where oral transmission rests on much more profound reasons ? There is really no need to stress this point further, and as for those profound reasons we have alluded to, the present is not a suitable moment for going into them ; we shall have an opportunity of saying something about them later on.

There remains one last point which we would like to mention in this chapter : while a particular period in the existence of an ancient people may be difficult to situate accurately in time, it is sometimes just as difficult, strange as this may seem, to situate it in space : whereby we mean that certain peoples may have migrated at various times from one place to another and that there is nothing to prove, for instance, that the works bequeathed by the ancient Hindus or Persians all originated in the countries where their descendants are now living. One can go further and say that the case is not proved, even when these works contain a mention of certain places, such as the names of rivers and mountains which are still familiar to us, for these same names might easily have been applied successively in the various regions where the people in question halted in the course of its migrations. There is nothing unnatural in this : are not present-day Europeans often in the habit of giving names borrowed from their own country to towns they have founded in their colonies or to other geographical features they may come across there ? It has sometimes been debated whether the Hellas of the Homeric age actually was the Greece of more recent times or whether Biblical Palestine really was the land we still refer to by that name ; discussions of this kind are perhaps not as pointless as is generally supposed, and it is at least justifiable to ask the question even if, as in the two examples just cited, it seems fairly probable that the answer should be given in the affirmative. On the other hand, in the case of Vedic India, there are many reasons for giving a negative reply to a question of this kind. The ancestors of the Hindus, at a time which remains undetermined, must have inhabited a very northerly region, since, according to certain texts, there were occasions when the sun circled the horizon without setting ; but when did they forsake that earliest abode, or at the end of how many stages did they reach the India of to-day ? These are interesting speculations from a certain point of view, but we must be content only to mention them here without embarking on their closer examination, as they do not enter into our subject. The questions we have so far been considering constitute no more than a mere preamble, which, however, appeared to us necessary before we could approach subjects relating directly to the interpretation of Eastern doctrines, and in connexion with these last-named questions, which are the principal object of our study, we have yet to draw attention to another kind of difficulty.

CHAPTER VI

Linguistic Difficulties

The most serious difficulties standing in the way of any correct interpretation of Oriental doctrines, are those arising from the essential differences between Eastern and Western ways of thinking ; we have already touched upon this matter, but we wish to go into it in further detail in the present chapter. The difference naturally shows itself in a corresponding difference between the languages destined to express the respective modes of thought, and thus another difficulty, derived from the first, arises when it comes to rendering certain ideas in the languages of the West, which are deficient in the appropriate terms and are, above all, metaphysically expressive only in a very small degree. Moreover, this is but an aggravation of the difficulties that attend every attempt at translation, and which are still to be met with, though in a less acute form, when passing from one language to another one that is closely related to it both philologically and geographically ; even in the latter case, terms that are considered to be synonymous, and which often have a common origin and derivation, are nevertheless in many cases very far from offering an exact equivalence of meaning. This is quite understandable, for it is evident that every language must be specially adapted to the mentality of the people speaking it, and each people has its own mental make-up, which differs more or less widely from that of other peoples.

This diversity in ethnic mentalities is much reduced, however, when one is dealing with peoples belonging to the same race or attached to the same civilization. In that case, the common mental features are certainly the most fundamental ones, but the secondary characteristics overlaying them may give rise to variations that are none the less quite considerable; and it might well be asked whether, among individuals speaking the same language, within the confines of a nation built up out of various racial elements, the words of that language do not possess shades of meaning that differ more or less from one district to another, and the more so since national and linguistic unification is often recent and somewhat artificial. There would be no cause for surprise if, for example, it were to be found that in each province the common language inherited certain peculiarities of the ancient dialect that it had come to supersede and had replaced more or less completely, and this would be true of the essence as well as of the form of the language. However, the differences we are referring to are naturally much more perceptible as between one people and another; if there can be several ways of speaking the same language, that is to say really several ways of thinking while using that language, then there is assuredly a particular way of thinking that is normally expressed in each distinct language; and this difference will attain its maximum in the case of languages that are unlike in every respect, or even in the case of languages which, although philologically akin, have been adapted to very different mentalities and civilizations, for philological affinities provide a much less certain basis for the establishment of real equivalences than mental resemblances. It is for this reason, as we pointed out at the very beginning, that the most literal translation is not always the most faithful one from the point of view of ideas, and that is also why the purely grammatical knowledge of a language is quite inadequate for a true understanding of it.

When we speak of the separation of peoples, and consequently of their languages, it must also be noticed that this can be a separation in time as well as space, so that the foregoing remarks apply with equal force to the understanding of ancient languages. Indeed, even in the case of a single people, if it should happen that its mental outlook undergoes considerable modifications in the course of its history, not only do new terms come to take the place of older ones in its language, but also the meaning of those terms that remain varies proportionally to the mental changes ; this is so true, that even where a language remains almost unchanged in its outward form, the same words really cease to correspond to the same concepts, so that a real translation becomes necessary in order to restore the sense, by substituting quite different words for words that nevertheless still remain in use ; a comparison between the French of the Seventeenth Century and that of our day would provide us with many examples. It should be added that this is especially true of Western peoples, whose mentality, as we were explaining earlier on, is extremely unstable and changeable ;

besides, there is another decisive reason why that kind of difficulty should not arise in the East, or rather should be reduced to a minimum; it is that in the East a sharp line of demarcation separates the vernacular tongues, which are bound to vary to some extent in response to current needs, from the languages that are used for purposes of doctrinal exposition, immutably fixed languages that are protected from all contingent variations by their object, a fact which incidentally still further diminishes the importance of questions of chronology.

Up to a point, something of this sort could have been found in Europe at the time when Latin was generally used in teaching and for intellectual intercourse; a language that is put to such a use cannot properly speaking be called a dead language, but it is a fixed language, wherein indeed lies its great advantage, not to mention its usefulness in international relations, for which purpose the artificial "auxiliary languages" advocated by the moderns are always bound to be a failure. If we are able to speak of unchangeable fixity, especially in the East, and of languages serving for the expression of doctrines that are purely metaphysical in essence, the reason is that these doctrines do not "evolve" in the Western sense of the word, a fact which moreover entirely precludes the application of any "historical method" to their study. However strange and incomprehensible this may appear in the eyes of modern Occidentals, who persist in believing in "progress" applied to every field, it is none the less a fact, and whoever fails to recognise it, condemns himself to a perpetual inability to understand the East in any of its aspects. There can be no question of metaphysical doctrines either altering their basis or even becoming perfected ; they can only undergo development according as they are regarded from different points of view, when they merely take on the forms of expression that are more particularly appropriate to each of these points of view, each successive formulation always remaining completely faithful to the traditional spirit. Under exceptional circumstances, should an intellectual deviation arise within a more or less restricted section of society, this deviation, if it is really serious, brings about, before long, the abandonment of the traditional language in the society in question ; by and by it is replaced by some idiom of popular origin, which, however, in its turn acquires a certain relative fixity, because the dissident doctrine tends of its own accord to constitute itself as an independent tradition, though one evidently deficient in regular authority. The Oriental, even when he has departed from the normal ways of his intellectuality, cannot exist without a tradition or something to take the place of one, and we shall later try to explain what tradition under all its various aspects means to him ; this moreover provides one of the deepest reasons for his disdain of the Westerner, who only too often appears to him as a being devoid of any traditional attachment.

We will now consider the difficulties we specially set out to discuss in the present chapter from another point of view and, as it were, in their principle. It can be said that any expression of a thought is necessarily imperfect in itself, for it limits and cramps the conception by enclosing it within a definite form, which can never hope to be completely adequate, inasmuch as a conception always contains something that surpasses its expression ; this applies with still greater force when metaphysical conceptions are in question, which always require a due allowance to be made for the inexpressible, since it is in their very essence to open the door to limitless possibilities. The passage from one language to another language less suited in its nature to such purposes can indeed only heighten the original and unavoidable defect ; but once one has to some extent succeeded in grasping the conception itself through its original expression, by identifying oneself as far as possible with the mental outlook of the person or persons whose thoughts it represents, it is evident that one can always make up largely for this disadvantage by resorting to an interpretation which, if it is to be intelligible, will have to be a commentary rather than a literal translation pure and simple. Fundamentally therefore, the real difficulty is the mental assimilation needed to arrive at this result ; there are certainly many minds that are quite incapable of it, and it is easy to gauge how far this effort transcends the scope of mere works of erudition. There is only one really profitable way of studying doctrines : in order to be understood they must be studied so to speak "from the inside," whereas the orientalists have always confined themselves to an investigation from the outside.

The kind of study referred to is, relatively speaking, easier in the case of doctrines that have been handed down regularly to the present day, and which still possess their authorised interpreters, than in the case of teachings that have only come down to us in a written or symbolic form, unaccompanied by the oral tradition that has long since died out. It is all the more regrettable that orientalists, through a prejudice that may have been partly involuntary but for that very reason all the more invincible, have always persisted in neglecting this help that is open to them—to those at least who embark on the study of still extant civilizations, if not to those others whose researches are concerned with extinct civilizations. Nevertheless, as we have already explained in an earlier context, even the latter, the Egyptologists and Assyriologists for example, could certainly spare themselves many a misunderstanding if they possessed a wider knowledge of the human mind and of the various modalities that it can assume ; but it is just this knowledge that can only be acquired by a genuine study of the Eastern doctrines, which could thus render the greatest service to the study of antiquity in all its branches, at least indirectly. However, even with this object in view (an object which is far from appearing of paramount importance in our eyes) something more is demanded than to bury oneself under an erudition which has little to offer in any case ; but this is doubtless the only field in which those who are unable to escape from the narrow limitations of the modern Western mentality find that they can exercise their activity without having to face too many awkward difficulties. It is this, we repeat once again, that constitutes the fundamental reason why the works of orientalists are utterly inadequate for bringing about the comprehension of any idea whatsoever, and they are at the same time useless, if not in some cases actually harmful, as a means towards promoting an intellectual understanding between East and West.

PART II

THE GENERAL CHARACTER OF EASTERN THOUGHT

CHAPTER I

The Main Divisions of the Eastern World

We have already said that though it is possible to contrast the Oriental mentality as a whole with that of the West, it would nevertheless be incorrect to speak of an Eastern civilization in the same way that one speaks of a Western one. There exist several quite distinct Eastern civilizations, each one of which possesses a principle of unity peculiar to itself and differing in essential respects from the corresponding principle governing each of the other civilizations, as we shall show presently; but however marked such differences may be, all the Eastern civilizations none the less exhibit certain characteristics in common, chiefly in regard to their ways of thinking, and it is this fact which allows of its being said, in a general way, that there exists a specifically Oriental mentality.

In undertaking any kind of study it always helps to make matters clearer if one starts off by establishing a classification based on the natural divisions into which the proposed subject of study falls. For this reason, it is necessary to explain before anything else how the various Oriental civilizations stand in relation to one another, keeping however to broad outlines and to the most general divisions, which are at least sufficient for a first approximation, since it is not our intention to enter here into a detailed survey of each of these civilizations taken separately.

With this end in view, the Orient may be divided

into three great regions, described respectively, according to their geographical relation to Europe, as the Near East, the Middle East and the Far East. The Near East, from our point of view, comprises the whole of the Islamic world ; the Middle East is essentially constituted by India ; as for the Far East, it corresponds to the regions usually denoted by that name, that is to say to China and Indo-China. It can be seen at a glance that these three general divisions do in fact correspond to three quite distinct and independent civilizations, which, even if they are not the only ones to be found in the East, are in any case the most important and cover the widest areas. Within each of these civilizations certain sub-divisions are recognizable, with variations comparable to those which, in the European civilization, exist between different countries ; only in this case it is not possible to assign national limits to these sub-divisions, since the notion of nationality answers to a conception that is, generally speaking, foreign to the East.

The Near East, which begins at the frontiers of Europe, extends not only over the neighbouring parts of Asia, but also over the whole of North Africa ; indeed it includes countries that geographically are situated just as far west as Europe itself. But Islamic civilization, despite the many directions in which it has spread, has none the less always preserved the essential characteristics which it owes to its Eastern origin, and it has imprinted its most typical features on many very different peoples, thus endowing them with a common outlook, though not to the point of depriving them of all originality. The Berber populations of Northern Africa have never fused with the Arabs inhabiting the same lands, and it is easy to distinguish them from the latter, not only by the special customs they have retained and by their physical appearance, but also by a kind of mental physiognomy which is peculiar to them ; for instance it is quite obvious that a Kabyle is in several respects more like a European than an Arab. But it nevertheless remains true to say that the civilization of North Africa, in so far as it possesses a unity of its own, is not only Moslem but even Arabian in essentials ; and it should be pointed out here that, in the Moslem world, what may be termed the Arab group holds a position of primary importance, not only because it is the group that gave birth to Islam, but also because its language is the traditional language of all Moslem peoples, irrespective of origin or race.

Besides the Arab groups, two other important groups are distinguishable, which might be called respectively the Turkish and the Persian, though these epithets are perhaps not quite strictly exact. The first group includes chiefly peoples of Mongolian race, like the Turks and the Tartars ; its mental as well as its physical traits distinguish it in a marked degree from the Arabs ; but being endowed with comparatively little intellectual originality of its own, it is fundamentally dependent on the Arabs in an intellectual sense ; moreover, even from the religious point of view, these two sections, the Arab and the Turkish, in spite of a few differences in respect of ritual and law, together form one single whole that can be opposed to the Persian group: and here we come to the deepest cleavage that exists in the Moslem world, a division which is usually expressed by saying that the Arabs and Turks are "sunnites" while the Persians are "shiites"; these descriptions however call for certain reservations, but this is not the place to enter into a discussion of them.

From the foregoing remarks it can be seen that geographical divisions do not always correspond exactly with the field of expansion of the corresponding civilizations, but only with their places of origin and their principal centres. In India, Moslem elements are to be found almost everywhere and the same may be said of China; but we need not take them into account when speaking of the civilizations of these two lands, because the Islamic civilization is not native to them. On the other hand, Persia ought by rights to be joined, racially and even geographically, to what we have called the Middle East; if we have not so included it, this is because its present inhabitants are entirely Moslem. In the Middle East two distinct civilizations should really be recognised, which however have both clearly issued from a common source: the first is that of India and the second that of the ancient Iranians; but nowadays the sole surviving representatives of the latter are the Parsis, who form a number of small and scattered groups, some in India, chiefly round Bombay, and others in the Caucasus; it is sufficient here to draw attention to the fact of their existence.

All that remains to be considered then, in the second of our main divisions, is Indian civilization proper, or Hindu civilization to be more exact, which embraces within its unity peoples of several different races ; between the various regions of India, and especially between the North and the South, there are ethnical differences at least as great as those to be found in the whole continent of Europe ; nevertheless, all these peoples share one civilization, and also a common traditional language, which is Sanskrit. Indian civilization spread at certain periods further to the East and left clear traces of its influence in various parts of Indo-China, such as Burma, Siam and Cambodia, and even in some of the Oceanic islands, notably in Java. On the other hand, this same Hindu civilization gave birth to the Buddhist civilization, which spread, under its different forms, over a large part of Central and Eastern Asia ; but the question of Buddhism calls for some additional explanations which will be given later on.

As for the civilization of the Far East, which is the only one where all the members really belong to the same race, it may properly be called the Chinese civilization ; it extends, as we have seen, to Indo-China, especially to Tongking and Annam, but the inhabitants of those regions are Chinese in race, either purely so, or else mixed with certain elements of Malay origin, which, however, are far from being preponderant. It must be stressed that the traditional language belonging to this civilization is essentially the written Chinese language, which is immune from the variations of the spoken tongue, whether these variations occur in time or in space ; a Chinaman from the North, a Southern Chinese and an Annamite may be unable to understand one another in conversation, yet the use of the same ideographic characters, with all that this really implies, none the less establishes between them a bond the strength of which is quite unsuspected by Europeans.

As for Japan, which we left out of our general classification, it is attached to the Far East in the measure in which it has been affected by Chinese influence, although in addition it possesses in *Shinto* a tradition of its own endowed with a very different character. It would be interesting to find out to what extent these various traditional elements have succeeded in maintaining themselves in the face of the modernization, that is to say of the Westernization, which has been imposed on the Japanese people by its leaders ; but that is too special a question for us to be able to dwell on it here.

To turn for a moment in another direction, it will be noticed that we have deliberately omitted all mention of the Tibetan civilization from our preceding survey, though it is very far from negligible, especially from the point of view that concerns us most. This civilization is connected in certain respects both with that of India and of China,[1] while exhibiting many other characteristics that are entirely its own ; but since it is far less familiar to Europeans than any of the other Eastern civilizations, it could not be discussed profitably without going into explanations that would be quite out of place in a work such as the present one.

[1] The Indian influence extends to the whole of the intellectual order, as well as to all those arts and sciences immediately dependent on it ; the Chinese contribution is more superficial, having chiefly affected social institutions and certain of the arts, and that to a limited extent. *Translator.*

Bearing in mind the reservations we have mentioned, we need therefore only consider three great Oriental civilizations, corresponding respectively to the geographical divisions previously referred to, namely the Islamic, Hindu and Chinese civilizations. In order to make clear the essential points in which these civilizations differ from one another, though without entering into too much detail, the most useful thing we can do will be to explain as briefly as possible the principles upon which the basic unity of each of them rests.

CHAPTER II

Principles of Unity of the Oriental Civilizations.

It is extremely difficult at the present time to discover a unifying principle in Western civilization ; it might even be said that its unity, while naturally still resting on a number of tendencies which have combined to form a common mentality, no longer amounts to anything more than a simple unity of fact, as lacking in principle as the civilization itself. This has been the case ever since the severing, at the time of the Renaissance and the Reformation, of the traditional bond derived from religion which provided the essential principle we have in mind and which gave to Western civilization in the Middle Ages its characteristic form of "Christendom." Western intellectuality, within the limits circumscribing its specifically restricted activity, could not have availed itself of any traditional attachment of a different order capable of replacing the one in question ; we mean by this that, apart from exceptions that could not become general in such an environment, tradition could not be conceived otherwise than in a religious mode. As for the European race, its unity, as we have already pointed out, is too relative and too vague to serve as a basis for the unity of a civilization. With the rupture of the fundamental unity of Christendom, therefore, a danger arose of several European civilizations coming into being, without any effective or conscious bond to unite them ; and in fact, it is from this moment that the secondary, fragmentary and reduced unities represented by the different "nations" were formed, after many vicissitudes and tentative efforts. Yet even in her mental deviation and as if in spite of herself, Europe preserved the traces of the single moulding she had received during the course of the preceding centuries ; the influences that produced the deviation worked everywhere in a similar manner, though in different degrees; thus there again emerged a common outlook and a civilization that continued to be shared by all in spite of many divisions ; but this new civilization, far from being based upon any legitimate principle, was henceforth vowed, if one might say so, to the service of an "absence of principle" which condemned it to a hopeless state of intellectual decadence. It might justifiably be argued that this was the price that had to be paid for the material progress towards which the Western world has been exclusively tending ever since, for there are certain paths of development that cannot be reconciled with one another ; but in any case, in our opinion, it was an exceedingly heavy price to pay for that much vaunted progress.

This very brief survey will make it plain why in the East there cannot exist anything comparable with the Western nations ; the reason is that the appearance of nations within a civilization is undoubtedly the sign of a partial dissolution due to the loss of the element which constituted its basic unity. Even in the West, it must be remembered, the conception of nations is a characteristically modern development ; nothing analogous was to be found in earlier times, whether it be in the Grecian cities, or in the Roman Empire which arose out of successive extensions of the original city, or in its more or less indirect Mediæval continuations, or in the confederations or tribal leagues after the Celtic model, or even in the states organised hierarchically on the feudal pattern.

On the other hand, what we have said about the former unity of "Christendom," an essentially traditional unity conceived according to the specifically religious mode, can also be applied fairly closely to the conception of unity in the Moslem world. Among Oriental civilizations, Islam is in fact the one that approaches closest to the West, and it might even be said in some respects to occupy an intermediary position between East and West, as regards its characteristic features no less than geographically. Furthermore its tradition can clearly be considered under two quite distinct modes, one being purely Oriental, while the other, which is the religious mode properly so-called, is common both to Islam and to Western civilization. Moreover Judaism, Christianity and Islam appear as three complementary branches of a single body of tradition, outside of which it is indeed difficult to apply the term " religion " correctly at all, that is if one wishes to preserve any precise and clearly defined meaning for it ; but in Islam, as we shall show later on, this purely religious side is really only its most external aspect. However that may be, taking its outward side alone into consideration for the moment, it will be seen that the whole organisation of the Moslem world rests on a tradition that may be described as religious : it is not a case, as in present-day Europe, of religion being one of the elements of the social order, but on the contrary the entire social order forms an integral part of religion, from which all legislation is inseparable, since it finds there both its principle and its justification. This is a point that has unfortunately never been grasped by those Europeans who have come into contact with Moslem peoples, with the consequence that this lack of understanding has led them into committing the crudest and most irretrievable political blunders ; but we do not intend to spend time over these matters and merely mention them in passing. We can, however, usefully make here two additional observations : firstly, the conception of the Caliphate, which alone could provide a possible basis for a really serious " Pan-Islamism," is in no wise to be assimilated to any form of national government whatsoever, and it is moreover well calculated to baffle Europeans, accustomed as they are to seeing an absolute separation, and even an opposition, between the " spiritual " and the " temporal " powers ; secondly, the pretension of setting up various national groups inside Islam, required all the ignorant self-conceit of certain " young "

Moslems, who so described themselves simply in order to advertise their own "modernism," and whose sense of tradition had been completely obliterated by the teachings of Western universities.

There is another point concerning Islam that should be stressed here, namely the unity of its traditional language: we have stated that this language is Arabic, but we must make it clear that by this we mean scriptural Arabic, which is to some extent distinct from vernacular Arabic, the latter representing an altered form and a grammatical simplification of the scriptural language. Here we see a difference that is somewhat reminiscent of that which exists between the written and spoken languages of China: scriptural Arabic alone possesses that fixity which is required if it is to fulfil its task as a traditional language, whereas spoken Arabic, like any other tongue in daily use, naturally goes through various changes in course of time and in different regions. Nevertheless, these variations are far from being as marked as is commonly supposed in Europe; they chiefly affect pronunciation and the use of certain more or less specialised terms, and they are insufficient to amount to a plurality of dialects, for all Arabic-speaking peoples are quite able to understand one another; in fact, even in the case of vernacular Arabic, there exists but one language, spoken from Morocco to the Persian Gulf, and the so-called Arabic dialects, with their greater or lesser variations, are largely an invention of the orientalists. As for the Persian language, though it does not play a fundamental part in the Moslem tradition, it is nevertheless employed in numerous *Sufi* writings and this gives it an undoubted intellectual importance in that portion of Islam lying farther East.

Passing now to the Hindu civilization, we find that its unity is also purely and solely of a traditional order ; it includes in fact elements belonging to very different races or ethnical groups, all of which can with equal justice be called " Hindu," in the strictest sense of the word, to the exclusion of certain other elements belonging to the same races, or at least to some of them. Certain people maintain that originally this was not the case, but their opinion rests on nothing better than the theory of a supposed " Aryan race," which is merely an invention of the over-fertile imagination of the orientalists. The Sanskrit term " *ārya*," which gave its name to this hypothetical race, was never really anything more than an epithet applied exclusively to the members of the first three castes, independently of their membership of this or that race, which is not in any way material here. It is true that the principles of caste, like many other things, have been consistently misunderstood in the West, so that it is not at all surprising to come across a confusion of this kind ; but we will return to this question at a later stage. What is important to grasp at the moment is the fact that Hindu unity rests entirely on the acknowledgment of a certain tradition, which also embraces the entire social order, but this time only as a simple application to a contingent realm ; the latter reservation is called for because the tradition in question is in no wise a religious one as in Islam, but is a more purely intellectual and essentially metaphysical tradition. The kind of twofold polarisation which we alluded to when speaking of the Islamic tradition is not to be found in India, so that we are precluded in the latter case from making comparisons with the West such as were rendered at least possible in the case of the external side of Islam; here we have absolutely nothing analogous to Western religions, and only superficial observers could maintain the contrary, thus proving their complete ignorance of Oriental modes of thought. As we are about to treat of the civilization of India in some detail, there is no point in going further into the subject at this moment.

The Chinese civilization, as we have already pointed out, is the only one the unity of which is essentially and in its very nature a unity of race; its governing feature, in this respect, is what the Chinese call *jen*, a conception that can without too great inexactitude be translated as "solidarity of race." This solidarity, implying both a perpetuity and a community of existence, is furthermore identified with the "idea of life," which is an application of the metaphysical principle of the "initial cause" to existing humanity; and it is the transposition of this notion into the social realm, with the continual application of all its practical consequences, that gives to Chinese institutions their exceptional stability. This same conception also explains why the whole social structure rests on the family, the essential prototype of the race; in the West something of the kind was to be found, to a certain extent, in the ancient city-state, the kernel of which was also the family, and where "ancestor worship" itself, with all that this really implies, played a part the importance of which is not easily appreciated to-day. Nevertheless, we do not believe that men anywhere except in China have gone so far in the direction of a family unity opposed to every kind of individualism, to the point for example of suppressing individual ownership and consequently individual inheritance, thus making life well-nigh impossible for any man who, whether of his own free will or not, found himself excluded from the community of the family. In Chinese society the family plays at least as important a part as caste does in Hindu society, and is comparable to caste in some respects, though its principle is quite a different one. Moreover, in China more than anywhere else, the properly metaphysical side of the tradition is sharply divided from the remainder, that is to say from its application to the various orders of relative things ; however, it goes without saying that though this separation may be deep, it does not amount to an absolute discontinuity, for this would have the effect of depriving the external forms of the civilization of any real principle. Such a state of things is only too apparent in the modern West, where the civil institutions, robbed of all traditional import, but still carrying with them a few relics of the past that no one understands any longer, sometimes present the appearance of a regular parody of ritual, devoid of all real significance, so that their retention really amounts to nothing but a " superstition " in the full force of the etymological meaning of that word.

We have said enough to show that the unity of each of the great Eastern civilizations is of a very different order from that of the present Western civilization, and rests on far more profound principles, which, being less dependent on historical contingencies, are eminently suited to assure to the civilizations in question both permanence and continuity.

CHAPTER III

What is Meant by Tradition

In the foregoing pages we have constantly had occasion to speak of tradition, of traditional doctrines or conceptions, and even of traditional languages, and this is really unavoidable when trying to describe the essential characteristics of Eastern thought in all its modalities ; but what, to be exact, is tradition ? To obviate one possible misunderstanding, let it be said from the outset that we do not take the word " tradition " in the restricted sense sometimes given to it by Western religious thought, when it opposes " tradition " to the written word, using the former of these two terms exclusively for something that has been the object of oral transmission alone. On the contrary, for us tradition, taken in a much more general sense, may be written as well as oral, though it must usually, if not always, have been oral originally. In the present state of things, however, tradition, whether it be religious in form or otherwise, consists everywhere of two complementary branches, written and oral, and we have no hesitation in speaking of " traditional writings," which would obviously be contradictory if one only gave to the word " tradition " its more specialised meaning; besides, etymologically, tradition simply means "that which is transmitted" in some way or other. In addition, it is necessary to include in tradition, as secondary and derived elements that are none the less important for the purpose of forming a complete picture, the whole series of institutions of various kinds which find their principle in the traditional doctrine itself.

Looked at in this way, tradition may appear to be indistinguishable from civilization itself, which according to certain sociologists consists of "the whole body of techniques, institutions and beliefs common to a group of men during a certain time"[1]; but how much exactly is this definition worth? In truth we do not think that civilization can be characterised generally by a formula of this type, which will always be either too comprehensive or too narrow in some respects, with the risk that elements common to all civilizations will be omitted or else that elements belonging to certain particular civilizations only will be included. Thus the preceding definition takes no account of the essentially intellectual element to be found in every civilization, for that is something which cannot be made to fit into the category known as "techniques," which, as we are told, comprises "those classes of practices specially designed to modify the physical environment"; on the other hand, when these sociologists speak of "beliefs," adding moreover that the word must be "taken in its usual sense," they are referring to something that clearly pre-supposes the

[1] E. Doutté, *Magie et Religion dans l'Afrique du Nord,* Introduction, page 5.

presence of the religious view-point, which is really confined to certain civilizations only and is not to be found in others. It was in order to avoid all difficulties of this kind that we were content at the start simply to describe a civilization as the product and expression of a certain mental outlook common to a more or less widespread group of men, thus making it possible to treat each particular case separately as regards the exact determination of its constituent elements.

However that may be, it remains none the less true, as far as the East is concerned, that the identification of tradition with the entire civilization is fundamentally justifiable. Every Eastern civilization, taken as a whole, may be seen to be essentially traditional, and this follows directly from the explanations given in the preceding chapter. As for Western civilization, we have shown that it is on the contrary devoid of any traditional character, with the exception of the religious element, which alone has retained it. Social institutions, to be considered traditional, must be effectively attached in their principle to a doctrine that is itself traditional, whether it be metaphysical or religious or of any other conceivable kind. In other words, those institutions are traditional which find their ultimate justification in their more or less direct, but always intentional and conscious, dependence upon a doctrine which, as regards its fundamental nature, is in every case of an intellectual order ; but this intellectuality may be found either in a pure state, in cases where one is dealing with an entirely metaphysical doctrine, or else it may be found mingled with other heterogeneous elements, as in the case of the religious or other special modes which a traditional doctrine is capable of assuming.

We have seen that in Islam, tradition exists under two distinct aspects, one of which is religious—it is upon this aspect that the general body of social institutions is dependent—while the other aspect, which is purely Oriental, is wholly metaphysical. In a certain measure something of the same sort existed in mediæval Europe in the case of the Scholastic doctrine, in which Arab influences moreover made themselves felt to an appreciable extent ; but in order not to push the analogy too far it should be added that metaphysic was never sufficiently clearly distinguished from theology, that is to say from its special application to the religious mode of thought ; moreover the genuinely metaphysical portion to be found in it is incomplete and remains subject to certain limitations that seem inherent in the whole of Western intellectuality ; doubtless these two imperfections should be looked upon as resulting from the double heritage of the Jewish and the Greek mentalities.

In India we are in the presence of a tradition which is purely metaphysical in its essence ; to it are attached, as so many dependent extensions, the diverse applications to which it gives rise, whether in certain secondary branches of the doctrine itself, such as that relating to cosmology, or in the social order, which is moreover strictly governed by the analogical correspondence linking together cosmic existence and human existence. A fact which stands out much more clearly here than in the Islamic tradition, chiefly owing to the absence of the religious point of view and of certain extra-intellectual elements that religion necessarily implies, is the complete subordination of the various particular orders relatively to metaphysic, that is to say relatively to the realm of universal principles.

In China, the sharp division we have already spoken of allows us to observe a metaphysical tradition on the one hand and a social tradition on the other, and these may at first sight appear not only distinct, as in fact they are, but even relatively independent of one another, all the more so since the metaphysical tradition always remained well-nigh exclusively the appanage of an intellectual elect, whereas the social tradition, by reason of its very nature, imposed itself upon all without distinction and claimed their effective participation in an equal degree. It is, however, important to remember that the metaphysical tradition, as constituted under the form of "Taoism," is a development from the principles of a more primordial tradition, formulated in the *Yi-king*, and it is from this primordial tradition that the whole of the social institutions commonly known under the name of "Confucianism" are entirely derived, though less directly and then only as an application to a contingent sphere. Thus the essential continuity between the two principal aspects of the Far Eastern civilization is re-established, and their true relationship made clear ; but this continuity would almost inevitably be missed if it were not possible to trace them back to their common source, that is to say to the primordial tradition of which the ideographical expression, as fixed from the time of Fo-hi onwards, has been preserved intact for almost fifty centuries.

We must now follow this general survey with a more detailed consideration of what really constitutes that special form of tradition known as religion, and we must also explain how pure metaphysical thought is to be distinguished from theological thought, that is to say from conceptions in religious mode, and furthermore how it differs from philosophical thought in the Occidental sense of the word. It is in these fundamental distinctions that we shall discover, by contrast with the chief types of intellectual or rather semi-intellectual conceptions current in the Western world, the basic characteristics of the general and essential modes of Eastern intellectuality.

CHAPTER IV

Tradition and Religion

It appears to be rather difficult to arrive at an agreement on an exact and strictly accurate definition of religion and its essential elements, and etymology, which often proves valuable in such cases, affords but little help in this instance, for the indications it has to offer are extremely vague. Religion, according to its verbal derivation, is "that which binds"; but is this to be taken in the sense of something that binds man to a superior principle, or something that binds men one to another? If we consider Græco-Roman antiquity, from which the word "religion" came down to us though not everything that the word stands for to-day, it is practically certain that the notion of religion included both the ideas we have mentioned and that the second more often than not played a preponderant part. In fact religion, or what was understood by that word at the time, was incorporated indissolubly in the body of social institutions, in which recognition of the "gods of the city" and observance of the lawfully established forms of worship played a fundamental part, providing them with a guarantee of stability; and it was this that conferred on these institutions a genuinely traditional character. Since those times however, at any rate during the classical period, men ceased to be fully aware of the principle on which their tradition should have been based intellectually; in this may be seen one of the earliest manifestations of the metaphysical incapacity common among Westerners, a deficiency that brings a strange confusion of thought as its fatal and unquestionable consequence. Among the Greeks especially, rites and symbols inherited from more ancient and already forgotten traditions rapidly lost their original and exact meaning; the imagination of that predominantly artistic people, freely expressing itself through the individual fancies of its poets, covered those symbols with an almost impenetrable veil, and that is the reason why philosophers like Plato openly declared that they did not know how to interpret the most ancient writings they possessed concerning the nature of the gods.[1] Symbols thus degenerated into mere allegories, and through the workings of an invincible tendency towards anthropomorphic personification they turned into "myths," that is to say fables about which everyone could believe

[1] *Laws*, Book X.

what he pleased, provided he continued in practice to maintain the conventional attitude prescribed by the legal ordinances.

Under these conditions hardly anything could survive except a formalism that became all the more purely external in proportion as it lost its meaning even for those who were charged to watch over its maintenance in accordance with the prescribed rules; thus religion, having forfeited its deeper significance, could not but become an exclusively social concern. This explains why a man who changed his city had at the same time to change his religion and could do so without the slightest scruple; he was expected to adopt the customs of those among whom he was about to settle, to whose laws he henceforth owed allegiance, and of these laws the established religion formed an integral part on exactly the same basis as governmental, judicial, military or other institutions. Over and above this conception of religion as a "social bond" among the inhabitants of the same city another more general religion was super-imposed, standing above local variations and common to all the Hellenic peoples, providing them with their only really effective and permanent connecting link; such a conception, while not corresponding to "State religion" in the sense that those words were to take on at a much later date, already suggests an obvious relationship with the latter idea, and it was certainly destined to contribute something towards its ultimate formation.

Among the Romans much the same conditions prevailed as in Greece, with the difference however that their incomprehension of the symbolical forms which they borrowed from the traditions of the Etruscans and other peoples did not arise as the result of an æsthetic tendency invading all the realms of thought, even those that should have been most firmly closed to it, but rather from a complete incapacity for anything of a really intellectual order. This rooted insufficiency of the Roman mind, turned as it was almost exclusively towards practical things, is too obvious and also too generally admitted for it to be necessary to dwell on it here; Greek influence, acting upon it later on, was only able to remedy the trouble to a very slight extent. However, in Rome also, the "gods of the city" occupied the chief position in public worship, a cult which was super-imposed on the family cults that always existed alongside of it, but perhaps without being any better understood as regards their deeper significance; and these "gods of the city," in consequence of successive extensions of their territory, ultimately became the "gods of the empire." It is clear that a cult such as that of the emperors, for example, could apply within the social sphere only, and we know that if Christianity was persecuted while so many other varied elements were incorporated without any difficulty in the Roman religion, it is because Christianity alone entailed, in practice as well as theoretically, a formal rejection of the "gods of the empire," thus striking at the very root of the established institutions. This rejection would however not have been necessary if the proper scope of what were purely social rites had been clearly defined and delimited; but it proved unavoidable on account of the many and various confusions that arose between the most different domains; these confusions, born of the misunderstanding of elements contained in those rites, some of which were derived from very distant sources, conferred on the rites the character of "superstitions," to use the word in the strict sense that we have already had occasion to give to it.

Our object in offering these comments has not been simply to show what was the conception of religion in the Græco-Roman civilization, which might in itself seem somewhat beside the point; we wished rather to show how profoundly that conception differed from the view held by present-day Western civilization, in spite of the identity of the expression used in both cases. It may be said that Christianity, or if one prefers it, the Judæo-Christian tradition, when it adopted this word "religion" together with the Latin language from which it is borrowed, imposed an almost entirely new meaning upon it; there are also other examples of changes of meaning of this kind, and one of the most striking is to be noticed in the case of the word "creation," to which we shall refer again later. The idea that will henceforth predominate is that of a link with a superior principle and no longer that of a social bond, though the latter notion will continue to be present to a certain extent, diminished in influence however, and reduced to a rank of secondary importance. But even now, what we have said only amounts to a first approximation; in order to determine the more exact meaning of religion according to the present-day conception of it, which is the one that we shall consider from now on under this name, it would evidently be useless to refer any more to etymology, because common usage has left it too far behind; it is only by a direct examination of what is effectively in existence that any precise information may be gathered.

It must be said from the outset that most of the definitions, or rather attempts at definition, proposed for the word "religion" suffer from the common defect of being applicable to things of markedly differing character, some of which really have nothing specifically religious about them. Thus for instance, there are certain sociologists who maintain that "what characterises religious phenomena is their force of obligation."[1] It might be pointed out that this obligatory character is far from belonging to all religious institutions in an equal degree, and that it can vary in intensity, either as regards practices and beliefs contained within the same religion or in a more general way from one religion to another; but even admitting that this feature is more or less common to all religious phenomena, it is far from being peculiar to them, and the most elementary logic teaches that a definition must fit not only "the whole of the thing defined" but also "nothing but that which is defined." As a matter of fact, obligation, imposed more or less strictly by an authority or a power of some sort or other, is an element that is to be found wherever there are social institutions properly speaking; for instance, is there anything that sets itself up as more rigorously obligatory than the idea of legality? Besides, whether legislation is directly bound

[1] E. Durkheim, *De la définition des phénomènes religieux.*

up with religion as in Islam, or whether it is on the contrary separate and independent of it as in the present-day European states, it still retains its character of obligation to an equal degree in either case, and it must always necessarily do so, because it is an indispensable feature of any form of social organisation whatsoever ; but who would seriously maintain that the juridical institutions of modern Europe are imbued with a religious character ? Such a suggestion is plainly absurd, and if we have perhaps given it more attention than it deserves, this is because we are now discussing theories that have acquired in certain circles an influence that is as considerable as it is unmerited. It is therefore not only in societies that are conventionally called " primitive "—wrongly so in our opinion—that " all social phenomena partake of the same constraining character " in a greater or lesser degree; a piece of observation that compels our sociologists, when speaking of these so-called "primitive" societies which they are so fond of invoking as evidence (especially since it is not easily verified), to assert that " here religion includes everything, unless one prefers to say that it is non-existent."[1] It is true that in the case of the second alternative, which indeed seems to us to be the right one, they hasten to add this qualification, " if one is prepared to regard religion as a special function " ; but if it is not a " special function " it is no longer religion at all.

We have not yet finished considering the phantasies of the sociologists : another favourite theory of

[1] E. Doutté, *Magie et religion dans l'Afrique du Nord*, Introduction, p. 7.

theirs consists in saying that religion is essentially characterised by the presence of a ritual element; this means in other words that wherever the existence of rites of any kind can be established, it may without further question be inferred that one is for that reason in the presence of religious phenomena. A ritual element admittedly is to be met with in all religions, but this element is not sufficient by itself to characterize religion as such; in this case, as in the previous one, the suggested definition is far too wide, because there exist rites, of more than one kind, that are in no wise religious.

In the first place there are rites that partake of a purely and exclusively social character, a civil character one might say. This would have been the case in the Græco-Roman civilization, were it not for the confusions we mentioned; it is actually the case in the Chinese civilization, where no such confusion has occurred, and where the ceremonies of Confucianism are in fact social rites, devoid of the slightest religious character; it is only in view of this fact that they are officially recognised, a thing that would have been inconceivable in China under any other conditions. This was well understood by the Jesuits who settled in China in the seventeenth century, and who felt no objection to taking part in these ceremonies, considering that they implied nothing incompatible with Christianity: they were certainly quite correct in holding this opinion, since Confucianism, in that it takes up a standpoint entirely outside the religious sphere and only concerns itself with those things which must normally be accepted by all members of a social body without distinction, is for that reason perfectly reconcilable with any and every religion, as well as with the absence of all religion. The present-day sociologists make exactly the same mistake as the former opponents of the Jesuits, who accused them of submitting to the practices of a religion foreign to Christianity : having observed that rites were involved, they quite naturally believed that such rites were religious in nature, like those they were familiar with in their European environment.

The Far Eastern civilization can also provide us with an example of non-religious rites of quite another kind ; Taoism in fact, which is, as we have said, a purely metaphysical doctrine, also possesses certain rites which are peculiar to it ; this means that there exist rites of which the character and purpose are essentially metaphysical, however astonishing such a thing may seem to Westerners. Since we do not wish to insist on this point at the moment, we will simply add that without going so far afield as China or India, such rites are to be found in certain branches of Islam, though it must be admitted that the Islamic tradition is almost as much a closed book to Europeans as all the rest of the East, largely by their own fault. After all, the sociologists might still be forgiven for being deceived about things that are quite strange to them, and they might with some show of reason believe that all rites are religious in their essence, if the Western world itself, about which they ought to be better informed, really had no other examples to offer them except rites of that type ; but though we do not propose to investigate their real nature here, it is permissible to ask whether the masonic rites, for instance, partake of a religious character in any degree whatsoever, even though they are quite unmistakably rites?

While considering this subject, we will take the opportunity of pointing out how the total absence of the religious point of view among the Chinese may have been the occasion of another misunderstanding, which is the converse of the preceding one, and which is due in this case to a reciprocal incomprehension on the part of the Chinese themselves. The Chinaman, who feels a great and, so to speak, natural respect for whatever belongs to the traditional order, is always ready, if transported into a foreign environment, to adopt the forms that will seem to him to constitute its tradition; now since in the West religion alone possesses this character he may thus be led to adopt it, but in a manner that is quite superficial and temporary. Returning to his native country, which he has never forsaken irrevocably, the "solidarity of the race" being too powerful an influence to allow him to do so, that same Chinaman will cease to trouble his head in the very least about the religion the customs of which he had provisionally followed; the reason being that this religion, which is a religion to others, could never have been conceived of by him in this fashion, since the religious viewpoint is foreign to his mentality; moreover, since he will never have come across anything in the West in the least degree metaphysical in character, religion is bound to appear to him as the more or less exact equivalent of a purely social tradition on the Confucian model. Europeans would thus be quite mistaken in taxing his attitude with hypocrisy, as sometimes happens; for the Chinaman it is simply a matter of courtesy, for politeness, as he conceives it, demands from a man that he should conform as far as possible to the customs of the country in which he is living, and the seventeenth century Jesuits were perfectly in order when they took rank in the official hierarchy of the *literati* during their sojourn in China, and offered to the Ancestors and Sages the ritual honours that are their due.

In the same order of ideas, there is a further interesting fact to be noted in the case of Japan, where *Shinto* in some measure can claim the same character and plays the same part as Confucianism in China; although it possesses other aspects that are less clearly defined, it is pre-eminently a ceremonial institution of the State, and its ministers, who are in no wise "priests," are quite at liberty to follow any religion they please or to follow none at all. We recall a passage in a manual of religious history which contained the strange comment that "in Japan as in China, faith in the doctrines of one religion does not in any way exclude faith in the doctrines of another"[1]; in reality different doctrines can only be compatible with each other on condition they do not cover the same ground, which in fact applies in this case, and this should be enough to prove that here there can be no question of religion. Indeed, apart from foreign importations that can never have had a very deep or extended influence, the religious point of view is as unknown to the Japanese as to the Chinese; in fact this is one of the few traits in common to be observed in the characters of these two peoples.

[1] *Christus*, Ch. V, page 198.

So far, we have only dealt with the negative aspects of our original question, for we have chiefly pointed out the inadequacy of certain definitions, an inadequacy that even involves downright falsity ; but now we must contribute, if not strictly speaking a definition, at least a positive conception of what really constitutes religion. It may be said that religion essentially entails the conjunction of three elements belonging to different orders, a dogma, a moral law and a cult or form of worship ; wherever one or other of these elements happens to be wanting, there can no longer be any question of religion in the proper sense of the word. We will add forthwith that the first element forms the intellectual part of religion, the second its social portion, while the third, which is the ritual element, participates in both these functions ; but this calls for further explanation.

The word " dogma " applies properly speaking to a religious doctrine ; without at present going further into the special characteristics of such a doctrine, we can say that though it is obviously intellectual as regards its profounder meaning, it does not belong to the purely intellectual order, for if it did so, it would not be religious but metaphysical. It follows then that this doctrine, in taking on the special form that is adapted to its point of view, must undergo the influence of extra-intellectual elements, for the most part of a sentimental order ; the very word " beliefs " which is commonly used to denote religious conceptions clearly reveals this character, for it is an elementary psychological observation that belief, taken in its most exact sense and in so far as it is opposed to certitude, which is an entirely intellectual condition, is a phenomenon wherein sentiment plays an essential part ; it amounts to a kind of inclination towards or sympathy for an idea, which moreover necessarily supposes that this idea is itself conceived with a more or less pronounced tinge of sentiment. The same sentimental factor, though a secondary one in the doctrine, becomes preponderant, and even overwhelmingly so, in morals, the dependence of which upon dogma considered as their principle is largely a theoretical assertion ; this moral aspect of religion, the justification of which can only be purely social, might be looked upon as a kind of legislation, the only kind that remains within the province of religion once the civil institutions have broken loose from it.

Lastly, the rites, which together constitute the cult or form of worship, possess an intellectual character in so far as they are looked upon as a symbolic and sensible expression of the doctrine, and a social character when considered as " practices " requiring the participation of all the members of the religious community in a manner that can be more or less binding. The name " cult " ought by rights to be reserved for religious rites only ; in actual practice however, it is fairly often used—though this is rather in the nature of an abuse—to denote other rites, for example purely social rites, as when people speak of the " cult of ancestors " in China. It should be observed that in a religion where the social and sentimental elements preponderate over the intellectual, both the dogma and the cult have their share reduced more and more, so that a religion of this kind tends to degenerate into "moralism" pure and simple, as is well exemplified in the case of Protestantism ; at the extreme limit, almost reached at the present day by a certain "liberal Protestantism," what remains is no longer a religion at all, since it has preserved only one of the essential factors ; it amounts simply to a kind of specialised philosophic thought. It should in fact be pointed out that morals may be conceived in two quite different ways : according to the religious mode, when they are attached to dogma as their principle and are subordinated to it, or else in the philosophic mode, when they are treated as independent ; we shall come back later to this second form.

It will now be understood why we said previously that the term "religion" is difficult to apply strictly outside the group formed by Judaism, Christianity and Islam, which goes to prove the specifically Jewish origin of the idea that the word now expresses. The reason is that in no other case are the three elements that we have just described found conjoined in one and the same traditional conception ; thus in China the intellectual and the social points of view are to be found, being represented moreover by two distinct bodies of tradition, while the moral point of view is totally absent, even in the social tradition. Likewise in India, it is that same moral point of view that is wanting ; if legislation here is not religious as in Islam, it is because it is entirely free from the sentimental element that can alone bestow on it the special character of a code of morals ; as for the doctrine, this is purely intellectual, that is to say metaphysical, without the least trace of the sentimental form that would be necessary in order to confer on it the character of a religious dogma, and without which the attachment of a moral code to a doctrinal principle would be quite inconceivable.

Thus it may be seen that the moral point of view, as well as the religious point of view, both essentially imply a certain element of sentimentality, which is highly developed among Westerners at the expense of intellectuality. We are therefore concerned with something which is in reality peculiar to Occidentals, with whom the Moslems should also be associated, but again with the great difference that in their case morals, kept in the secondary place that belongs to them, have never come to be looked upon as existing for their own sake. This is true even apart from the extra-religious aspect of the Islamic doctrine ; the Moslem mental outlook is incapable of accepting the notion of an "autonomous morality," that is to say a philosophical morality, an idea which formerly arose among the Greeks and Romans, and which has once again become widely accepted in the West at the present time.

One last remark is called for here : we in no wise admit the opinion held by the sociologists that religion is purely and simply a social fact ; we merely say that it contains a constituent element belonging to the social order, which is clearly not the same thing at all, since this element is normally secondary in relation to the doctrine, belonging as this does to quite a different order; and thus religion, though social on a the one side, is at the same time something more. Moreover, in practice, there are cases where all that pertains to the social order is bound up with and, as it were, dependent upon religion ; such is the case in Islam, as we have already had occasion to explain, and also in Judaism, where legislation is no less essentially religious, but with this special feature that it only applies to a particular people ; the same is equally true of a conception of Christianity that might be called "integral" and which formerly found effective realization.

The sociological opinion only corresponds to the present state of Europe, and even then only by leaving out of account all doctrinal considerations, which however have really only lost their primary importance among the Protestant nations ; strange to say, this theory has been used to justify the conception of a "State religion," that is to say of a religion that has become more or less completely a department of the State, and which as such is in great danger of being turned into a political instrument. This is a conception that in some ways brings us back to Græco-Roman religion, according to the description of it we have already given. Such an idea is evidently diametrically opposed to that of "Christendom" : the latter, being anterior to the formation of nations, could neither continue to exist nor be re-established after they had once been constituted, except on condition of being essentially "supra-national" ; on the other hand State religion is always looked upon in fact, if not by right, as national, whether it be entirely independent or whether it recognizes an attachment to other similar institutions by a sort of federal bond, which in any case only leaves to the superior and central authority an influence considerably reduced. The first of these two conceptions, that of "Christendom," is essentially identified with Catholicism, in the etymological sense of the word ; the second conception, that of a "State religion," finds its logical expression, as the case may be, either in a Gallicanism after the style of Louis XIV, or in Anglicanism and in certain forms of the Protestant religion, which in general does not seem to find such a degradation distasteful. In conclusion it may be added that of these two Western ways of conceiving religion, the first one alone, taking the special features pertaining to the religious mode into account, is capable of fulfilling the conditions of a real tradition, as the Oriental mind has always conceived it.

CHAPTER V

Essential Characteristics of Metaphysic

While the religious point of view necessarily implies the intervention of an element drawn from the sentimental order, the metaphysical point of view is exclusively intellectual ; but although for our part we find such a remark sufficiently clear, to many people it might seem to describe the metaphysical point of view inadequately, unfamiliar as it is to Westerners, so that a few additional explanations will not come amiss. Science and philosophy, such as they are to be found in the Western world, also in fact have pretensions towards intellectuality ; if we do not admit that these claims are well-founded and if we maintain that a gulf separates all speculations of this kind from metaphysic, this is because pure intellectuality, as we understand it, is a very different thing from the rather vague ideas that ordinarily pass under that name.

It should be explained first of all that in adopting the term " metaphysic " we are not greatly concerned with the historical origin of the word, which is open to some doubt, and which would even have to be regarded as purely accidental if one were prepared to admit the opinion, a decidedly improbable one in our view, according to which the word was first used to denote that which came " after physics " in the collected works of Aristotle. Likewise we need not concern ourselves with various other rather far-fetched interpretations that certain authors have thought fit to attach to this word at different times ; these are not reasons, however, for giving up its use, for, such as it is, it is very well suited for what it should normally be called upon to express, at least so far as any term borrowed from the Western languages ever can be. In actual fact, taken in its most natural sense, even etymologically, it denotes whatever lies " beyond physics " ; the word " physics " must here be taken to denote the natural sciences viewed as a whole and considered in quite a general manner, as they always were by the ancients ; it must on no account be taken to refer to one of those sciences in particular, according to the restricted acceptation in vogue at the present day. It is therefore on the basis of this interpretation that we make use of the term " metaphysic," and we must make it clear once for all that if we persist in using it, this is solely for the reasons just given and because we consider that it is always undesirable to have recourse to neologisms except in cases of absolute necessity.

It may now be stated that metaphysic, understood in this way, is essentially the knowledge of the Universal, or if preferred, the knowledge of principles belonging to the universal order, which moreover alone can validly lay claim to the name of principles ; but in making this statement we are not really trying to propose a definition of metaphysic, for such a thing is a sheer impossibility by reason of that very universality which we look upon as the foremost among its characteristics, the one from which all the others are derived. In reality only something that is limited is capable of definition, whereas metaphysic is on the contrary by its very nature absolutely unlimited, and this plainly does not allow of our enclosing it within a more or less narrow formula; a definition in this case would be all the more inaccurate the more exact one tried to make it.

It is important to note that we have spoken of knowledge and not of science ; our purpose in so doing is to emphasize the radical distinction that must be made between metaphysic, on the one hand, and the various sciences in the proper sense of the word, on the other, namely all the particular and specialised sciences which are directed to the study of this or that determinate aspect of individual things. Fundamentally, this distinction is none other than that between the universal and the individual orders, a distinction that must not however be looked upon as an opposition, since there can be no common measure nor any possible relationship of symmetry or co-ordination between its two terms. Indeed, no opposition or conflict of any sort between metaphysic and the sciences is conceivable, precisely because their respective domains are so widely separated ; and exactly the same thing applies to the relationship between metaphysic and religion. It must however be understood that the division in question does not so much concern things themselves as the points of view from which they are considered ; and this is a specially important point to note in connection with what we shall have to say later on about the different branches of the Hindu doctrine and the precise nature of their inter-relationship. It is easy to see that the same subject can be studied by different sciences under different aspects ; similarly, anything that may be examined from an individual and particular point of view can, by a suitable transposition, equally well be considered from the universal point of view (which is not to be reckoned as a special point of view at all), and the same applies in the case of things incapable of being considered from any individual standpoint whatsoever. In this way, it may be said that the domain of metaphysic embraces all things, which is an indispensable condition of its being truly universal, as it necessarily must be ; but the respective domains of the different sciences remain none the less distinct from the domain of metaphysic, for the latter, which does not occupy the same plane as the specialised sciences, is in no wise analogous to them, so that there can never be any occasion for making a comparison between the results arrived at by the one and by the others.

On the other hand, the metaphysical realm certainly

does not consist of those things of which the various sciences have failed to take cognizance simply because their present state of development is more or less incomplete, as is supposed by certain philosophers who can hardly have realized what is in question here; the domain of metaphysic consists of that which, of its very nature, lies outside the range of those sciences and far exceeds in scope all they can legitimately claim to contain. The domain of every science is always dependent upon experimentation, in one or other of its various modalities, whereas the domain of metaphysic is essentially constituted by that of which no external investigation is possible: being "beyond physics" we are also, by that very fact, beyond experiment. Consequently, the field of every separate science can, if it is capable of it, be extended indefinitely without ever finding the slightest point of contact with the metaphysical sphere.

From the preceding remarks it follows that when reference is made to the object of metaphysic it must not be regarded as something more or less comparable with the particular object of this or that science. It also follows that the object in question must always be absolutely the same and can in no wise be something which changes or which is subject to the influences of time and place; the contingent, the accidental and the variable belong essentially to the individual domain; they are even characteristics which necessarily condition individual things as such, or, to speak still more precisely, which condition the individual aspect of things in its manifold modalities. Where metaphysic is concerned, all that can alter with time and place is, on the one hand, the manner of expression, that is to say the more or less external forms which metaphysic can assume and which may be varied indefinitely, and on the other hand, the degree of knowledge or ignorance of it to be found among men ; but metaphysic in itself always remains fundamentally and unalterably the same, for its object is one in its essence, or to be more exact "without duality," as the Hindus put it, and that object, again by the very fact that it lies "beyond nature" is also beyond all change : the Arabs express this by saying that "the doctrine of Unity is unique."

Following the same line of argument, we may add that it is absolutely impossible to make any "discoveries" in metaphysic, for in a type of knowledge which calls for the use of no specialised or external means of investigation all that is capable of being known may have been known by certain persons at any and every period ; and this in fact emerges clearly from a profound study of the traditional metaphysical doctrines. Moreover, even admitting that the notions of evolution and progress might have a certain relative value in biology and sociology, though this is far from having been proved, it is none the less certain that they cannot possibly find a place in metaphysic ; besides, such ideas are completely foreign to the Orientals, just as they were foreign even to Westerners until almost the end of the eighteenth century, though people in the West now take it for granted that they are essential to human thought. This also implies, be it noted, a formal condemnation of any attempt at applying the "historical method" to the metaphysical order ; in fact the metaphysical point of view is itself radically opposed to the historical point of view, or what passes for such, and this opposition will be seen to amount not only to a question of method, but also, what is far more important, to a real question of principle, since the metaphysical point of view, in its essential immutability, is the very negation of the notions of evolution and progress. One might say in fact that metaphysic can only be studied metaphysically. No notice must be taken of contingencies such as individual influences, which are strictly inexistent from this point of view and cannot affect the doctrine in any way ; the latter, being of the universal order, is thereby essentially supra-individual, and necessarily remains untouched by such influences. Even circumstances of time and space, we must repeat, can only affect the outward expression but not the essence of the doctrine ; moreover there can be no question here, as there is in the relative and contingent order, of "beliefs" or "opinions" that are more or less variable and changing precisely because they are more or less open to doubt ; metaphysical knowledge essentially implies permanent and changeless certitude.

Indeed, from the very fact that it in no wise shares in the relativity of the sciences, metaphysic is bound to imply absolute certainty as one of its intrinsic characteristics, not only by virtue of its object, which is certitude itself, but also by virtue of its method, if this word can still be used in the present context, for otherwise this method, or whatever else one cares to call it, would not be adequate to its object. Metaphysic therefore of necessity excludes every conception of a hypothetical character, whence it follows that metaphysical truths, in themselves, cannot in any way be contestable. Consequently if there sometimes is occasion for discussion and controversy, this only happens as a result of a defect in exposition or of an imperfect comprehension of those truths. Moreover, every exposition possible in this case is necessarily defective, because metaphysical conceptions, by reason of their universality, can never be completely expressed, nor even imagined, since their essence is attainable by the pure and "formless" intelligence alone; they vastly exceed all possible forms, especially the formulas in which language tries to enclose them, which are always inadequate and tend to restrict their scope and therefore to distort them. These formulas, like all symbols, can only serve as a starting point, a "support" so to speak, which acts as an aid towards understanding that which in itself remains inexpressible; it is for each man to try and conceive it according to the extent of his own intellectual powers, making good, in proportion to his success, the unavoidable deficiencies of formal and limited expression; it is also evident that these imperfections will be at their maximum when the expression has to be conveyed through the medium of certain languages, such as the European languages and especially the modern ones, which seem particularly ill-adapted to the exposition of metaphysical truths. As we said previously in connection with the difficulties of translation and adaptation, metaphysic, because it opens out a limitless vista of possibilities, must take care never to lose sight of the inexpressible, which indeed constitutes its very essence.

Knowledge belonging to the universal order is of necessity beyond all the distinctions that condition the knowledge of individual things, of which the distinction between subject and object is the general and basic type ; this also goes to show that the object of metaphysic is in no wise comparable with the particular object of any other kind of knowledge whatsoever, and indeed it can only be referred to as an object purely by analogy, because, in order to speak of it at all, one is forced to attach to it some denomination or other. Likewise, when one speaks of the means of attaining metaphysical knowledge, it is evident that such means can only be one and the same thing as knowledge itself, in which subject and object are essentially unified ; this amounts to saying that the means in question, if indeed it is permissible to describe it by that word, cannot in any way resemble the exercise of a discursive faculty such as individual human reason. As we have said before, we are dealing with the supra-individual and consequently with the supra-rational order, which does not in any way mean the irrational : metaphysic cannot contradict reason, but it stands above reason, which has no bearing here except as a secondary means for the formulation and external expression of truths that lie beyond its province and outside its scope. Metaphysical truths can only be conceived by the use of a faculty that does not belong to the individual order, and which, by reason of the immediate character of its operation, may be called "intuitive," but only on the strict condition that it is not regarded as having anything in common with the faculty which certain contemporary philosophers call intuition, a purely instinctive and vital faculty that is really beneath reason and not above it. To be more precise, it should be said that the faculty we are now referring to is intellectual intuition, the reality of which has been consistently denied by modern philosophy, which has failed to grasp its real nature whenever it has not preferred simply to ignore it ; this faculty can also be called the pure intellect, following the practice of Aristotle and his Scholastic successors, for to them the intellect was in fact that faculty which possessed a direct knowledge of principles. Aristotle expressly declares[1] that "the intellect is truer than science," which amounts to saying that it is more true than the reason which constructs that science ; he also says that "nothing is more true than the intellect," for it is necessarily infallible from the fact that its operation is immediate and because, not being really distinct from its object, it is identified with the truth itself.

Such is the essential basis of metaphysical certainty ; it may thus be seen that error can only enter in with the use of reason, that is with the formulation of the truths that the intellect has conceived, and this follows from the fact that reason is obviously fallible in consequence of its discursive and mediate character. Furthermore, since all expression is bound to be imperfect and limited, error is inevitable in its form, if not in its content : however exact one tries to make the expression, what is left out is always much greater than what is included ; but this unavoidable error in expression contains nothing positive as such and simply amounts to a lesser truth, since it resides

[1] *Posterior Analytics*, Book II.

merely in the partial and incomplete formulation of the integral truth.

It now becomes possible to grasp the profound significance of the distinction between metaphysical and scientific knowledge: the first is derived from the pure intellect, which has the Universal for its domain; the second is derived from reason, which has the general for its domain since, as Aristotle has declared, "there is no science but that of the general." One must on no account confuse the Universal with the general, as often happens among Western logicians, who moreover never really go beyond the general, even when they erroneously apply to it the name of universal. The point of view of the sciences, as we have shown, belongs to the individual order; the general is not opposed to the individual, but only to the particular, since it is really nothing else than the individual extended; moreover the individual can receive an indefinite extension without thereby altering its nature and without escaping from its restrictive and limiting conditions; that is why we say that science could be indefinitely extended without ever joining metaphysic, from which it will always remain as completely separate as ever, because metaphysic alone embraces the knowledge of the Universal.

We think we have now sufficiently discussed the nature of metaphysic, and we could hardly say more without entering upon an exposition of the doctrine itself, for which this is not the place; however, these remarks will be amplified in succeeding chapters, especially when we come to discuss the difference between metaphysic and what generally goes by the name of philosophy in the modern West. All that we have just said can be applied, without reservation, to every one of the traditional doctrines of the East, in spite of great differences in form which might conceal their fundamental identity from the eyes of a casual observer: this conception of metaphysic is equally true of Taoism, of the Hindu doctrine, and also of the inward and extra-religious aspect of Islam. Now, is there anything of the kind to be found in the Western world? If one were only to consider what actually exists at the present time, it would certainly not be possible to give any but a negative answer to this question, for that which modern philosophical thought is sometimes content to label as metaphysic bears no relation whatsoever to the conception just put forward; however we shall presently have to return to this point. Nevertheless, what we said about Aristotle and the Scholastic doctrine at least shows that metaphysic really existed in the West to a certain extent, if incompletely; and in spite of this necessary reservation, one can say that here was something which is without the slightest equivalent in the modern mentality and which seems to be utterly beyond its comprehension. On the other hand, if the above reservation is unavoidable, it is because, as we said earlier on, there are certain limitations that seem to be innate in the whole of Western intellectuality, at least from the time of classical antiquity onwards; we have already noted, in this respect, that the Greeks had no notion of the Infinite. Besides, why do modern Westerners, when they imagine they are conceiving the Infinite, always represent it as a space, which can only be indefinite, and why do they persist in confusing eternity, which abides essentially in the "timeless," if one may so express it, with perpetuity, which is but an indefinite extension of time, whereas such misconceptions do not occur amongst Orientals? The fact is that the Western mind, being almost exclusively inclined to the study of the things of the senses, is constantly led to confuse conceiving with imagining, to the extent that whatever is not capable of sensible representation seems to it to be actually unthinkable for that very reason; even among the Greeks the imaginative faculties were preponderant. This is evidently the very opposite of pure thought; under these conditions there can be no intellectuality in the real sense of the word and consequently no metaphysic. If another common confusion be added as well, namely that of the rational with the intellectual, it becomes evident that the supposed Western intellectuality, especially among the moderns, in reality amounts to no more than the exercising of the exclusively individual and formal[1] faculties of reason and imagination; it can then be understood what a gulf separates it from Eastern intellectuality, which regards no knowledge as real or valuable excepting that knowledge which has its deepest roots in the Universal and the formless.

[1] It should be pointed out that M. Guénon uses the terms "form" and "formal" with their ordinary and not with their Scholastic meaning. *Translator.*

CHAPTER VI

The Relations between Metaphysic and Theology

The question we are now about to consider does not arise in the East, because of the absence of the specifically religious point of view, in which the theological mode of thought is naturally inherent; or rather it could only arise in connection with Islam, where it would assume the form of an inquiry into the proper relationship between the two aspects of the tradition, religious and extra-religious, which could with equal justice be called the theological and metaphysical aspects. In the West on the other hand, it is the absence of the metaphysical point of view that prevents this question from being generally raised; in actual practice it only affects the Scholastic doctrine, which was in fact both theological and metaphysical, though, as we said before, it was restricted in scope in this second respect; but it does not appear as if a very definite solution of the question was ever arrived at. Its discussion in quite general terms therefore is of all the greater interest, since essentially it implies a comparison between two different modes of thought, namely the purely metaphysical and the specifically religious modes.

As we have said, the point of view of metaphysic is alone universal and therefore limitless; accordingly every other point of view is more or less specialised and of its own nature subject to certain limitations. We have already shown that this applies to the scientific point of view for example, and we shall also show that it applies to various other points of view that are usually classed under the common and rather vague heading of philosophy, which do not greatly differ, however, from the scientific point of view properly so-called, though they are put forward with greater, if quite unjustifiable, pretensions. Now this essential limitation, which may evidently be either more or less narrow, even applies to the theological point of view; in other words, the latter is also a specialised point of view, although not in the same sense as the sciences, neither are its limits such as to enclose it within so narrow a field; but it is precisely because theology, in one sense, comes closer to metaphysic than do the sciences, that it requires a more subtle perception to distinguish it from metaphysic, so that confusions can arise here more easily than in any other case. Such confusions indeed have not failed to arise, and they have gone so far as to bring about a reversal of the relations that should normally exist between metaphysic and theology; thus, even in the Middle Ages, which nevertheless was the only period when Western civilization enjoyed a truly intellectual development, metaphysic came to be treated merely as a dependency of theology, besides being insufficiently detached from various considerations of a purely philosophical nature; that this should have been possible is due simply to the fact that metaphysic, as conceived by the Scholastic doctrine, had remained incomplete, with the result that its universal character, implying as it does the absence of every limitation, was never fully grasped; metaphysic was effectively conceived only within certain limits, and the existence of further possibilities of conception, transcending those limits, remained unsuspected. This fact provides sufficient excuse for the misunderstanding which arose at that time, and it is almost certain that the Greeks, to the extent to which they cultivated true metaphysic, would have been deceived in exactly the same way had they possessed anything occupying the same place as theology in the Judæo-Christian religions ; this brings us back to what we have already said, namely that Westerners, including even those who were true metaphysicians up to a certain point, have never known metaphysic in its entirety. Nevertheless there may have been individual exceptions, for, as we pointed out before, nothing in principle precludes the existence, at any period or in any country, of men capable of attaining to complete metaphysical knowledge ; and this would even be possible in the present Western world, though doubtless unlikely by reason of the general tendencies governing men's outlook, which create as unfavourable a background as can well be imagined. In any case, it is only right to point out that if such exceptions ever did exist, no written evidence has been found to prove it, nor do the generally known facts reveal traces of their influence ; this absence of direct evidence however proves nothing in a negative sense, nor should it occasion any surprise, for if cases of this sort did in fact occur, it can only have been thanks to very special circumstances of a nature that we cannot profitably discuss here.

To return to the question that chiefly concerns us

at present, we shall remind the reader that we have already pointed out the most essential difference between a metaphysical doctrine and a religious dogma; whereas the metaphysical point of view is purely intellectual, the religious point of view implies as a fundamental characteristic the presence of a sentimental element affecting the doctrine itself, which does not allow of its preserving an attitude of entirely disinterested speculation ; this is indeed what occurs in theology, though to a degree that is more or less strongly marked according to the particular branch under consideration. This emotional element nowhere plays a bigger part than in the "mystical" form of religious thought ; and let us take this opportunity of declaring that contrary to a far too prevalent opinion, mysticism, from the very fact that it is inconceivable apart from the religious point of view, is quite unknown in the East. In the very wide-spread confusion which consists in lending a mystical interpretation to ideas that have nothing mystical about them, one can observe yet another example of the persistent tendency among Westerners to find all over the world pure and simple equivalents of modes of thought that are in reality peculiar to themselves ; but we will not enter into this question in greater detail here, for to do so would lead us too far afield.

The influence of sentimental elements obviously impairs the intellectual purity of the doctrine, and it is only right to say that it does in fact represent a certain falling away from the standpoint of metaphysical thought ; this falling away, in the region where it took place generally and extensively, that is to say in the

Western world, was in many ways inevitable and in a sense even necessary, if the doctrine was to be adapted to the mentality of the men for whom it was being specially framed, men in whom feeling was stronger than intelligence in virtue of a predominance that has reached its climax in modern times. Nevertheless, it remains true that feeling is but a relative and contingent thing, so that any doctrine that makes an appeal to it and on which it reacts in its turn is bound to be relative and contingent ; and this is especially noticeable in regard to the need for "consolations" with which the religious point of view is closely bound up. Truth, in itself, has no need to be consoling ; if anyone finds it so, so much the better for him, certainly, though the consolation he feels does not emanate from the doctrine, but purely from himself and from the particular predispositions of his own sentimentality.

It follows that a doctrine which adapts itself to the requirements of sentimental beings and which must therefore itself put on a sentimental dress can henceforth no longer be identified with absolute and total truth ; the profound change produced in the form of the doctrine by the introduction of a consolatory principle corresponds to an intellectual falling off on the part of the human collectivity to which its message is addressed. Looked at from another angle, it is this characteristic that gives birth to the inevitable diversity of religious dogmas ; hence their incompatibility, for whereas intelligence is one, and truth, in whatever measure it is understood, can be understood in one way only, the same does not apply to feeling, so that religion, in seeking to satisfy the demands of feeling, cannot avoid trying to adapt its form as far as possible to its multiple modes, which vary largely according to race and period. This does not mean, however, that all religious forms, in their doctrinal part, suffer the dissolving action of sentimentalism to an equal degree, with its resultant need for change; a comparison between Catholicism and Protestantism, for example, is particularly instructive in this connection.

It can now be seen that the theological point of view is but a particularisation of the metaphysical point of view, implying a proportional alteration; it is an application of it to contingent conditions, one might say, the mode of adaptation being determined by the nature of the conditions to which it must respond, since these special exigencies, after all, furnish the only reason for its existence. From this it follows that every theological truth, by means of a transposition dissociating it from its specific form, may be conceived in terms of the metaphysical truth corresponding to it, of which it is but a kind of translation, though this does not mean that there is effective equivalence between the two orders of conception: the reader should recall our earlier observation that everything which can be considered from the individual point of view can also be considered from the universal point of view, without the two being however any the less widely separated on that account.

If things are now examined in an inverse sense, it must be said that certain metaphysical truths are capable of being translated into theological language, though not all, for in this case it is important to take into consideration many things which cannot be included under any individual point of view whatsoever, and which therefore belong exclusively to the realm of metaphysic ; the Universal in its entirety cannot be compressed within any particular point of view, neither can it be enclosed within any form, which really amounts to saying the same thing. Even in the case of such truths as are suited to undergo the translation in question, that translation, like every other formulation, cannot but always remain incomplete and partial, and what it omits gives the precise measure of the difference between the points of view of theology and of pure metaphysic. This could be illustrated by numerous examples ; but these examples themselves, if they are to be understood, would necessitate doctrinal developments that cannot be entered into here: one such example, to mention a typical case among many others, may be found in a comparison of the metaphysical conception of "Deliverance" in the Hindu doctrine, with the theological conception of "Salvation" in the Western religions ; these two conceptions are essentially different, and it is only the lack of comprehension of some of the orientalists that is responsible for attempts to assimilate them, in a way that remains, however, a mere matter of words. Let it also be noticed in passing that a case like this should serve as a warning against another very real danger : if a Hindu, to whom Western concepts are foreign, is told that Europeans mean by the word "salvation" exactly what he means by the word *moksha*, he will certainly have no reason for contradicting this assertion or for doubting its accuracy, so that later on, at least until he becomes better informed, he may himself be led into employing this word "salvation" in order to describe a conception that is in no wise theological in character; in that case the misunderstanding will be mutual, and the confusion will thus be rendered still more inextricable. The same applies to the misconceptions that spring from the no less mistaken assimilation of the metaphysical point of view to the points of view of Western philosophy: we have in mind the case of a Moslem who readily accepted, as quite natural, the expression "Islamic pantheism" when applied to the metaphysical doctrine of the "Supreme Identity;" but the moment it was explained to him what pantheism really stood for in the true sense of the word, as for example in Spinoza, he rejected such a designation with horror.

To show what is implied by the translation of metaphysical truths into theological language, we will confine ourselves to one extremely simple and elementary example: the immediate metaphysical truth "Being is," when expressed according to the religious or theological mode, will give rise to another proposition, namely that "God exists"; but the two statements would not be strictly equivalent except on the double condition of conceiving God as Universal Being, which is far from always being the case in fact, and of identifying existence with pure Being, which is metaphysically inexact. Doubtless this example, because of its too great simplicity, does not entirely do justice to the deeper aspects of theological conceptions; but even such as it is, it can be found instructive, because it is precisely out of the misunderstanding of the implications of the two formulas just cited, resulting from a confusion of the two corresponding points of view, that there arose the endless controversies connected with the famous " ontological argument," which is itself but a product of this confusion.

Another important point that may be noted concerning the same example is that theological conceptions, not being beyond the reach of individual variations, as are pure metaphysical conceptions, can vary from one individual to another, and these variations are inevitably centred around divergencies concerning the most fundamental conception of all, namely the very conception of Divinity : those who discuss such matters as the " proofs of God's existence," if they hope to understand one another, should first of all make sure that in uttering the same word " God " they really are intending to express an identical conception ; they would often discover that this is far from being the case, so that they have no better chances of reaching agreement than if they were speaking different languages. It is especially in this realm of individual variations, for which official and instructed theology must however in no wise bear the blame, that a pre-eminently anti-metaphysical tendency is revealed, commonly to be found among Westerners, and which properly speaking constitutes " anthropomorphism " ; but this subject calls for a few additional explanations, which will enable us to consider the question from another angle.

CHAPTER VII

Symbolism and Anthropomorphism

The word "symbol," in its most general sense, can be applied to every formal expression of a doctrine, whether verbal, visual or otherwise; a word can have no other function or justification but that of symbolising an idea, which amounts to saying that it gives, as far as such a thing is possible, a sensible and moreover purely analogical representation of the idea. Taken in this sense, symbolism, which is but the employing of forms or images as signs of ideas or of supra-sensible things, is evidently natural to the human mind, and therefore necessary and spontaneous; language provides a simple example of this process. There exists also, in a more special sense, a deliberate, calculated symbolism, that to some extent crystallizes the doctrinal teachings in figurative representations; and indeed, between these two kinds of symbolism there is, truth to tell, no precise dividing line, for it is quite certain that writing, at its origin, was everywhere ideographic, that is to say essentially symbolical, even in the more special sense just referred to, though it is only in China that it can be said to have remained in this state always and exclusively. Howbeit, symbolism, as usually understood, is in much more constant use for the expression of Oriental than of Western thought; and this is quite understandable when it is realized that it constitutes a much less narrowly limited means of expression than ordinary language;

suggesting as it does far more than it expresses, it provides the support that is best adapted to possibilities of conception that lie beyond the power of words.

Indeed symbolism, in which conceptual indefinitude in no wise precludes an absolutely mathematical exactness, thus reconciling apparently contradictory qualities, is, as one might say, the natural language of metaphysic; moreover symbols that were originally metaphysical can become religious symbols as well, by a process of secondary adaptation running parallel to that of the doctrine itself. All rites, for example, possess a pre-eminently symbolical character, whatever realm they may be attached to, and it is always possible to transpose the meaning of religious rites in a metaphysical sense, as well as that of the theological doctrine to which they are linked; even in purely social rites, if one wishes to discover the deeper reasons for their existence, it is necessary to pass from the sphere of applications, which contains their immediate governing conditions, to the sphere of principles, that is to say to their traditional source, which is metaphysical in its essence. We are not trying to suggest, however, that rites are nothing but pure symbols; they are symbolical no doubt, and they cannot but be so, for they would otherwise be quite devoid of meaning, but they must at the same time be conceived of as possessing an efficacy of their own, as means of realization operating in view of the end for which they have been instituted and to which they are subordinated. Here, on the religious plane, may be recognised the Catholic conception of the virtue of the "sacraments," while from the metaphysical point of view one discovers the principle underlying certain ways of realization to which we shall refer later on, and it is this which has enabled us to speak of specifically metaphysical rites. Moreover, it might be said that every symbol, in so far as it must essentially serve as a support to a conception, is also endowed with a very real efficacy ; and the religious sacrament itself, in so far as it is a sensible sign, does indeed play a similar part as support of the "spiritual influence" which will turn the sacrament into an instrument of immediate or deferred psychical regeneration ; just as in the parallel case the intellectual potentialities included in the symbol are able to awaken either an effective or simply a virtual conception, according to the receptive capacity of each individual. From this point of view, a rite is still only a particular kind of symbol : it is, one might say, a symbol "enacted," but only if the symbol is taken for what it really is and not merely considered in its outward or contingent appearance : here, as in the study of texts, one must learn to look beyond the "letter" in order to discover the "spirit."

This, however, is precisely what Westerners usually fail to do : the faulty interpretations of the orientalists provide us with characteristic examples, for they quite frequently take the form of distorting the symbols which are the objects of study, in the same way that the Western mind in general spontaneously distorts any symbols that it happens to come across. The determining cause of the error in this case is the predominance of the sensible and imaginative faculties : to mistake the symbol itself for what it represents, through an incapacity to rise to its purely intellectual purport, is the fundamental confusion to be found at the root of all "idolatry," giving to this word its strictest sense such as is brought out with especial clarity by Islam. When nothing of a symbol remains but its outward form, both its justification and its actual virtue have alike disappeared; the symbol has then become nothing but an "idol," that is to say a vain image, and its preservation amounts to mere "superstition"—so long, that is, as no one appears who is endowed with an understanding capable of effectively restoring to it, either partially or wholly, whatever it had lost, or at least those elements which it no longer contains save in a state of latent possibility. This applies to the traces left behind by every tradition the real meaning of which has fallen into oblivion, and especially to any religion that has been reduced by the general incomprehension of its votaries to a mere external formalism; we have already mentioned what is perhaps the most striking example of such a degeneration, in the case of Greek religion. It is also among the Greeks that a tendency was to be found in its most extreme form which appears to be inseparable from "idolatry" and the materialisation of symbols, namely the tendency towards anthropomorphism: they did not look on their gods as representing certain principles, but they pictured them really as beings with human forms, affected by human feelings and acting after the manner of men; and these gods, for the Greeks, no longer possessed anything whereby to distinguish them from the forms in which poetry and art had clothed them, so that they were literally nothing apart from the form itself.

Such complete reduction to a human perspective could alone serve as a pretext for the theory that has been called "Euhemerism," after the name of its inventor, according to which the gods were originally nothing more than illustrious men; it would indeed be impossible to go further in the direction of gross incomprehension, grosser even than that of certain moderns who refuse to see in the ancient symbols anything more than a figuring or an attempted explanation of various natural phenomena; the all too famous theory of the "solar myth" is the best known example of the latter kind of interpretation. "Myths," like "idols," have never been anything else but symbols misunderstood: the one corresponds in the order of speech to what the other is in the visual order; among the Greeks, poetry gave rise to the first just as art produced the second; but among peoples to whom, as to the Orientals, naturalism and anthropomorphism are equally foreign, neither the one nor the other could arise save in the imagination of Westerners who wished to set themselves up as interpreters of things they quite failed to understand. The naturalistic interpretation really reverses the normal relationships: a natural phenomenon, like anything else belonging to the sensible order, can be taken to symbolise an idea or a principle, and a symbol has no use or justification except in virtue of the fact that it belongs to an order inferior to the thing symbolised. Similarly, there is doubtless a general and natural tendency in man to employ the human form for symbolical purposes; but the practice, which in itself is not open to objection any more than the use of a geometrical figure or any other method of representation, in no wise constitutes anthropormorphism, so long as man does not become a dupe of the figuration he has adopted.

In China and in India there has never been any parallel with what occurred in Greece, and symbols based upon the human figure, though commonly used, were never turned into " idols " ; and in this connection it may also be noted how opposed symbolism is to the Western conception of art : nothing is less symbolical than " classical " Greek art and nothing is more so than the Oriental arts ; but where art is regarded solely as a means of expression to serve as the vehicle of certain intellectual conceptions, it obviously could not be taken for an end in itself, as only happens among peoples of a predominantly sentimental turn of mind. It is to such peoples that anthropomorphism comes naturally, and it should be noticed that these are the peoples among whom, for the same reason, the religious point of view properly so-called was able to establish itself ; religion, however, has always tried to react against the anthropomorphic tendency and to combat it in principle, even when a more or less garbled conception of religion in the popular mind sometimes helped to develop it in practice. The peoples called Semitic, such as the Jews and Arabs, are in this respect akin to the Western peoples : there is in fact no other reason to account for the prohibition of symbols under a human form which is common both to Judaism and Islam, but with this exception, that in Islam it was never so strictly applied among the Persians, for whom the employment of symbols of this kind offered less dangers because, being more completely Oriental than the Arabs, and moreover of quite a different race, they were much less prone to slip into anthropomorphism.

These last remarks provide us with the opportunity to say a few words about the idea of "creation." This conception, which is as foreign to the Orientals, the Moslems only excepted, as it was to Græco-Roman antiquity, appears to be specifically Jewish in its origin ; the word denoting it is indeed Latin in form, but it did not originally bear the meaning that Christianity gave to it later, since *creare* at first meant nothing else but "to make," a sense that the verbal root *kri*, which is identical with the root of the Latin word, has always preserved in Sanskrit ; the change of meaning which took place was a profound one and, as we have pointed out, similar to the alteration undergone by the term "religion."

It is clearly from Judaism that this idea passed over into Christianity and Islam ; and the reason for this is essentially the same as that which gave rise to the prohibition of anthropomorphic symbols. In practice, a tendency to conceive God as "a being," more or less analogous to individual and especially to human beings, wherever it is to be found, is certain to produce as a natural corrollary a tendency to attribute to God simply a "demiurgic" function, that is to say an activity exercised upon a "matter" which is looked upon as external to Him and which is the mode of action proper to individual beings. Under these conditions, in order to safeguard the notion of the Divine Unity and Infinity, it became necessary to declare expressly that God "made the world from nothing," which amounts to saying "from nothing that was external to Himself," for the other supposition would result in limiting Him by giving birth to a radical dualism. In this case the theological heresy amounts to the expression of a metaphysical absurdity, which is moreover usually the case ; but this danger, quite non-existent as regards pure metaphysic, became a very real one from the religious point of view, because in this derived form the absurdity was no longer immediately apparent. The theological conception of "creation" is an appropriate translation of the metaphysical conception of "universal manifestation," being the one that is best adapted to the mentality of Western peoples ; there is however no real equivalence between these two conceptions, given that they must necessarily be separated by the whole difference that separates the points of view to which they respectively refer : this is a further example illustrating the question we were discussing in the preceding chapter.

CHAPTER VIII

Metaphysical Thought and Philosophical Thought Compared

We have stated that metaphysic differs profoundly not only from science, but also from everything that Westerners, and especially the moderns, refer to by the name of philosophy, under which heading moreover many heterogeneous and even quite dissimilar elements are assembled together. It is of little importance in the present instance to consider what notions the Greeks originally may have meant to include in the term philosophy, which appears at first to have comprised for them, in a rather indistinct way, the whole of human knowledge within the limits in which they were able to conceive it ; we only propose to deal with what actually passes under this name at the present day. First of all however, it should be noted that whenever true metaphysic has made its appearance in the West, people have always tried to link it up with questions appertaining to special and contingent points of view, in order to include it together with these questions in one whole, bearing the name of philosophy ; this goes to prove that in the West the essential characteristics of metaphysic, whereby it is distinguished from every other kind of knowledge, never emerged with sufficient clearness. One may go even further and say that to treat metaphysic as a branch of philosophy, either by placing it thus on a level with relative sciences of any kind or even by qualifying it as the "foremost philosophy," as Aristotle did, implies a profound misunderstanding of its real scope and of its character of universality : the absolute Whole cannot form a part of something nor can anything else whatsoever enfold or comprise the Universal. This in itself, then, is clear evidence of the incompleteness of Western metaphysic, which furthermore is to all intents and purposes limited to the doctrine of Aristotle and the Scholastics, for, with the exception of a few fragments scattered here and there and of certain things about which not enough is known to speak of them with any great degree of certainty, no other doctrine of a truly metaphysical character is to be met with in the West, at least from the time of classical antiquity onwards, not even if every allowance is made for the admixture of scientific, theological or other contingent elements ; we do not include the Alexandrians, however, upon whom Oriental influences came to be exercised in a direct manner.

If modern philosophy be considered as a whole, it may be said, quite generally, that its point of view does not differ in any essential way from that of science : the point of view in either case is a rational one, or at least pretends to be, and all knowledge that is confined to the domain of reason, whether or not it is called philosophical, is strictly speaking scientific knowledge ; if it aspires to being something else, it thereby loses all value, even of a relative kind, through arrogating to itself a scope and importance which do not legitimately belong to it : this is the case of what might be termed pseudo-metaphysic. Furthermore, the distinction between the provinces of philosophy and science is all the less justifiable in that the former includes among its numerous constituents certain sciences which are just as special and restricted as any others, and which do not possess characteristics distinguishing them in a way that would entitle them to a privileged position ; sciences of this sort, such as psychology or sociology, for example, are only called philosophical as the result of custom not based upon any logical argument ; philosophy, in short, possesses only a purely fictitious unity, historical if one wishes, and it is difficult to say why it is no longer customary, as in former times, to include in it various other sciences as well. On the other hand, certain sciences at one time classed as philosophical are no longer considered to be so at the present day ; the fact that they have received a wider development has proved a sufficient reason for separating them from this ill-defined assemblage, although intrinsically their nature has not altered in the very least ; if some sciences still remain under the heading of philosophy, no more should be seen in this than a survival of the extended meaning which the Greeks originally had given to philosophy, whereby it in fact included all the sciences.

From what we have said it is evident that true metaphysic cannot have a closer nor a different relationship with psychology, for example, than it can have with physics or physiology : these are all alike natural sciences, that is to say physical sciences in the primary and general sense of the word. Still less can metaphysic be considered as in any way dependent upon any such special science : to pretend to give it a psychological basis, as certain philosophers have tried to suggest, having no other excuse for such an attitude but their own complete ignorance of what metaphysic really is, amounts to trying to make the universal depend upon the individual, the principle upon its more or less remote or indirect consequences, and it also inevitably entails ending up with an anthropomorphic, and therefore eminently anti-metaphysical conception. Metaphysic must of necessity be self-sufficing, since it is the only kind of knowledge which is really direct, and it cannot be based on anything other than itself from the very fact that it consists of the knowledge of universal principles from which all else is derived, including the subject matter of the various sciences. If the above-mentioned sciences have isolated their subject matter from these principles in order to consider it from their own special points of view, such a procedure is certainly legitimate on their part, for were they to do otherwise and refer their subject-matter to universal principles, they could not but go beyond the limits of their own particular fields. This last observation also shows that there can be no question of basing these sciences directly upon metaphysic ; the very relativity of the points of view that they represent assures them of a certain autonomy, and to misunderstand this can only lead to quite unnecessary conflicts ; this error, which weighs heavily upon all modern philosophy, was in the first instance committed by Descartes, whose metaphysic moreover was really no more than a pseudo-metaphysic, and who only interested himself in it in order to provide an introduction to his physics, to which he thought in this way to give a more solid foundation.

If we turn now to logic, we will find that it is not in quite the same position as the sciences we have so far been considering, all of which may be called experimental sciences, since they are based upon the results of observation. Logic is also a special science, being essentially a study of the conditions properly pertaining to human understanding ; but its connection with metaphysic is more direct, in the sense that what are called logical principles are simply applications and specifications in a determinate sphere of the true principles which belong to the universal order : this enables a transposition to be effected in respect of them similar to that which we indicated as possible when speaking of theology. The same considerations are equally applicable in the case of mathematics : this science, although necessarily limited in its range by reason of being exclusively confined to the realm of quantity, applies in its own special sphere certain relative principles which may be regarded as constituting a direct particularisation of certain universal principles. Thus, taking the field of science as a whole, logic and mathematics may be said to be the two sciences having the most real affinity with metaphysic ; but from the very fact that they come within the general definition of scientific knowledge, being confined within the limits of reason and within the category of individual conceptions, it follows that they are still radically separated from pure metaphysic. It is this separation which prevents any effective value being attached to points of view represented as being more or less of a blend of logic and metaphysic, such as the "theories of knowledge" which have played such a prominent part in modern philosophy ; reduced to what may be considered as their legitimate elements, these theories are only logic pure and simple, and to the extent that they claim to go beyond logic, they are merely pseudo-metaphysical fantasies devoid of any substance. In a traditional doctrine logic can only occupy the place of a secondary and dependent branch of knowledge, and it is effectively regarded as such both in China and in India ; like cosmology, which was studied in the West during the Middle Ages, as well as in the East, but which is ignored by modern philosophy, it is in fact, as we have already seen, only an application of metaphysical principles to a particular point of view and in a determinate sphere ; we will however return to this point later when dealing with the Hindu doctrines.

What has just been said concerning the relationship between metaphysic and logic will perhaps seem surprising to those who are accustomed to regard logic as in a sense dominating all possible knowledge, on the grounds that no speculation of any order whatsoever can be valid unless conforming strictly to its laws ; nevertheless it is quite evident that metaphysic, always by reason of its universality, can no more be dependent upon logic than upon any other science ; the error in that case may be said to consist in conceiving knowledge as lying solely within the sphere of reason. However, it is necessary at this point to make a distinction between metaphysic itself, as purely intellectual conception, and its formal expression ; while the former is entirely free from individual limitations, and therefore from those of reason, the latter, in the measure in which it is possible, can at best amount to a sort of translation of metaphysical truths into the discursive and rational mode, for the simple reason that the very constitution of all human language does not permit of its being otherwise. Logic, like mathematics, is exclusively a rational science ; metaphysical exposition may assume an analogous aspect with regard to its form, but with regard to its form only, and if it must then comply with the laws of logic, that is because these laws themselves rest on an essentially metaphysical basis, without which they would have no validity ; at the same time, however, if it is to possess a truly metaphysical bearing, this exposition must, as we have already shown, always be formulated in such a way as to leave open possibilities of conception as limitless as the domain of metaphysic itself.

As for morality, or ethics as it is now called, we have already partly explained what it implies in the course of our discussion of the constituent elements of religion, but we have yet to refer to its specifically philosophical conception, in so far as this is clearly distinguishable from the religious conception. There is nothing in the entire realm of philosophy more relative and contingent than ethics ; indeed it no longer even represents knowledge of a restricted order, being merely a more or less coherent mass of considerations the aim and scope of which can only be purely practical, notwithstanding the illusions too commonly cherished on this subject. In fact, it is solely a matter of formulating rules applicable to human action, the need for doing so moreover being found exclusively within the social order, since these rules would have no sense were it not for the fact that human individuals live gregariously, in more or less organised groups ; furthermore these rules, instead of being regarded from the purely social standpoint as is the case with the Orientals, are formulated in conformity with that specifically moral point of view which is foreign to the greater part of mankind. We have seen how it was possible for this point of view to find a place among religious conceptions, through a linking up of the social order with a doctrine that had been subjected to influences of a sentimental kind ;

but apart from this particular case, it is not easy to see wherein lies its justification.

Outside the religious viewpoint, which gives to ethics a legitimate meaning, everything connected with this order of things should logically be reduced purely and simply to a body of conventions, established and obeyed solely with the object of making social life possible and tolerable ; but if this conventional character of ethics were frankly recognised and acted upon accordingly, there would no longer be any question of philosophical ethics. It is sentimentality once again which has stepped in here, and which, in order to find material for the satisfaction of its own special needs, contrives to take these conventions and to cause them to be taken for other than what they really are ; hence the development of many different theories, some of which remain clearly sentimental in form as well as in substance, while others are disguised under a more or less rational appearance. Moreover, if ethics, like everything else bound up with social contingencies, vary greatly according to circumstances of time and place, the ethical theories making their appearance in a given society, however opposed they may appear to be on the surface, all alike tend to justify the very same practical rules, which are always those commonly observed in the society in question. This in itself should suffice to show that these theories are devoid of any real value, being built up by each individual philosopher solely as a belated justification for his own conduct and that of his fellow men—or at least of those who are most in sympathy with him—in accordance with his own views, and above all with his own feelings.

It is noticeable that ethical theories of this kind come to light chiefly during periods of intellectual decadence, doubtless because this decadence is itself correlated with or consequent on the expansion of sentimentalism, and perhaps also because, by plunging in this way into illusory speculations, at least a faint semblance of thinking is preserved. This phenomenon occurred notably amongst the Greeks, after their intellectuality had yielded up, with Aristotle, the last contribution of which it was capable ; in the later philosophical schools, such as the Epicurean and the Stoic, everything was subordinated to the moral point of view, and it was to this that they owed their success among the Romans, for whom all speculation of a higher order would have been difficult of attainment. The selfsame phenomenon has recurred at the present day, when "moralism" has become unusually rampant, but this time primarily through a degeneration of religious thought, as is clearly shown by the example of Protestantism ; it is natural, moreover, that those peoples whose mentality is purely practical, and whose civilization is wholly material, should seek to satisfy their sentimental aspirations through that false mysticism which finds one of its expressions in philosophical ethics.

We have now passed under review all those branches of philosophy which possess a clearly defined character; but the field of philosophical thought also contains a variety of more or less indeterminate elements which cannot properly be included under one or other of these headings, and which are not held together by any characteristics inherent in their own nature, but solely by reason of their being grouped within the same systematized conception. For this reason, after separating metaphysic completely from the so-called philosophical sciences, there is a further need to distinguish it no less radically from the many philosophical systems which most commonly originate, as we have already seen, from someone's attempt at intellectual originality ; the individualism expressed by such a pretension is manifestly opposed to the traditional spirit, and it is also incompatible with all conceptions of a truly metaphysical order.

Pure metaphysic necessarily excludes all systematization, because a system cannot avoid being a closed and limited conception, contained in its entirety within more or less narrowly defined boundaries, and as such is in no wise reconcilable with the universality of metaphysic ; besides, a philosophical system is always the system of some particular person, that is to say a construction the value of which can only be purely individual. Furthermore every system is necessarily erected upon some more or less special and relative foundation, being really nothing more than the development of a hypothesis, whereas metaphysic, which possesses the character of absolute certainty, cannot admit anything hypothetical. This does not mean to say that a system may not contain a certain element of truth in respect of this or that particular point ; but it is illegitimate in so far as it is a system, and it is in the systematic form itself that the radical falsity of the conception taken as a whole is inherent. Leibnitz was right in saying that " every system is true in what it affirms and false in what it denies," which really amounts to saying that its falsity is the greater in proportion as it is more narrowly limited or in other words systematic, since a conception of this kind leads inevitably to the negation of everything lying outside its scope. In all fairness this must be applied to Leibnitz himself, no less than to other philosophers, in so far as his own philosophy assumes a systematic character ; moreover such true metaphysic as it contains is borrowed from the Scholastics, and even this he has often distorted by failure to understand it aright. As regards the statement that a system is true in what it affirms, this should not be taken as the expression of any sort of eclecticism ; it simply amounts to saying that a system is true to the extent that it leaves the way open for less narrowly limited possibilities of conception ; this is indeed obvious, but it implies precisely the condemnation of the system as such. Metaphysic on the other hand, lying as it does outside and beyond relative things all of which belong to the individual order, for that very reason eludes all systematization, just as, for the same reason, it cannot be enclosed within any formula.

It should now be quite clear what we mean by the term pseudo-metaphysic : it includes everything in a philosophical system which lays claim to a metaphysical character, any such pretension being totally unjustified by reason of the systematic form itself, which is sufficient to rob theories of this kind of all real significance. Indeed, some of the problems commonly engaging the attention of philosophical thought appear to be deprived, not only of all importance, but of any meaning as well ; a host of problems arise resting solely upon some ambiguity or upon a confusion of points of view, problems which only exist in fact because they are badly expressed, and which normally should not arise at all. In most cases therefore, it would in itself be sufficient to set these problems forth correctly in order to cause them to disappear, were it not that philosophy has an interest in keeping them alive, since it thrives largely upon ambiguities. There exist a number of other questions also, belonging moreover to widely differing orders of ideas, which may quite justifiably be raised, but in regard to which a precise and exact formulation would lead to an almost immediate solution, the difficulties involved being much more verbal than real. If it happens that amongst these questions some are of such a nature as to be capable of having a certain metaphysical bearing, they lose this entirely upon inclusion within a system : it is not enough that a question should be of a metaphysical character, it is necessary in addition that, being recognized as such, it should be conceived and treated metaphysically. It is evident, in fact, that one and the same question may be treated from a metaphysical point of view or in a variety of other ways ; and whether the subjects to which the majority of philosophers have seen fit to devote themselves be considered interesting or not, one thing is certain, namely that there is nothing metaphysical about them. It is a matter at least for regret that the lack of clarity which is so characteristic of modern Western thought, and which is apparent quite as much in the ideas themselves as in their expression, by permitting as it does indefinite and random discussion without ever solving anything, leaves the way open for a mass of hypotheses, which certainly have the right to be called philosophical, but which have absolutely nothing in common with true metaphysic.

In this connexion, it may also be observed in a general way that questions which arise as it were accidentally, and only possess a particular and momentary interest, like many of those to be met with in the history of modern philosophy, are thereby clearly deprived of all metaphysical character, or in other words are lacking in the character of universality; moreover most questions of this kind usually fall into the category of problems enjoying a purely artificial existence. The truly metaphysical, let us repeat once more, can only be that which is absolutely stable, permanent and independent of all contingencies and in particular of historical contingencies; that alone is metaphysical which does not change, and it is also this universality of metaphysic which constitutes its essential unity, precluding the multiplicity of philosophical systems and religious dogmas alike, and hence which confers on it its profound immutability.

From all that has been said, it also follows that metaphysic bears no relation to conceptions such as idealism, pantheism, spiritualism and materialism, which are all stamped with the systematic character of Western philosophical thought; and this point is all the more important to note here since orientalists commonly suffer from the obsession of trying at all costs to force Eastern thought into these narrow frames which were never made for it; we shall have occasion later to draw special attention to the misuse thus made of these ineffectual labels or at least of some of them. For the moment there is only one point upon which it is necessary to insist, namely that the quarrel between spiritualism and materialism, around which almost all philosophical thought has revolved since the time of Descartes, has nothing to do with pure metaphysic ; here, in fact, is an example of one of those questions of a purely temporary nature to which we have previously referred. Actually the duality "spirit-matter" had never been put forward as absolute and irreconcilable prior to the Cartesian conception ; indeed the notion of matter, in the modern sense of the word, was completely foreign to the ancient peoples, the Greeks included, and it is still equally foreign to the majority of Orientals at the present day ; in Sanskrit no word exists even remotely answering to it. The conception of a duality of this kind has the sole merit of representing in a fairly adequate way the outward appearance of things ; but precisely because it stops short at appearances it remains entirely superficial and, being based on a special and purely individual point of view, it leads to the negation of all metaphysic as soon as an attempt is made to attribute an absolute value to it by affirming the irreducibility of its two terms—an affirmation which constitutes dualism in the proper sense of the word. Moreover the opposition between spirit and matter only represents one particular example of dualism, since the two terms of the opposition might well be quite other than these two relative principles, and it would be equally possible to imagine in the same manner an indefinite series of pairs of correlative terms besides this one, in reference to other more or less particularized determinations.

Speaking quite generally, dualism is characterized by the fact that it stops short at the antithesis between two more or less particular terms. This opposition doubtless really does exist from a certain point of view, and herein is to be found the element of truth that dualism contains ; but by treating it as irreconcilable and absolute, whereas it is really quite relative and contingent, all possibility of going beyond the two contrasted terms is precluded ; thus it is that dualism is seen to be limited by its own systematic nature. If this limitation is not accepted and there is a desire to resolve the opposition to which dualism clings so obstinately, it is possible to put forward several different solutions ; and two solutions do in fact appear in those philosophical systems which may be grouped together under the common heading of monism. It may be said that monism is essentially characterized by a refusal to admit the existence of an absolute irreducibility and a wish to surmount the apparent opposition, leading to an attempt to achieve this result by reducing one of the two terms to the other ; we therefore find, in the particuar case of the opposition between spirit and matter, spiritualistic monism on the one hand, which claims to reduce matter to spirit, and on the other hand materialistic monism, which claims on the contrary to reduce spirit to matter. Of whatever kind it may be, monism is right in maintaining that there is no absolute opposition, for in this respect it is less narrowly limited than dualism, and it represents at least an effort to penetrate further to the heart of things ; but it ends almost inevitably by falling into another error, through completely neglecting, if not altogether denying, the opposition in question which, even if only an appearance, none the less deserves to be recognized as such : here once again it is the exclusiveness of the system which is responsible for its principal defect. On the other hand, by wishing to reduce one of the two terms directly to the other, it is never possible to escape completely from the alternative set up by dualism, since nothing is considered outside those two terms, which are treated as its basic principles ; and seeing that these two terms are correlative, it might even be asked whether either has any justification for existing apart from the other, or if it is logical to preserve the one while suppressing the other. Indeed we find ourselves in the presence of two solutions which are really much nearer to being equivalent than they appear on the surface ; the fact that spiritualistic monism affirms that everything is spirit, whereas materialistic monism affirms on the contrary that everything is matter, is really of little importance, particularly since each finds itself obliged to attribute to the principle which it retains the most essential properties of the one it suppresses. It is evident that discussion between spiritualists and materialists carried out on this basis must rapidly degenerate into a mere battle of words : the two opposed monistic solutions represent in reality but two sides of a double solution, and one moreover that is wholly inadequate.

It is here that a different solution must be propounded : but whereas, with dualism and monism, we were only concerned with two different types of systematized conception of a purely philosophical order, we shall now be considering a doctrine the viewpoint of which, on the contrary, being a purely metaphysical one, has consequently received no name in Western philosophy, which can but ignore it. We will call this doctrine "non-dualism," or better still, the "doctrine of non-duality," in order to translate as exactly as possible the Sanskrit term *advaita-vāda*, which has no recognised equivalent in any European language. The first of these two expressions has the advantage of being more concise than the second, and for this reason we are quite prepared to adopt it; it is true that it suffers from the presence of the ending "ism," which in philosophical language is ordinarily attached to the names of systems, but it might justifiably be argued that the negation bears upon the word "dualism" in its entirety, including its ending, implying that the negation embraces dualism precisely in so far as it is a systematic conception. Non-dualism, while not admitting an absolute irreducibility any more than monism, differs profoundly from the latter in that it does not for this reason claim that one of the two terms of the opposition is purely and simply reducible to the other; both terms are considered simultaneously within the unity of a common but more universal principle, in which both are equally contained, no longer as opposites in the ordinary sense of the word, but as complements, by a kind of polarisation which in no wise affects the essential unity of this common principle.

Thus the intervention of the metaphysical point of view has the effect of immediately resolving the apparent opposition, and moreover it alone is able to accomplish this where the philosophical point of view has proved itself impotent to do so; and what is true of the distinction between spirit and matter, is equally true for any other of the distinctions, indefinite in number, which one might likewise choose to establish between various more or less special aspects of Being. If it is moreover possible to view simultaneously an indefinite series of such distinctions, all equally true and legitimate from their respective points of view, this is because we are no longer confined within a systematization limited to one of these distinctions to the exclusion of all the others; thus "non-dualism" is the only type of doctrine that corresponds to the universality of metaphysic. In general the various philosophical systems may be attached, in one respect or another, either to dualism or to monism; but non-dualism, such as we have described it in principle, is capable of immeasurably surpassing the scope of all philosophy, because it alone is genuinely and exclusively metaphysical in its essence, or in other words because it is an expression of the most essential and fundamental character of metaphysic itself.

If it has seemed necessary for us to develop these questions at such length, this is on account of the habitual ignorance existing in the West concerning everything connected with true metaphysic, and also because such considerations are directly connected with our subject, whatever some perple may choose to think, since it is metaphysic that is at the heart of all the doctrines of the East, so that it is impossible to understand anything at all about them without having acquired a notion of metaphysic sufficient at least to dispel all possible confusion. In tracing the wide difference separating metaphysical thought from philosophical thought, we have shown how the classical problems of philosophy, even those which it regards as most general, have literally no place at all in pure metaphysic: the transposition from one point of view to the other, which has moreover the effect of bringing to light the profound meaning of certain truths, causes these pretended problems quite simply to disappear, a clear indication that they possess no deep significance. On the other hand, these explanations have provided us with an opportunity for bringing out the meaning of "non-duality," an understanding of which, essential for all metaphysic, is not less indispensable in interpreting the Hindu doctrines in particular; this follows naturally from the fact that these doctrines are purely metaphysical in essence.

There remains one further remark to be made which is of the utmost importance: not only is it impossible to limit metaphysic by the consideration of any duality composed of complementary aspects of Being—whether it be a question of such special aspects as spirit and matter, or, on the contrary, of aspects that are as universal as they can be, such as those represented by the terms "essence" and "substance",—but it cannot even be limited by the conception of pure Being in all its universality, since it must not be limited by anything whatsoever. Metaphysic cannot be defined exclusively as "knowledge of Being," as Aristotle defined it: strictly speaking this is only ontology, which undoubtedly falls within the province of metaphysic, but which nevertheless does not constitute the whole of metaphysic ; and it is in this respect that the metaphysic of the West has always remained incomplete and insufficient, as also in another respect which will be indicated further on. Being is not really the most universal of all principles, as it would have to be for metaphysic to coincide with ontology, because even if Being is the most primordial of all possible determinations, it is none the less clearly a determination, and every determination is a limitation at which the metaphysical point of view cannot stop short. A principle obviously possesses proportionately less universality the greater its degree of determination, carrying with it a corresponding degree of relativity ; to use the language of mathematics, it may be said that a determinative "plus" is equivalent to a metaphysical "minus."

This absolute indetermination of the most universal principles, of those principles which should therefore be considered before all others, is a cause of considerable difficulty, not as regards their conception, except perhaps for those who are not accustomed to it, but at least in the exposition of the metaphysical doctrines relating to them, so that it often becomes necessary to resort to expressions which in their exterior form are purely negative. It is thus, for example, that the idea of the Infinite (which in reality is the most positive idea of all, since the Infinite can only be the absolute whole which, being limited by nothing, leaves nothing outside itself) can only be expressed by a term negative in form, because in language every direct affirmation is of necessity the affirmation of something, that is to say a particular and determinate affirmation ; but the negation of a determination or of a limitation is properly the negation of a negation, and therefore a real affirmation, so that the negation of all determination is equivalent in reality to affirmation total and absolute. What we have said of the idea of the Infinite can equally well be applied to many other extremely important metaphysical conceptions, but this example is sufficient for present purposes ; however it should never be forgotten that pure metaphysic is in itself absolutely independent of all the more or less imperfect terminologies in which we try to clothe it in order to make it more accessible to human understanding.

CHAPTER IX

Esoterism and Exoterism

In the course of our preliminary remarks we have had occasion to refer to the distinction which is fairly generally known to have existed in certain philosophical schools of ancient Greece, if not in all of them, between what is called esoterism and exoterism, that is to say between two aspects of a single doctrine, the one more interior and the other relatively exterior: such in fact is the whole literal meaning of these two terms. Exoterism, comprising the more elementary and easily understandable part of the teaching, which was consequently more readily brought within everybody's reach, is the only aspect to be expressed through the writings that have come down to us in a more or less complete form. Esoterism, being more profound and of a higher order, addressed itself as such only to regular disciples of the school who were specially prepared to receive it, and was the subject of a purely oral teaching, concerning which it has obviously not been possible to preserve very precise indications. Moreover, since we are here only concerned with a single doctrine regarded under two different aspects and having as it were two different levels of teaching, it should be clearly understood that these aspects could not in any way be opposed or contradictory, but must rather have been complementary to one another. The esoteric branch, by bringing to light the deeper meaning which the exoteric branch contained only virtually, developed and completed the doctrine which the latter had expounded in a rather vague, over-simplified and sometimes more or less symbolic form, although with the Greeks the symbol too often came to possess a purely literary and poetical character which caused it to degenerate into mere allegory. On the other hand, it goes without saying that within the school itself, esoterism was in its turn capable of being subdivided into several grades of teaching of varying profundity, the disciples passing successively from one grade to another according to their state of preparedness, with the possibility of going just as far as their intellectual aptitudes permitted ; but that is about all that can be said for certain.

This distinction between esoterism and exoterism has in no wise been maintained in modern philosophy, which is really nothing more than it appears to be on the surface, and which assuredly has no need of any sort of esoterism for what it teaches, since everything really profound totally escapes its limited viewpoint. Now the question arises whether this conception of two complementary aspects of a single doctrine was peculiar to Greece ; in truth, it would be very surprising if a division that seems so natural in principle had remained so exceptional, and in fact such is not the case. First of all, there are known to have existed in the West, since an early date, certain schools, generally very inaccessible and little known for that reason, which were in no sense philosophical schools ; their doctrines only found outward expression under the veil of certain symbols which necessarily remained very obscure to those who did not possess the key to them ; and this key was only given to adherents who had taken certain pledges, and who had given sufficient assurance of their discretion as well as of their intellectual capacity. This state of affairs, which manifestly implies the existence of doctrines sufficiently profound to be completely foreign to the common mentality, seems to have been especially prevalent during the Middle Ages, and this is one of the reasons why it is always necessary, when speaking of the intellectuality of that period, to make due reservations for anything that may then have existed over and above what is known to us for certain ; indeed, as in the case of Greek esoterism, it is evident that many things must have been lost through never having been taught otherwise than orally, a circumstance which, as we have already indicated, accounts also for the almost total disappearance of the doctrines of the Druids.

As an example of the schools just referred to, mention may be made of the alchemists, whose doctrines were primarily of a cosmological order, although cosmology must always have for its foundation a more or less extensive body of metaphysical conceptions. It might be said that the symbols contained in the alchemical writings constituted in this instance the exoteric aspect of the doctrine, while the interpretations set apart for the use of the adepts constituted the esoteric aspect ; but the part played by exoterism is in that case much reduced, and seeing that it has no real reason for existing except in relation to esoterism, it is even questionable whether these two terms can any longer be applied legitimately. In point of fact, esoterism and exoterism, being words comparative in form, are essentially correlatives, so that where there is no exoterism, there is no longer any occasion to speak of esoterism either ; the latter term, if one wishes to preserve to it its proper meaning, cannot therefore be applied indiscriminately to any and every doctrine which is set apart for the exclusive use of an intellectual elect.

It would no doubt be possible, though in a much wider sense, to envisage both an esoteric and an exoteric aspect in any particular doctrine, in so far as the conception is to be distinguished from its expression, the first being wholly interior while the second represents only an exteriorisation of it ; it may thus be said, though by straining the usual meaning of the words somewhat, that the conception represents the esoteric aspect and the expression the exoteric aspect, necessarily so and in a manner resulting from the very nature of things. Looked at in this way, there is something peculiar to metaphysical doctrines which must always be esoteric, and this is the inexpressible element which, as we have explained, all conceptions of a truly metaphysical order necessarily contain ; it represents something which each person can only conceive for himself, with the aid of words and symbols which simply serve as points of support for his conception, and his understanding of the doctrine will be more or less complete and profound according to the measure in which he will conceive it effectively. Even in doctrines of a different order, the meaning of which does not extend to what is really and truly inexpressible (which is the "mystery" in the etymological sense of the word), it is equally certain that the expression is never completely adequate to the conception, so that here also something analogous occurs, although on a much reduced scale; he who possesses true understanding is always the person who is able to see beyond the words, and it may be said that the "spirit" of any doctrine is of an esoteric nature, while the "letter" is exoteric. This is notably the case with all the traditional texts, which moreover usually present a plurality of meanings of varying profundity, corresponding to as many different points of view; but, instead of seeking to penetrate these meanings, people commonly prefer to devote themselves to barren exegetical researches and "textual criticism," following the methods laboriously worked out by the most modern scholarship; and such work, however wearisome it may be and whatever patience it may demand, is much easier than the other, for it at least lies within the reach of everyone's intelligence.

A noteworthy example of this plurality of meanings is furnished by the interpretation of the ideographic characters which go to make up Chinese writing. All the various meanings of which these characters are capable may be grouped around three principal ones corresponding to the three fundamental degrees of knowledge, the first belonging to the sensory order, the second to the rational order, and the third to the purely intellectual or metaphysical order; thus, to take a very simple case, the same character may be used analogically to represent at one and the same time the sun, light, and the truth, the context alone making it possible to know which of these meanings is to be adopted—whence manifold errors on the part of Western translators. It may be understood from this how the study of the ideograms, the real significance of which so completely escapes Europeans, can serve as the foundation for a truly integrated teaching, by permitting the development and co-ordination of all possible conceptions in all the different orders; this study can therefore be resumed from different standpoints at all the successive levels of instruction, from the most elementary to the most lofty, giving an opportunity each time for new possibilities of conception; it is therefore an instrument admirably adapted to the exposition of a traditional doctrine.

Let us return now to the question of whether the distinction between esoterism and exoterism, understood this time in the precise sense, is applicable to the Oriental doctrines. In the first place, in Islam, the tradition appears under a double form, religious and metaphysical, as we have already explained; the religious side of the doctrine, which is in fact the most exterior side and the one that lies within reach of all, may justly be qualified in this instance as exoteric, while the metaphysical side, which contains its innermost meaning, and which is moreover regarded as the doctrine of an elect, may be qualified as esoteric; the precise force of the distinction is well preserved here, since these are two sides of one and the same doctrine. It may also be noted that something analogous is to be found in Judaism, where esoterism is represented by what is called *Kabbala*, a word the primary meaning of which is simply "tradition," and which is concerned with the study of the more profound meanings of the sacred texts, while the exoteric or popular doctrine is confined to their most exterior and literal meaning. However, the *Kabbala* is in general less purely metaphysical than Moslem esoterism, and it remains to some extent affected by the influence of the strictly religious point of view, in which respect it is comparable to the metaphysical part of the Scholastic doctrine, which did not keep sufficiently free of theological considerations. In Islam, on the contrary, the distinction between the two points of view is usually very sharp, apart from the case of certain schools which are more or less tinged with mysticism, and in which orthodoxy is moreover less strict than that of the other esoteric schools ; it is possible to see here more clearly than anywhere else, by reason of the connexion between the exoteric and the esoteric side of the tradition, how theological conceptions can receive a deeper meaning through metaphysical transposition.

To pass now to the doctrines of more easterly traditions, the distinction between esoterism and exoterism can no longer be applied in the same fashion ; indeed in some cases it cannot even be applied at all. Doubtless in the case of China, it might be said that the social tradition, which is common to all, appears to be exoteric, while the metaphysical tradition, the doctrine of the elect, is esoteric as such. However, this would only be strictly exact if one were to consider these two doctrines in relation to the primordial tradition from which both are derived ; but notwithstanding this common source, they are in reality too sharply differentiated to be regarded as aspects of one and the same doctrine, which would have to be the case before one could speak of esoterism and exoterism. One of the reasons for this separation lies in the absence of that sort of combined domain associated with the religious viewpoint, in which a union takes place, in so far as this is possible, between the intellectual and the social points of view, always however at the expense of the purity of the former ; but the absence of such a domain does not always entail consequences so clearly marked as in China, and this is shown by the case of India, where there is similarly nothing that can properly be called religious but where all the branches of the tradition form none the less a single and indivisible whole.

It is precisely of India that it now remains for us to speak, and there least of all is it possible to make a distinction such as that between esoterism and exoterism, because the tradition is in fact too completely unified to appear either in two separate bodies of doctrine or even under two complementary aspects of this kind. The only distinction that can really be made is between the essential doctrine, which is wholly metaphysical, and its various applications, which constitute so many secondary branches of it ; but it is quite clear that this is in no way equivalent to the distinction we have in mind. The metaphysical doctrine itself provides no esoterism other than that which is inherent in it in the very wide sense we have already alluded to, and this is natural and inevitable in every doctrine of this kind : all may be admitted to the teaching in all its degrees, on the sole condition of being intellectually qualified to derive effective benefit from it. We are naturally speaking here only of admission to the different degrees of teaching, and not to the exercise of different functions, since other additional qualifications may be required in that respect ; but it necessarily happens that among those who receive the same doctrinal teaching, as among those who read the same text, each one understands it and assimilates it more or less completely and more or less profoundly according to the extent of his own intellectual possibilities. For these reasons it is quite incorrect to speak of "esoteric Brahmanism," as certain people have done, applying this denomination principally to the teaching contained in the *Upanishads ;* it is true that others, speaking in their turn of an "esoteric Buddhism," have made matters still worse, for under this label they have merely presented quite imaginary conceptions, derived neither from authentic Buddhism nor from any real esoteric doctrine.

In a text-book on the history of religions, which we have already referred to, and which, although distinguished from other works of the same kind by the spirit in which it is written, contains nevertheless many of the usual confusions and in particular that which consists in treating things as religious that cannot in any way be regarded as such, we have come across the following observation : "An Indian conception rarely finds its exact equivalent outside India ; or, to put it less broadly, ways of regarding things which elsewhere are esoteric, individual and extraordinary, are in Brahmanism and in India, common, general and normal."[1] This is fundamentally correct, but it calls nevertheless for certain reservations, since one can by no means qualify as individual, whether in India or elsewhere, conceptions which, being of a metaphysical order, are on the contrary essentially supra-individual. Moreover these conceptions find their equivalent, although under different forms, wherever a truly metaphysical doctrine exists, that is to say in all Eastern countries, and it is only in the West that there is nothing to be found corresponding to them even remotely. The truth is that conceptions of this kind are nowhere so widespread as in India, because nowhere else does a people exist endowed so generally and to such an extent with the requisite aptitudes, although these aptitudes are also commonly met with amongst all Orientals, notably amongst the Chinese, whose metaphysical tradition has nevertheless remained much more inaccessible. It is the purely traditional character of Hindu unity that has contributed more than anything else to the development of such a mentality; it is impossible really and effectively to participate in this unity without assimilating the tradition, and since the tradition is metaphysical in essence, it may be said that if every Hindu is naturally a metaphysician, he must be one almost by definition.

[1] *Christus,* Ch. VII, page 359, note.

CHAPTER X

Metaphysical Realization

When describing the essential features of metaphysic, we said that it constitutes an intuitive, or in other words, immediate knowledge, as opposed to the discursive and mediate knowledge which belongs to the rational order. Intellectual intuition is even more immediate than sensory intuition, for it is beyond the distinction between subject and object which the latter allows to subsist ; it is at once the means of knowledge and the knowledge itself, and in it subject and object are identified. Indeed, no knowledge is really worthy of the name except in so far as it has the effect of bringing about such an identification, although in all cases other than that of intellectual intuition this identification always remains incomplete and imperfect ; in other words there is no true knowledge except that which participates to a greater or less extent in the nature of pure intellectual knowledge, which is the supreme knowledge. All other knowledge, being more or less indirect, has at best only a symbolic or representative value ; the only genuinely effective knowledge is that which permits us to penetrate into the very nature of things, and if such a penetration may be effected up to a certain point in the inferior degrees of knowledge, it is only in metaphysical knowledge that it is fully and totally realizable.

The immediate consequence of this is that knowing and being are fundamentally but one and the same thing; they are, so to speak, two inseparable aspects of a single reality, being no longer even really distinguishable in that sphere where all is "without duality." This in itself is enough to show how purposeless are all the various "theories of knowledge" with metaphysical pretensions which occupy such a prominent place in modern Western philosophy, sometimes even going so far, as in the case of Kant for example, as to absorb, or at least to dominate, everything else. The only reason for the existence of such theories arises from an attitude of mind shared by almost all modern philosophers and originating in the Cartesian dualism; this way of thinking consists in artificially opposing knowing and being, an opposition which is the negation of all true metaphysic. Modern philosophy thus ends by wishing to substitute the theory of knowledge for knowledge itself, which amounts to an open confession of impotence on its part; nothing is more characteristic in this respect than the following declaration of Kant: "The chief and perhaps the only use of all philosophy of pure reason is, after all, exclusively negative, since it is not an instrument for extending knowledge, but a discipline for limiting it."[1] Do not such words amount purely and simply to saying that the only aim of philosophers should be to impose upon everyone else the narrow limits of their own understanding? Here we see an inevitable consequence of the systematic outlook, which, let it be repeated once more, is anti-metaphysical in the highest degree.

Metaphysic affirms the fundamental identity of

[1] *Kritik der reinen Vernunft,* ed Hartenstein, page 256.

knowing and being, which can only be questioned by those who are ignorant of the most elementary metaphysical principles ; and since this identity is essentially implied in the very nature of intellectual intuition, it not merely affirms it but realizes it as well. This is true at least of integral metaphysic ; but it must be added that such metaphysic as there has been in the West seems always to have remained incomplete in this respect. Nevertheless, Aristotle clearly laid down the principle of identification by knowledge, when he expressly declared that " the soul is all that it knows."[1] But neither he himself nor his successors ever seem to have given this affirmation its full significance, or to have extracted all the consequences implied in it, so that for them it has remained something purely theoretical. Certainly this is better than nothing, but it is nevertheless very inadequate, and thus Western metaphysic appears to have been doubly incomplete : it is already so theoretically, as previously explained, in that it does not proceed beyond Being ; on the other hand it only considers things, to the extent that it does consider them, in a purely theoretical light. Theory is regarded as if it were in some way self-sufficient, an end in itself, whereas it should normally be looked upon as nothing more than a preparation, indispensable as such we admit, leading to a corresponding realization.

It is necessary to say something at this point about the way in which we use the word " theory " : etymologically its primary meaning is " contemplation," and if it is taken thus, it might be said that metaphysic

[1] *De anima.*

in its entirety, including the realization which it implies, is theory in the fullest sense ; but usage has given the word a rather different and above all a much narrower meaning. In the first place, it has become usual to oppose theory and practice, and in its original sense, this antithesis, which meant the opposition of contemplation to action, would still be justifiable here, since metaphysic is essentially beyond the sphere of action, which is the sphere of individual contingencies ; but the Western mentality, being turned almost exclusively towards action and being unable to conceive of any realization outside the sphere of action, has come to oppose theory and realization in a general sense. It is therefore this last opposition that we shall in fact accept, so as not to depart from common usage and in order to avoid any confusion which might arise owing to the difficulty of separating these terms from the meaning which rightly or wrongly is ordinarily attached to them ; we will not go so far however as to qualify metaphysical realization as "practical," for in current speech this word has remained inseparable from the idea of action which it originally expressed, and which is in no wise applicable here.

In all doctrines that are metaphysically complete, as are those of the East, theory is always accompanied or followed by an effective realization, for which it merely provides the necessary basis ; no realization can be embarked upon without a sufficient theoretical preparation, but theory is ordained entirely with a view to this realization as the means towards the end, and this point of view is presupposed, or at least tacitly implied, even in the exterior expression of the doctrine. On the other hand, in addition to theoretical preparation and subsequent to it, other means of effective realization of a very different kind may be brought into play ; but these means also are destined simply to furnish a support or a point of departure, playing the part of "aids" only, however important they may be in actual practice : this is indeed the reason for the existence of rites possessing a genuinely metaphysical character and import, to which we have already alluded. However, these rites, unlike theoretical preparation, are never regarded as an indispensable means, since they are only accessory and not essential, and the Hindu tradition, where they nevertheless hold an important place, is quite explicit in this respect ; but they are capable none the less, by virtue of their own efficacy, of markedly facilitating metaphysical realization, that is to say the transformation of this virtual knowledge, which is all that theory amounts to, into effective knowledge.

Certainly these considerations are likely to appear very strange to Western people, who have never even considered the possibility of anything of this kind ; and yet, to be exact, a partial, though rather distant, analogy with metaphysical realization is to be found in the West in what may be called mystical realization. What we mean is that in the mystical states, using the word "mystical" in its current sense, there is present an effective element which makes of them something more than purely theoretical knowledge, although a realization of this nature is always inevitably limited. The very fact that such realization is of a purely religious character shows thereby that it is confined entirely to the individual domain ; the mystical states are in no way supra-individual, since they only imply a more or less indefinite extension of purely individual possibilities ; nevertheless these possibilities are incomparably greater than is commonly supposed, going far beyond anything that the psychologists in particular are capable of conceiving, notwithstanding all that they try to force into their idea of the "subconscious." Realization of this kind cannot have a universal or metaphysical bearing, and it always remains subject to the influence of individual elements, chiefly of a sentimental order ; this indeed is the essential characteristic of the religious point of view, only here it is more accentuated than anywhere else ; and it must furthermore be pointed out that the confusing of the intellectual and the sentimental orders is likely to prove a frequent source of illusions. Finally, it should be noted that this realization, always fragmentary and rarely controlled, does not presuppose any theoretical preparation : religious rites certainly do play the same part of "supports" in relation to it as is played elsewhere by the metaphysical rites, but in itself it is independent of religious theory, that is to say of theology ; nevertheless it can be said that those mystics who possess some theological knowledge are able to avoid many of the errors committed by others who lack it, and they are also to some extent more capable of controlling their imagination and sentimentality. Such as it is, mystical or religious realization, with its essential limitations, is the only mode of realization now known to the West ; as we have just said, this is by no means negligible, though nevertheless still far removed from true metaphysical realization.

It was necessary to give some description of the point of view of metaphysical realization, because it is essential to all Oriental thought and common to the three great civilizations of which we have spoken : nevertheless, we do not wish to dwell upon it to any great extent in the present work, which must necessarily remain rather elementary. We shall therefore only take it into consideration, when treating more particularly of the Hindu doctrines, in so far as it is unavoidable to do so, since, for the great majority of Western people, this point of view is probably more difficult to understand than any other. Furthermore, it should be added that if theory may always be expounded without reserve, or at least up to the point of meeting the truly inexpressible, the same cannot be said in respect of matters touching on realization.

PART III

THE HINDU DOCTRINES

CHAPTER I

On the Exact Meaning of the Word Hindu

Everything that has been said up to now might serve as a general introduction to the study of all Oriental doctrines; what follows will relate more closely to the Hindu doctrines in particular, adapted as they are to modes of thought which, while retaining those characteristics common to Eastern thought as a whole, also exhibit certain distinctive features of their own, with corresponding differences in the forms of expression. These differences arise even when strict identity exists with other traditions as regards the basis of the doctrine, which in fact must always remain the same when it is a question of pure metaphysic, for reasons we have already explained. At this point in our treatise it is important, before passing on to anything else, to indicate the exact meaning of the word "Hindu," for the more or less haphazard manner in which it has been used has given rise to frequent misunderstandings in the West.

In order to define clearly what is Hindu and what is not Hindu, we cannot avoid recalling briefly certain points which we have touched on already. In the first place, this word cannot denote a race, since it is applied without distinction to persons belonging to various races; still less can it denote a nationality, since nothing of the kind exists in the East. India considered as a whole is more comparable to the whole continent of Europe than to any single European state, not only because of its size or the numerical strength of its population, but also because of the variety of ethnical types to be found there ; from the north to the sóuth of India the differences are at least as great in this respect as from one extremity of Europe to another. Moreover, no governmental or administrative bond exists between the various regions, other than that recently established in an entirely artificial way by the Europeans. This administrative unity, it is true, had already been achieved before them by the Mughal emperors, and perhaps even before that by others, but it never had a more than transitory existence in relation to the permanence of Hindu civilization, and it is noteworthy that it was nearly always the result of a foreign domination, or in any case the work of non-Hindu influences ; furthermore it never went so far as completely to suppress the autonomy of the separate states, the intention being rather to include them in a federal organization. On the other hand, there exists nothing in India comparable to the kind of unity which is achieved elsewhere by the recognition of a common religious authority, which may either be represented by a single individual, as in Catholicism, or by a plurality of distinct functions, as in Islam. Though the Hindu tradition in no wise partakes of a religious character, there is yet no reason why it should not possess a more or less analagous organization, but such is not actually the case despite the gratuitous assumptions which certain people make in this respect, because they are unable to understand how unity can be effectively achieved simply by the inherent power of the traditional doctrine itself. That is certainly very different from anything obtaining in the West, but nevertheless it is a fact : Hindu unity, as we have already emphasized, is a unity of a traditional order purely and exclusively and has no need to depend upon any more or less exterior form of organization, or upon the support of any authority other than that of the doctrine itself.

From these facts the following conclusions may be drawn : Hindus are those who adhere to the Hindu tradition, on the understanding that they are duly qualified to do so really effectively, and not simply in an exterior and illusory way ; non-Hindus, on the contrary, are those who, for any reason whatsoever, do not participate in the tradition in question. This is, for example, the case of the Jains and the Buddhists; it is also, in more modern times, the case of the Sikhs, who moreover were subject to Moslem influences, the mark of which is clearly to be seen in their particular doctrine. Such is the true distinction, and there can be no other, although it is admittedly a rather difficult one for Western people to grasp, accustomed as they are to judging by quite different standards, which are entirely absent here. Under these circumstances it is absurd to speak, for example, of "Hindu Buddhism," as has actually been known to occur ; if one wishes to refer to Buddhism as it formerly existed in India, the only appropriate expression is "Indian Buddhism," just as one speaks of "Indian Moslems," that is to say the Moslems of India, who are in no sense Hindus. The true gravity of an error of the kind indicated above, and the reason why we look upon it as something more than a mere fault of detail, lies in the fact that it implies a profound misunderstanding of the essential nature of Hindu civilization ; but the remarkable thing is not that such ignorance should be widespread in the West, but that it should even have been known to occur among professional orientalists.

Certain evidences that we have already mentioned go to show that the tradition in question was brought to the country now known as India, at a comparatively remote date which it would be very difficult to determine exactly, by men who came from the North ; nevertheless it has never been proved that these men, who must have settled successively in various regions, ever formed what could properly be called a people, in the beginning at least, or that they belonged originally to a single race. At all events, the Hindu tradition, or at least the tradition now bearing this name—since it may at that time have had a different name or even have had no name at all—when it became established in India, was adopted sooner or later by the majority of the descendants of the indigenous populations ; the latter, the Dravidians for example, consequently became Hindus as it were by adoption, but once they had been admitted into the unity of the traditional civilization, they were just as genuinely Hindus as those who had always been so, even though some traces of their origin may still have persisted in the form of particular modes of thought and action, always provided that these were compatible with the spirit of the tradition.

Prior to its establishment in India, this particular tradition belonged to a civilization which we do not intend to call Aryan, having already explained why this word is devoid of meaning, but for which, in the absence of a better term, the name Indo-Iranian may be accepted, not because the place of development of the tradition is any more likely to have been in Iran than in India, but simply to indicate that it subsequently gave birth to two civilizations, distinct and even opposed in certain respects, namely the Hindu and the Persian civilizations. At some period or other therefore, a rupture must have occurred not unlike that brought about by Buddhism at a later date, and the separated branch, constituting a deviation from the primordial tradition, then became what is known as "Iranism," eventually destined to form the basis of the Persian tradition, known also as Mazdeism. We have already drawn attention to the tendency, often met with in the East, for such doctrines as were at first opposed to the regular tradition to become established in their turn as independent traditions; and there is no doubt that this happened in the case under consideration long before the tradition was codified in the *Avesta* under the name of *Zarathustra* or "Zoroaster," which moreover should not be taken for the name of a man but rather as denoting a collectivity, as is often the way in such cases: the examples of Fo-hi in China, Vyāsa in India and Thoth or Hermes in Egypt show this very clearly. On the other hand a very distinct mark of the deviation has survived in the Persian language itself, where certain words have taken on an exactly contrary meaning to the one they bore originally and which is the meaning they still preserve in Sanskrit; the word *deva* is the best known example, but it would be possible to cite others (such as the name *Indra*) which cannot be due to pure accident. The dualistic character usually attributed to the Persian tradition, if it were a fact, would also be a manifest proof of an alteration in the doctrine, though it must be stated that this character appears to have become attached to it only as the result of a false or incomplete interpretation ; another more serious proof consists in the presence of certain sentimental elements, but there is no need to insist upon this point here.

Starting from the moment when the separation of which we have just been speaking occurred, the regular tradition may properly be called Hindu, wherever the region may have lain in which it was first established and whether or not this name was actually given to it at that time. The use of this name, however, should on no account give rise to the idea that the tradition had undergone some profound and essential change ; any modifications that may from time to time have taken place are attributable merely to a natural and normal development of the primordial tradition. This leads us to point out another error committed by orientalists, who, understanding nothing of the essential immutability of the doctrine, have imagined the existence, subsequent to the Indo-Iranian period, of three successive and supposedly distinct doctrines, to which they give the names of Vedism, Brāhmanism and Hinduism respectively. If this classification were only intended to refer to three periods in the history of Hindu civilization, it would no doubt be admissible, notwithstanding the fact that the names are very inappropriate and that it is extremely difficult to fix the limits of these periods and to relate them chronologically. Even if it were only intended to state that the traditional doctrine, while always remaining fundamentally the same, received successively several more or less different forms of expression in order to adapt itself to the particular mental and social conditions of such and such a period, this again, with similar reservations, would be admissible. But this is not the sole contention of the orientalists : in using a plurality of denominations, they expressly assume a series of deviations or alterations, which are not only incompatible with traditional regularity, but have never existed save in their own imaginations.

In reality, the entire Hindu tradition is founded upon the *Veda* ; it always was so and has never ceased to be so ; it might therefore quite legitimately be called Vedism, and the name Brāhmanism also would be equally applicable to it at all periods. The name actually preferred is really a matter of little importance, provided one clearly understands that, under one or several names, it is always the same thing that is being referred to ; and this can only be the development of the doctrine contained in principle in the *Veda*, a word which literally means traditional knowledge without further qualification. There is therefore no such thing as Hinduism in the sense of a deviation from traditional thought, since that which is correctly and purely Hindu is just that which, by definition, admits of no such deviation ; and if, notwithstanding, certain more or less grave irregularities have sometimes occurred, the power of the tradition has always kept them within certain limits, or else has rejected them entirely from the unity of Hindu civilization, and in any case has prevented them from acquiring any real authority ; but to be properly understood, this calls for further explanation.

CHAPTER II

Perpetuity of The Veda

The name *Veda*, the proper meaning of which has just been explained, is applied in a general way to all the basic scriptures of the Hindu tradition ; these are divided into four collections known respectively as the *Rig-Veda*, the *Yajur-Veda*, the *Sāma-Veda* and the *Atharva-Veda*. The question of the date when these collections were composed is one of those that worry orientalists the most, and they have never managed to agree on its solution, even when confining themselves to a very approximate computation of their antiquity. Here as everywhere else may be observed the usual tendency to refer everything to a period as little remote in time as possible, and likewise to contest the authenticity of such and such parts of the traditional writings, the whole argument being based on a minute analysis of texts, accompanied by dissertations that are as endless as they are superfluous on the use of a word or of a certain grammatical form. These are in fact the habitual preoccupations of orientalists, and the general purpose, in the minds of those who occupy themselves with such things, is to show that the text under discussion is not as old as was believed, that it cannot be the work of the author to whom it had hitherto been ascribed (if indeed it ever had an author), or at least that it has been "interpolated" or has suffered some alteration or other at a comparatively recent date; anyone who is acquainted with the products of "Biblical criticism" can form a clear enough idea of the nature of these proceedings. It is hardly surprising that researches undertaken in such a spirit only lead to the piling up of volumes of tedious discussions, and that the pitiful results of this undermining "criticism," when they come to the knowledge of Orientals, contribute substantially to inspiring them with a contempt for the West. In fact, it is always questions of principle that escape the orientalists, and as it is precisely this knowledge which is essential to a proper understanding (seeing that everything else is derived from it and should logically be deduced from it), these scholars are led to neglect the one essential thing through their inability to grasp its primary importance; the consequence is that they lose their way hopelessly in a maze of the most insignificant details or in a tangle of quite arbitrary theorizing.

The question of the date when the different portions of the *Veda* may have been composed appears to be truly insoluble; it is not however a matter of any real importance because, prior to the more or less distant epoch when the text was written down for the first time, it is necessary to consider a period of oral transmission of indeterminate length, as we have already pointed out. It is probable that the origin of writing in India in fact dates from considerably earlier than is usually admitted; furthermore it is most unlikely that the Sanskrit characters have been derived from a Phœnician alphabet, which they resemble neither in shape nor arrangement. However that may be, one thing is certain, namely that nothing more than an ordering and final codifying of pre-existing traditional texts is to be seen in the work attributed to Vyāsa, a name which in reality does not refer to an historical person, still less to a "myth," but denotes an intellectual collectivity, as we mentioned before. This being the case, the determining of the epoch of Vyāsa, even admitting that such a thing were possible, is only of interest as a simple historical fact, devoid of any doctrinal implication; moreover it is obvious that this epoch may comprise a period of several centuries, or may even never have been completed, so that the question of its starting-point alone is open to discussion; this however does not mean that it can of necessity be answered, least of all by resorting to the methods favoured by Western scholarship.

The preceding oral transmission is often indicated in a text, though without the addition of any chronological data, by what is called the *vansha* or traditional filiation; this is the case for example in most of the *Upanishads*. As regards the origin, however, it is always necessary to refer back to a direct inspiration, likewise implied in the *vansha*, for here there is no question of an individual work; it makes little difference that the tradition has been expressed or formulated by such and such an individual, for this does not make him its author, given that the tradition belongs essentially to the supra-individual order. That is why the origin of the *Veda* is said to be *apaurusheya* or "non-human": historical circumstances exert no more influence on the essence of the doctrine than any other contingent factors, since it is endowed with an immutable and entirely timeless character, and it is moreover clear that the inspiration just referred to can manifest itself at any period. Perhaps the only difficulty here is to get Westerners to accept the theory of inspiration and especially to make them understand that this theory is neither mystical nor psychological, but can only be purely metaphysical ; to pursue this question would however necessitate developments which do not fit in with our present scheme. These few explanations should suffice to give at least some idea of what the Hindus mean when they speak of the perpetuity of the *Veda*. From another point of view this doctrine is also correlated with the cosmological theory of the primordial place of sound among the sensory qualities, though we cannot undertake to expound this theory here ; this last point may provide a clue to the fact that even after the adoption of writing, the oral transmission of the doctrine has always continued to play a preponderant part in India.

Since the *Veda* represents traditional knowledge unqualified, it therefore constitutes the principle and common basis of all the more or less secondary and derived branches of the doctrine ; and even in their case, the question of chronological development is of small importance. The tradition has to be considered in its entirety, and there is no point in asking which part of it is or is not primitive, since we are dealing with a perfectly coherent whole (which does not mean a systematic whole), and since all the points of view included in it can be considered simultaneously just as well as successively; consequently it is of no great interest to ascertain the historical order in which they were actually unfolded. Indeed such a proceeding is all the less interesting because one can do no more than trace the actual development of the points of view in question as formulated in those works which are available to us ; once one has learned to look beyond texts and has begun to penetrate further into the nature of things, one is bound to recognise that the various points of view have always been conceived as co-existing simultaneously in the unity of their principle ; that is why a traditional text is capable of manifold interpretations or applications corresponding to these different points of view. It is not possible to assign a definite author to this or that portion of the doctrine any more than to the Vedic texts themselves, in which the doctrine in its entirety is contained synthetically, at least in so far as it is capable of expression ; and if such and such a known author or commentator has expounded a certain more or less special point, that certainly does not imply that no one else had done so before him, and still less that no one had previously thought about it, even if until then it had not been formulated in a definite text.

Undoubtedly the exposition can be modified in its external form in order to be adapted to circumstances ; but—and we can never repeat it too often—the foundation always remains absolutely identical and its outward modifications in no wise touch or affect the essence of the doctrine. These considerations, by raising the question to the plane of principles, serve to show the chief reasons for the embarrassment of the chronologists, as well as the pointlessness of their researches; and since these reasons, which they are unfortunately unaware of, are inherent in the very nature of things, it would assuredly be better if they resigned themselves to the inevitable and stopped debating insoluble questions; indeed they would have no hesitation in following this course once they realized that these inquiries were without serious import: this is the point we were more particularly concerned to clear up in the present chapter, since it was not possible to treat the main theme fully and in its more profound aspects.

CHAPTER III

Orthodoxy and Heterodoxy

Orthodoxy and heterodoxy may be considered not only from the religious standpoint, as is usually the case in the West, but also from the much more general standpoint of tradition in all its modes; indeed, with regard to India it is only in the latter way that it is possible to understand these terms, since nothing of a properly religious nature exists there, whereas in the West, on the contrary, there is nothing genuinely traditional outside religion. So far as metaphysic and everything which derives more or less directly from it is concerned, the heterodoxy of a conception is at bottom nothing more or less than its falsity, resulting from its disagreement with fundamental principles; more often than not this falsity even appears as a manifest absurdity, once the question is reduced to essentials: it could hardly be otherwise, since metaphysic, as we have already explained, excludes everything of a hypothetical character, only admitting those things the comprehension of which involves immediate certitude. Under these circumstances, orthodoxy becomes one with true knowledge, since it consists in an unbroken accord with the principles; and since these principles, in the case of the Hindu tradition, are contained in essence in the *Veda*, it is evidently agreement with the *Veda* that is here the criterion of orthodoxy. Only it should be understood that it is not so much a question of having recourse to the authority of the written texts, as of observing the perfect coherence of the traditional teaching as a whole; agreement or disagreement with the Vedic texts is after all only an exterior sign of the intrinsic truth or falseness of a conception; it is this truth or falseness which really constitutes its orthodoxy or heterodoxy. It will be objected perhaps that if this is so, then why is it not sufficient to speak quite simply of truth or falsity? The reason is that the unity of the traditional doctrine, with all the power inherent in it, furnishes the most trustworthy guide for preventing individual aberrations from being carried too far; moreover the influence diffused by the tradition itself is sufficient for this purpose, without there being a need for the restraining influence of any authority more or less analogous to a religious authority: this follows from what has been said on the subject of the real nature of Hindu unity. The confusion brought about by an unbridled development and expansion of the most hazardous and contradictory opinions, in circumstances where this power of the tradition is lacking and where there is not even an external authority able in some measure to take its place, is illustrated only too well by the example of modern Western philosophy; if false conceptions arise so easily in the West and even succeed in forcing themselves upon the minds of the people in general, it is because a reference to principles is no longer possible, since no principles in the true sense of the word are any longer recognized. On the contrary, in an essentially traditional civilization, the principles are never lost sight of and it only remains to apply them, directly or indirectly, in whatever sphere it is desired to do so. Consequently deviations occur much more rarely and are even exceptional; if they do nevertheless arise sometimes, they are never very widely accredited: they always remain the anomalies they were in the first instance, and if they become serious to the point of incompatibility with the most essential principles of the tradition, they finish by being rejected on this account from the civilization in which they arose.

To illustrate the point just mentioned we will take the case of atomism, to which we shall also have to refer again later: this conception is clearly heterodox, since it is in formal disagreement with the *Veda*, and furthermore its falsity may easily be demonstrated since it contains certain self-contradictory elements; fundamentally, therefore, heterodoxy and absurdity are really synonymous. In India, atomism appeared first of all in the cosmological school of Kanāda, and it may be noted here that it would hardly be possible for heterodox conceptions to arise in the schools devoted to purely metaphysical speculation, because in the realm of principles absurdity is much more immediately apparent than in the realm of secondary applications. So far as the Hindus are concerned this atomist theory never represented anything but a simple anomaly of no great importance, so long at least as nothing more serious came to be added to it; thus it only enjoyed a very limited success, especially in comparison with the influence it was to acquire later with the Greeks, where, because the traditional principles were already in default, it was readily accepted by various schools of "physical philosophy"; Epicureanism, in particular, gained for it a widespread recognition, giving it an influence which is still to be felt in the modern West.

To return to India, atomism was at first only put forward as a special cosmological theory, therefore quite limited in its scope; but for those who accepted this theory, heterodoxy on that particular point logically entailed heterodoxy on many other points also, since everything is closely linked together in a traditional doctrine. Thus, the conception of atoms as constitutive elements of things has as its corollary the idea of a void in which these atoms can move; there was therefore a likelihood of a theory of "the universal void" arising sooner or later, this expression being taken not in a metaphysical sense as referring to the Unmanifest, but on the contrary in a physical or cosmological sense. That is what actually happened in certain Buddhist schools, which came to identify this void with *ākāsha* or ether. Thence they were naturally led on to a denial of the existence of ether as a corporeal element, so that they no longer admitted five, but only four such elements. It must also be noted, in this connection, that the majority of the Greek philosophers also admitted only four elements, like the Buddhist schools in question ; if, nevertheless, some of them spoke of ether, they only did so in a rather restricted sense, giving it a much more special and also much less clear acceptation than the Hindus.

We have already indicated to which side borrowing must be attributed when concordances such as this come to be noticed, especially when the borrowing is made in an incomplete form, which is perhaps the most revealing evidence of all. It cannot be objected that the Hindus "invented" ether at a subsequent date for more or less plausible reasons analogous to those which cause it to be fairly generally accepted by modern physicists. In the first place, their reasons are of quite another order and are not the result of experiment ; moreover, as we have already explained, there is no such thing as an "evolution" of traditional conceptions, and the testimony of the Vedic texts is in fact just as explicit on the subject of ether as of the four remaining corporeal elements. It seems therefore that the Greeks, when they came into contact with Hindu thought, in many cases only received that thought deformed and mutilated, and moreover it is probable that they did not always expound it exactly as they had received it ; it is also possible, as we mentioned before, that in the course of their history they were in closer and more continuous touch with some of the Buddhists than with the Hindus.

However that may be, it must be understood, as regards atomism, that its principal danger lies in the fact that it can easily be made to serve as the foundation of a "naturalism" which runs entirely counter to the ways of Oriental thought, though it frequently appears in Western conceptions, under more or less explicit forms; in fact it can be said that if all naturalistic theories are not necessarily atomic, atomism is always more or less naturalistic, at least in tendency. When it is incorporated in a philosophical system, as it was with the Greeks, it even becomes mechanistic, which does not necessarily mean materialistic, for materialism is something entirely modern. This is of little importance here, however, since in India there is no question of philosophical systems any more than of religious dogmas; even the deviations of Hindu thought have never been either philosophical or religious in nature, and this also holds good of Buddhism even though, in all the East, its doctrine is the one which at first sight might appear to approach closest to Western points of view in certain respects; and that is the very reason why it lends itself all the more easily to those false assimilations that are so dear to orientalists. For this reason, although the study of Buddhism does not really form part of our subject, we must nevertheless say a few words about it, if only to dispel certain confusions that are commonly entertained in the West.

CHAPTER IV

Concerning Buddhism

Compared with other doctrines of the East, Buddhism, as we have just explained, in some ways appears to be nearer to, or shall we say less remote from Western conceptions, and causes it to be regarded as an easier field of study for Westerners ; this also probably accounts for the marked preference displayed towards it by orientalists. The latter do in fact believe that there is to be found in Buddhism something that can be made to fit into the framework of their own outlook, or at any rate something that does not lie entirely outside it, since here they do not encounter a barrier of utter incomprehensibility as happens with the other doctrines, an obstacle which they must sense vaguely even if they do not admit it openly. At least this is the feeling they experience when studying certain forms of Buddhism, for, as we shall show presently, there are many distinctions to be made even in this respect ; and it is perhaps natural that they should be at pains to prove that those forms which they find most accessible represent the primitive and true Buddhism, whereas the remaining forms, according to them, are but comparatively late corruptions.

But Buddhism of whatever kind it be and even under the most "simplified" aspects that may have been displayed by certain of its subdivisions, remains none the less an Oriental doctrine ; besides, the orientalists go much too far in discovering assimilations with Western points of view, for example when they wish to turn Buddhism into the equivalent of a religion in the European sense of the word, an intention which furthermore sometimes lands them in a strange embarrassment : for have not some of them, without recoiling from a contradiction in terms, declared

Buddhism to be "an atheistical religion"? In reality however, it is no more "atheistical" than it is "theistic" or "pantheistic"; all that need be said of it is that it does not adopt a point of view where these various terms have any meaning; but if it does not do so, it is precisely because it is not a religion. Thus by their interpretations the orientalists succeed in distorting even those features which might appear to be least foreign to their mentality and this they do in more ways than one, for when they would make a philosophy of Buddhism they scarcely denature it more than when they attempt to turn it into a religion; for instance when they speak of "pessimism," as often happens, it is not Buddhism that is thus qualified or rather it is only Buddhism as viewed through the philosophy of Schopenhauer; authentic Buddhism is neither pessimistic nor optimistic, for things are not really regarded by it in this fashion; but certain people doubtless find it annoying not to be able to attach Western labels to every doctrine.

The truth is that Buddhism is neither a religion nor a philosophy, although, in comparison with the Hindu traditional doctrines, it comes closer to both in some respects, especially in the case of those forms of it which find most favour with orientalists. In point of fact these forms belong to schools which, having cut adrift from the regular tradition and having in consequence lost sight of the real metaphysic, were inevitably led into substituting for it something resembling the philosophical point of view in a certain measure, but only in a certain measure. One may even occasionally come across speculations which, if examined superficially, might seem to suggest psychology ; but, quite clearly, they do not belong to psychology as we know it, for the latter is an entirely Western invention and even in the West it is quite recent, since it actually goes no further back than Locke; it would be wrong to attribute to the Buddhists an outlook which arose specifically out of the modern empiricism of the Anglo-Saxons. For the comparison to be legitimate it must not proceed as far as an assimilation ; and likewise, where religion is concerned, Buddhism is not effectively comparable to it except as regards a single feature, of importance no doubt, but not sufficiently so to establish an identity of thought : the feature referred to is the appearance in it of a sentimental element, which however can in any case be explained by the need for adaptation to the special conditions of the period that saw the birth of those doctrines that were affected by it ; this fact is therefore far from implying that all doctrines of this kind necessarily fall into one and the same category. A real difference of points of view can be much more essential than a resemblance which, after all, chiefly affects the forms of expression of the doctrines concerned ; this is the point that is missed by those who speak of "Buddhist morality" : what they mistake for a moral code, all the more easily since its sentimental side might render such a confusion plausible, is really viewed from a totally different angle and springs from quite other causes which are not even of an equivalent order : the well-known formula "may beings be happy" concerns the universality of beings without any restriction, and not human beings alone ; this is an extension which the moral point of view, even by definition, in no wise admits of. The Buddhist " compassion " is not the same thing as Schopenhauer's " pity " ; rather should it be compared to the " cosmic charity " of the Moslems, which is moreover quite capable of being transposed outside all sentimentalism. However it must be recognised that Buddhism is beyond question invested with a certain sentimental form which, though it does not go to the point of " moralism," nevertheless constitutes one of the characteristic elements of the Buddhist doctrines ; this should be borne in mind, especially as it is one of the features that sharply distinguish Buddhism from the Hindu doctrines ; it is the presence of this element which also goes to show that Buddhism is farther removed than Hinduism from the tradition in its " primordial " state.

Another point can usefully be noted in the same connection, namely, that there is a fairly close link between the sentimental form of a doctrine and its tendency to wide diffusion, a tendency that is to be found both in the religions and in Buddhism, as is proved by its expansion over the greater part of Asia ; but here again, likenesses should not be over-stressed, and it is perhaps not quite accurate to speak of Buddhist " missionaries " who went out from India at certain periods, for apart from the fact that here one is only dealing with a small number of isolated individuals, the word " missionary " is almost bound to call to mind methods of propaganda and proselytism which are peculiar to Westerners. What is furthermore remarkable is the fact that alongside this process of distant diffusion, Buddhism was losing ground in India itself, till it finally disappeared from that country altogether, after having in its last stages given birth, incidentally, to certain degenerate and clearly heterodox schools which are frequently referred to in Hindu works contemporary with this closing phase of Indian Buddhism ; the writings of Shankarāchārya, for example, never mention these schools except in order to refute their theories in the name of the traditional doctrine, without however ascribing any of their errors to the founder of Buddhism himself, which goes to prove that it was nothing more than a case of degeneration. Strange to say, it is precisely such shrunken and aberrant forms which, in the opinion of a considerable number of orientalists, are supposed to represent as nearly as possible the true original Buddhism.

We shall return to this point later ; but before proceeding further it is important to state quite plainly that India never was really Buddhist, contrary to a commonly expressed opinion, which would make of Buddhism the very pivot of all that affects India and its history : India before Buddhism, India after Buddhism—such is the clear division that orientalists believe themselves to have established, implying by this statement moreover that Buddhism, even after its complete disappearance, left behind it a deep impression on the lands of its origin, which is untrue for the reasons we have just given. It is true that these writers, who fancy that the Hindus must have borrowed from Greek philosophy, are equally capable of maintaining, with no greater degree of probability, that they also are indebted to Buddhism ; and we are not quite sure whether such is not perhaps the substance of their thought. It must however be admitted that there have been some honourable exceptions ; thus Barth declared that "Buddhism only had the importance of an episode," a statement that is strictly accurate as far as India is concerned ; but nevertheless, contrary opinions have not ceased to prevail among scholars, not to mention the complete ignorance of the European public, which is even sometimes led to believe that Buddhism still actually reigns in India. The truth of the matter is that about the time of King Ashoka, that is to say towards the Third Century B.C., Buddhism in India enjoyed a period of wide extension, while at the same time it was beginning to overflow outside India, this period being moreover quickly followed by that of its decline ; but even during that period, if one wished to discover some parallel in the Western world, one would have to say that this extension was rather comparable to the spread of a monastic order than to the propagation of a religion addressing its message to the whole body of a population ; this comparison, though not perfect, is probably the least inexact of all.

But we have not yet done with all the fantasies of the orientalists ; we find some of them, like Max Müller, claiming to discern the germs of a Buddhism imagined after their own fashion, that is to say the germs of heterodoxy, even in the *Upanishads*[1] which, forming as they do an integral portion of the *Veda*, are therefore among the essential foundations of Hindu

[1] *The Upanishads,* Volume II, Introduction, pages xxvi-xxvii and l-lii.

orthodoxy ; it would indeed be difficult to push absurdity further or to give proof of greater incomprehension. Whatever picture may be formed of Buddhism, it is nevertheless quite easy to understand that it must always have shared many features with Hinduism, even after it had separated from it, given the fact that it arose in a Hindu environment and was in a way an offshoot of Hinduism, and it is this fact which fully explains whatever is found to be common to both ; M. Roussel has doubtless exaggerated in an opposite direction by insisting on the complete lack of originality of the Buddhist doctrine, though his opinion is more plausible than Max Müller's and at least expresses no contradiction ; and it should be added that this opinion would express praise rather than criticism for those who, like ourselves, take up the traditional standpoint, since differences between doctrines, in order to be legitimate, can only be a mere matter of adaptation, modifying the more or less external forms of expression but in no wise touching the principles themselves ; the introduction of the sentimental form is itself only a case in point, always provided that it allows metaphysic to be preserved intact at the centre of the doctrine.

Having said this much, we must now ask ourselves how far it is justifiable to refer to Buddhism in general terms, as is customary, without incurring the danger of various misunderstandings ; in order to avoid them, it is on the contrary necessary to make clear which Buddhism is being referred to, for in point of fact it included and still does include a large variety of branches and schools and one must beware of attributing to all indiscriminately features that are really confined to one or other among them. These schools, viewed as a whole, can be made to fall under the two main headings of *Mahāyāna* and *Hīnayāna*, titles which are usually translated by " Greater Vehicle " and " Lesser Vehicle," but which would perhaps both more exactly and more clearly be rendered by the names " Great Way " and " Little Way " ; it is much better to keep these names, which are the ones they bear authentically, than to replace them by epithets such as " Northern " or " Southern " Buddhism, which have only a geographical bearing, rather vague at that, and which do not in any way describe the doctrines concerned. It is the *Mahāyāna* which can unquestionably be regarded as constituting a complete doctrine in the fullest sense, including the properly metaphysical elements which go to form its higher or central part ; on the other hand, the *Hīnayāna* appears to be a doctrine that in some ways stops short at comparatively external aspects without proceeding beyond those things that are accessible to the ordinary run of people, and this accounts for the name it has been given ; it is but natural that this more restricted branch of Buddhism, of which the Buddhism of Ceylon is the most typical present-day representative, should have given rise to the deviations we referred to earlier on. It is here that the orientalists really reverse the normal relations, for they will insist that the most aberrant schools, those which have carried heterodoxy furthest, are the most authentic expressions of the *Hīnayāna* and that the *Hīnayāna* itself is really the primitive form of Buddhism or at least its regular continuation, to the exclusion of the *Māhayāna* which, according to them, is but the product of a series of alterations and borrowings. In upholding this opinion they do no more than obey the anti-traditional trend of their own mentality which prompts them naturally to sympathise with all that is heterodox ; more particularly they conform to the false conception, held pretty generally by modern Westerners, that whatever is simplest, one might even say most rudimentary, must always for that reason pass for being most ancient ; with such prejudices, it does not so much as cross their minds that the truth might be the exact opposite. Under the circumstances one might well ask what sort of a weird caricature has been represented to Westerners as being the real Buddhism, such as its founder preached, and one can almost smile at the idea that this travesty has become an object of admiration for many people in the West, who have been so fascinated by it that some have not even hesitated to proclaim their conversion—a conversion moreover which remains quite theoretical and "ideal"—to this Buddhism which they discover to be so extraordinarily similar to their own "rationalist" and "positivist" outlook !

Of course, when one says that the *Māhayāna* should be included in Buddhism from the beginning, this must only be taken as referring to what might be called its essence, independently of the more or less special forms belonging to its various schools ; these forms are only secondary, but they are all that the "historical method" allows itself to take into account and it is this fact which lends an appearance of justification to the statements of the orientalists when they try to argue that the *Māhayāna* is "late" or that it only represents an "altered" form of Buddhism. The question is further complicated by the fact that Buddhism, when it came out of India, was modified considerably and in several different ways, as indeed it was bound to be modified in order to adapt itself to quite different surroundings; all that is important is to know how far these modifications go, a question that does not seem very easy to decide, especially for those who have practically no idea of the traditional doctrines with which it came into contact. This applies especially to the Far East, where Taoism clearly has influenced certain branches of the *Māhayāna*, at least as regards their modes of expression; the school of *Zen*, in particular, adopted methods which are quite plainly of Taoist inspiration. This fact finds its explanation in the special character of the Far Eastern tradition, with the sharp cleavage existing between its two portions, inner and outer, that is to say between Taoism and Confucianism; under these conditions Buddhism appears to have been called upon to occupy a realm intermediate between the two; in certain cases it even seems to have provided what was really an "outer covering" for Taoism, thus allowing the latter to remain a very closed preserve much more easily than would otherwise have been the case. This also explains how Far Eastern Buddhism came to assimilate certain symbols of Taoist origin, as for example when it identified *Kuan-yin* with a *Bodhisattva* or, to be more exact, with a feminine aspect of *Avalokiteshwara*, by reason of the "providential" function common to both; and this, be it noted, has been the occasion of a further mistake on the part of some orientalists, who as regards

Taoism as often as not know little more than its bare name ; they were led into believing that *Kuan-yin* properly belonged to Buddhism, and they seemed to ignore her essentially Taoist origin completely.

Furthermore, whenever they come across something of which the character or the origin cannot be exactly determined by them, it is quite in accordance with their mental habits to settle the difficulty by attaching to it a Buddhist label ; this provides a rather convenient means of disguising their conscious or unconscious embarrassment and they have recourse to it all the more readily because, in virtue of the practical monopoly of information that they have succeeded in acquiring, they are pretty sure that no one is going to contradict them ; what fear of criticism can people feel who start off by laying down the principle that, in the line of study concerned, no real competence is admissible except such as is to be gained in their own school ? Moreover it goes without saying that all those things that they thus label as Buddhist to their heart's content, as well as those things that really are Buddhist, represent in their eyes nothing but a "corrupted Buddhism." In a manual of the history of religions that we have already quoted, containing a chapter on China that in very many ways reveals a most regrettable lack of understanding, it is stated that "of primitive Buddhism there is no longer a trace in China" and that the doctrine now to be found there "retains nothing of Buddhism but the name"[1]; if by this primitive Buddhism is meant that which orientalists put forward as such, the statement is quite correct, but first of all

[1] *Christus,* Chapter IV, page 187.

it would be necessary to decide whether their conception of it is acceptable or whether, on the contrary, it is that conception which in actual practice represents nothing but a corrupted Buddhism.

The question of the relations of Buddhism and Taoism is comparatively easy to settle, provided of course that one knows something about Taoism ; but it must be admitted that there are also other and more difficult problems : this is especially true when one is no longer dealing with elements belonging to traditions foreign to India, but actually with Hindu elements, concerning which it may be hard to tell whether they were always more or less clearly associated with Buddhism in virtue of its Indian origin, or whether they came to be integrated into certain of its forms after the event. This applies, for instance, to the Shivaite elements that occupy so large a place in Tibetan Buddhism, the form which is commonly known by the rather misleading name of " Lamaism " ; this feature is moreover not confined exclusively to Tibet, since in Java a *Shiva-Buddha* is to be met with, exemplifying a similar association but carried this time to the farthest possible limit. In fact, a solution of this question might be arrived at through a study of the relations between Buddhism, even at the outset, with the Tantric doctrines ; but the latter are so little known in the West that it would be almost impossible to consider them without being led off into lengthy discussions than can find no place here ; we will therefore stop short at the mere suggestion, for the same reason that decided us, when writing the chapter on the main divisions of the East, to confine ourselves to a passing mention of the Tibetan civilization, despite its great importance.

One last point now remains to be discussed at least in brief: for what reason did Buddhism expand so far and with such success outside its original country, whereas in that same country it declined so rapidly till it disappeared entirely? Does not this diffusion outside India constitute the real justification of Buddhism itself? What we mean to say is that Buddhism seems to have been really destined for non-Indian peoples; nevertheless it was necessary for it to arise out of Hinduism itself, in order that it might be the recipient of those elements that were to be carried elsewhere after undergoing the required process of adaptation; but this task once accomplished, it was but natural for it to disappear from India where it had no enduring task to fulfil: in this particular respect, but in this respect only, it would not be altogether unreasonable to compare the situation of Buddhism with regard to Hinduism, with that of Christianity in relation to Judaism, on condition, of course, of constantly bearing in mind those differences of points of view which we stressed earlier on. In any case, this consideration is the only one which permits of recognising in Buddhism, without falling into an illogicality, the character of a traditional doctrine, a character which the *Mahāyāna* at least undeniably possesses—for one must equally be ready to admit the heterodoxy of certain late and deviated forms of the *Hīnayāna*; and it is also the same reasons that explain what the mission of the Buddha himself really was. Had he taught the heterodox doctrines attributed to him by orientalists it would be impossible to explain the fact that a large number of orthodox Hindus do not hesitate to look on him as an *Avatāra*, that is to say as a "divine manifestation," a function of which the records of his life in fact reveal all the characteristic features; it is true that the orientalists, who make a point of excluding whatever belongs to the "non-human" order, maintain that the events of his life are only part of "a legend," that is to say a story devoid of any historical value, and that these legendary features are also foreign to "primitive Buddhism"; but if these features are done away with, what after all remains of the founder of Buddhism in the sense of a purely human individuality? It would indeed be hard to say; but Western "criticism" makes no bones over so small a matter, and in compiling a life of the Buddha according to its own views, it goes so far as to lay it down as a principle, following Oldenberg, that the "Indo-Germans" do not admit miracles; it is difficult to keep serious in the face of such assertions. This so-called "historical reconstitution" of the Buddha's life is worth about as much as that of his "primitive" doctrine, and is entirely a product of the same prejudices; in either case the principal aim is the suppression of anything that offends the modern outlook, and it is by means of this eminently naive proceeding that these people hope to arrive at the truth.

We will say no more on the subject, since Buddhism is not the object of our present study; it is sufficient to have "situated" it on the one hand with regard to the Hindu doctrine and on the other in relation to those Western theories which people have tried to assimilate to it with greater or less abuse. Having digressed thus far we can now return to the examination of properly Hindu conceptions, but before doing so we will permit ourselves one last comment which can serve as a conclusion to all that has been said above : if orientalists have fallen into such grave errors on the subject of Buddhism, in which they have so to speak "specialised," what value is to be attached to their statements concerning other doctrines which, compared with Buddhism, have been regarded by them as secondary and almost incidental objects of study ?

CHAPTER V

The Law of Manu

As an example of the kind of idea that is apt to cause confusion in the minds of Western people, through the absence of any equivalent term in their own vocabulary, one might cite the conception denoted by the Sanskrit word *dharma* ; orientalists have certainly proposed any number of translations for the word, but most of these are only rough approximations or even completely erroneous, owing as usual to the confusion of points of view which we have alluded to before. Thus attempts are sometimes made to translate *dharma* by "religion," though the religious point of view is here quite inapplicable ; furthermore it should at the same time be realized that it is not the conception of a doctrine, wrongly supposed to be religious, that this word properly designates. On the other hand, if it be a question of the accomplishment of rites, which likewise are not religious in character, these are described in their entirety by the word *karma*, the general meaning of which is "action," but which is here taken in a special and, as it were, technical sense. For those who wish at all costs to see a religion in the Hindu tradition, there would still remain what they believe to be a moral aspect, and it is this more especially that they would call *dharma* ; hence, according to circumstances, several more or less secondary interpretations have arisen, such as "virtue," "justice," "merit" and "duty," all of which are in fact exclusively moral ideas and for this very reason do not in any way express the idea in question. The moral point of view, apart from which these ideas have no meaning, does not belong to India ; we have already sufficiently insisted on this point, and we have even observed that Buddhism, which alone might perhaps have been thought likely to introduce it, never made any such advance along the path of sentimentality. Furthermore, we may note in passing that these same ideas are not all equally essential to the moral point of view itself ; that is to say, there are some of them which are not common to all moral conceptions : for example, the idea of duty or obligation is absent from most ancient codes of morality, among others from that of the Stoics, and it is only recently, and especially since Kant, that it has come to play such a preponderant part. An important thing to notice in this connexion, since it is one of the most frequent sources of error, is that ideas or points of view which have become habitual tend for that very reason to appear essential ; that is why attempts are made to introduce them into the interpretation of every kind of conception, even those most remote in time or space, although there would often be no need to go back very far to discover their real source.

Having said this much by way of dealing with the false interpretations most commonly met with, we will try and show as clearly as possible what should really be understood by *dharma*. As the meaning of the verbal root *dhri*, from which it is derived, indicates, this word, in its most general sense, simply denotes "manner of being"; it is, so to speak, the essential nature of a being, comprising the sum of its particular qualities or characteristics, and determining, by virtue of the tendencies or dispositions it implies, the manner in which this being will conduct itself, either in a general way or in relation to each particular circumstance. The same idea may be applied, not only to a single being, but also to an organized collectivity, to a species, to all the beings included in a cosmic cycle or state of existence, or even to the whole order of the Universe; it then, at one level or another, signifies conformity with the essential nature of beings, which is realized in the ordered hierarchy where all beings have their place, and it is also, in consequence, the fundamental equilibrium or integral harmony resulting from this hierarchical disposition, which is moreover precisely what the idea of "justice" amounts to when stripped of its specifically moral character.

Considered in this way, as a principle of order, and therefore as an inherent organization and disposition either of a being or group of beings, *dharma* may in one sense be regarded as opposed to *karma*, which is simply the action by which this disposition will be manifested outwardly, always provided the action is normal, or in other words provided it conforms to the nature of beings and the states of existence to which they belong, and to the relationships arising in consequence. Under these circumstances, that which is *adharma*, or contrary to *dharma*, is not "sin" in the theological sense of the word, neither is it "evil" in the moral sense, since both these ideas are equally foreign to the Hindu mind; it is simply "non-conformity" with the nature of beings, disequilibrium, a rupture of harmony, a destruction or upsetting of hierarchical relations. Without doubt, in the universal order, the sum total of all particular disequilibriums always goes to make up the total equilibrium, which nothing can destroy; but at each point regarded separately and by itself, disequilibrium is both possible and conceivable, and whether it occurs in the social sphere or elsewhere, there is absolutely no need to attribute to it anything of a moral character when defining it as something that is contrary, within its own sphere, to the "law of harmony" which governs at the same time both the cosmic and the human orders. The meaning of "law" being thus defined, and care being taken to distinguish it from all the particular and derivative applications to which it can give rise, we may accept the word "law" as a translation of *dharma*,[1] no doubt

[1] Another possible translation of *dharma*, which has much to recommend it, is by means of the word "norm"; the advantage of this rendering lies in the fact that it is entirely free from any kind of ethical or social associations, which nowadays even the word "law" does not entirely escape. Thus a "normal"

an imperfect one, but less inexact than other terms borrowed from Western languages; it must be emphasized once more, however, that it is not a moral law that is here in question; while the notions of scientific law and social or juridical law, even by definition, only refer to special cases.

The "law" may be regarded in principle as a "universal will," by an analogical transposition, which however does not allow anything personal to subsist in the conception, nor, for still stronger reasons, anything anthropomorphic. The expression of this will in each state of manifested existence is called *Prajāpati* or the "Lord of produced beings"; and in each particular cosmic cycle, this same will manifests itself as the *Manu* who gives the cycle its proper law. *Manu* should not therefore be taken for the name of a mythical, legendary, or historical personage; it is properly speaking the name of a principle, which can be defined, in accordance with the meaning of the verbal root *man*, as "cosmic intelligence" or "thought reflecting the universal order." On the other hand, this principle is also regarded as the prototype of man, who is called *manava* in so far as he is considered essentially as a "thinking being," characterized by the possession of *manas*, the mental or rational faculty; the concept of *Manu* is therefore equivalent, at least in certain respects, to what other traditions, notably the Hebrew *Kabbala* and Islamic esoterism, refer to as

existence, whether for a single being or a natural grouping of beings or for a whole universe, is the development of its possibilities in full conformity with its *dharma*; "abnormality" (*adharma*) being any departure from conformity to its essential nature.—*Translator*.

Universal Man, or what Taoism calls "the King." We have seen previously that the name *Vyāsa* does not denote a man but a function ; in that case, however, the function is in a general way an historical one, while *Manu* represents a cosmic function which can only become historical when specially applied to the social order, but without this in itself pre-supposing any kind of "personification." In fact, the law of *Manu*, for any cycle or collectivity whatsoever, is nothing else but the observance of the natural hierarchical relations existing between the beings subject to the special conditions of that cycle or collectivity, together with the whole body of precepts normally pertaining thereunto. We do not propose to dwell here on the subject of cosmic cycles, especially as rather lengthy explanations would be necessary to make the theory plainly intelligible; we will simply point out that the connexion between them is not chronological but logical and causal, each cycle being determined in its entirety by the preceding cycle and determining in its turn the following one, through a continuous production governed by the "law of harmony" which establishes the fundamental analogy between all the modes of Universal Manifestation.

When it comes to applying it to the social sphere, the "law," which then takes on its specifically juridical acceptation, may be formulated in a *shastra* or code, which, in so far as it expresses the "cosmic will" at that particular level, is referred to *Manu*, or, more precisely, to the *Manu* of the actual cycle ; but it is evident that this attribution does not make *Manu* the author of the *shastra*, at least not in the ordinary sense in which something purely human is said to be the work of such or such an author. Here again, as in the case of the Vedic texts, there is no definitely assignable historical origin, and indeed, as we have already explained, the question of such an origin is of no consequence from the doctrinal point of view. However, an important distinction is to be noted between the two cases: while the Vedic texts are described by the term *shruti*, as being the fruit of direct inspiration, the *dharma-shastra* only belongs to the class of traditional writings called *smriti*, the authority of which is of a less fundamental character; among the writings of this class are also included the *Purānas* and the *Itihāsas*, which Western scholars take to be mythological or epic poems only, having failed to grasp the profound symbolism which makes of them something quite other than "literature" in the ordinary sense of the word. Fundamentally, the distinction between *shruti* and *smriti* is equivalent to that between pure and direct intellectual intuition, on the one hand, and reflected consciousness of the rational order on the other hand, the former applying exclusively to the domain of metaphysical principles, the latter exercising itself upon objects of knowledge in the individual sphere, as must necessarily be the case where social or other applications are in question. Despite this, the traditional authority of the *dharma-shastra* does not in any way derive from the human authors whose task it has been to formulate it, doubtless orally at first and later on in writing, and that is why these writers have remained unknown and unidentified; its authority derives exclusively from the fact that it represents a true expression of the law of *Manu*, that is to say from its conformity with the natural order of the existences it is destined to govern.

CHAPTER VI

Principles Governing the Institution of Caste

In order to complete what has been said in the preceding chapter, we may usefully add a few explanations on the subject of caste, which is of primary importance in the law of *Manu* and which has been persistently misunderstood by Europeans in general. First of all we will give the following definition : caste, which the Hindus describe indifferently by one or other of the two words *jāti* and *varna*, is a social function determined by the particular nature of each human being. The word *varna* in its original sense means " colour," and some people have attempted to see in this a proof, or at least an indication, of the supposed fact that the distinction between the castes was originally founded upon racial differences ; but this is not a tenable view, for the same word bears by extension the meaning of " quality " in general, whence its analogical use to denote the particular nature of a being, or what might be called its " individual essence " ; and it is in fact the latter which determines caste, racial considerations intervening merely as one of the elements capable of exercising an influence upon the constitution of the individual nature. As for the word *jāti*, its proper meaning is " birth," and some have therefore concluded from this that caste is essentially hereditary, but this again is an error. If it is most often hereditary in actual practice, it is not strictly so in principle, for although the part played by heredity in the formation of the individual nature may be preponderant in the majority of cases, it is by no means exclusive ; this however calls for some supplementary explanations.

The individual being is regarded in its totality as a compound of two elements, called respectively *nāma*, name, and *rūpa*, form, which in effect represent the "essence" and the "substance" of the individuality, or what the Aristotelian school calls "form" and "matter" ; these last two terms however have a technical meaning very different from their ordinary ones, and it should be observed in particular that the word "form," instead of denoting the element which we have so named to translate the Sanskrit *rūpa*, denotes on the contrary the other element, which is properly speaking the "individual essence." It should be added that the distinction we have just pointed out, although analogous to that made in the West between soul and body, is far from being its exact equivalent : the form referred to is not an exclusively corporeal form, although we cannot at present insist on this point ; as for the name, it represents the sum of all the being's characteristic qualities or attributes. A further distinction is to be made within the individual essence itself : *nāmika*, "that which refers to the name" in a more restricted sense, or "that which the particular name of each individual should express," is the sum of the qualities properly belonging to the individual, without his deriving them from anything other than himself ; *gotrika*, "that which belongs to the race or family," is the sum of the qualities which the being derives from his heredity. An analogical representation of this second distinction may be observed in the attribution to an individual, on the one hand, of a prenomen belonging exclusively to himself and, on the other hand, of a family name. Much might be said about the original significance of names and what they should normally be intended to express; but since questions of this kind do not fall within the scope of the present work, we will only point out that the determination of the true name is bound up in principle with the determination of the individual nature itself. Birth, within the meaning of the Sanskrit word *jāti*, is properly speaking the resultant of the two elements *nāmika* and *gotrika*: allowance must therefore be made for the part played by heredity, and this may be considerable, but account has also to be taken of those qualities by which the individual is distinguished from his parents and other members of his family. It is clear, in fact, that no two beings possess exactly the same qualities, either physical or psychic: apart from what they have in common, there are also certain distinguishing characteristics, and those people who try to ascribe everything in the individual to the influence of heredity would undoubtedly have considerable difficulty in applying their theory to any particular case; this influence is undeniable, but there are other elements to be taken into account, and allowance is in fact made for them in the theory we are explaining.

The particular nature of each individual necessarily comprises from the beginning all the tendencies and aptitudes which will be developed and manifested in the course of his existence, and which, for instance, will determine his qualification for this or that social function, this being the point that more especially concerns us here. Knowledge of the individual nature should therefore make it possible to assign to each human being the function for which his nature fits him, or in other words to assign him the place which he should normally occupy in the social organization. It will be easily understood that we have here the basis of an organization that is truly hierarchical, that is to say in conformity with the nature of beings, following the interpretation we have given of the notion of *dharma* ; errors of application are no doubt always possible, especially in periods when the light of tradition has grown dim, but they do not in any way affect the validity of the principle, and it can be said that to deny it implies theoretically, if not always in practice, the overturning of every legitimate hierarchy. At the same time it can be seen how absurd is the attitude of those Europeans who feel indignant because a man cannot pass from his own caste into a higher one : in effect this would imply nothing more nor less than a change of individual nature, or in other words a man would have to cease being himself in order to become another man, which is manifestly an absurdity ; a being will remain throughout the whole of his individual existence what he is potentially at the time of his birth. The question why a being is himself and not another is a pointless one : the truth is that every being, each according to his own nature, is a necessary element in the total and universal harmony. It is only too clear, however, that considerations of this kind are completely foreign to people living in societies such as are to be found in the West to-day, the constitution of which is without principle and does not rest upon any hierarchy ; in these societies any man may exercise almost indifferently the most diverse functions, including those for which he is not in the least fitted, while material riches are generally accepted as the only real mark of superiority.

From what has been said about the meaning of *dharma*, it follows that the social hierarchy ought to reproduce analogically, in accordance with its own conditions, the constitution of "Universal Man" ; by this we mean that there is a correspondence between the cosmic and the human orders, and that this correspondence, which finds natural expression in the organization of the individual, whether the latter is regarded integrally or even simply corporeally, should also be realized in an appropriate manner in the organization of society. The conception of a "social organism," with organs and functions comparable to those of a living being, is already familiar to modern sociologists ; but the latter have gone much too far in this direction, forgetting that correspondence and analogy do not mean assimilation and identity, and that in any legitimate comparison between the two cases allowance would necessarily have to be made for differences in the respective modes of application ; furthermore, being ignorant of the profound reasons for the analogy, they have never been able to draw any valid conclusions concerning the establishment of a true hierarchy. It is clear from these reservations that expressions which may appear to indicate an assimilation must only be understood in a purely symbolical sense, in the same way that designations borrowed from different parts of the human individual are applied analogically to "Universal Man."

These indications will be sufficient to explain the meaning of the symbolical description of the origin of castes, as it is to be found in numerous texts, notably in the *Purusha-sukta* of the *Rig-Veda* from which the following quotation is taken: "of *Purusha*, the *Brāhmana* was the mouth, the *Kshatriya* the arms, the *Vaishya* the thighs; the *Shūdra* was born under his feet."[1] Here is to be found the enumeration of the four castes the differentiation of which constitutes the basis of the social order, and which are susceptible of more or less numerous secondary subdivisions: the *Brāhmanas* represent essentially the spiritual and intellectual authority; the *Kshatriyas*, the administrative prerogative comprising both the judicial and the military offices, of which the royal function is simply the highest degree; to the *Vaishyas* belongs the whole varied range of economic functions in the widest sense of the word, including the agricultural, industrial, commercial and financial functions; as for the *Shūdras*, they carry out the tasks necessary to assure the purely material subsistence of the community. It should be added that the *Brāhmanas* are not "priests" in the Western and religious sense of the word: no doubt their functions include the accomplishment of various kinds of rites,

[1] *Rig-Veda*, X, 90.

because they must possess the knowledge necessary to make them fully effective ; but they also include, above everything else, the conservation and regular transmission of the traditional doctrine. Indeed the function of teaching, represented by the mouth in the symbolism we have just mentioned, was regarded by nearly all ancient peoples as the highest priestly function, because their civilizations were based in their entirety upon a doctrinal principle. For the same reason deviations from the doctrine were generally bound up with a subversion of the social hierarchy, as can be seen, for example, in the repeated attempts made by the *Kshatriyas* to throw off the overlordship of the *Brāhmanas*, an overlordship the justification of which will be apparent from all that has been said concerning the real nature of Hindu civilization.

These summary remarks would not be complete without some reference to the traces which these traditional and primordial conceptions have left in the ancient institutions of Europe, notably in connection with the conferring of the Divine Right upon kings, whose function was originally regarded as being essentially that of regulators of the social order, as the root of the word *rex* indicates ; but we can only note these things in passing, without dwelling upon them as much as would be necessary to bring out their full significance.

Participation in the tradition is only fully effective for the members of the first three castes ; this is expressed by the various designations exclusively reserved for them, such as *ārya*, of which mention has already been made, and *dwija* or "twice born" ;

the idea of a "second birth," understood in a purely spiritual sense, is indeed common to all traditional doctrines, and Christianity itself provides an equivalent in religious mode in the rite of Baptism. For the *Shūdras*, participation is primarily indirect and as it were virtual, for in a general way it only results from their relations with the superior castes; moreover, to revert to the analogy of the "social organism," the part they play does not properly speaking constitute a vital function, but an activity which is in some sense mechanical, and this is why they are represented as springing, not from a part of the body of *Purusha* or "Universal Man," but from the earth beneath his feet, which is the element in which the substances of bodily nourishment are compounded. In connexion with this same representation, it may also be noted that the distinction between the castes is sometimes applied by analogical transposition not merely to the whole human collectivity, but to the totality of beings, both animate and inanimate, as comprised within Nature in its entirety, since all these beings are likewise said to be sprung from *Purusha*: it is thus that the *Brāhmana* is regarded as the type of immutable beings, that is to say of those which are above change, and the *Kshatriya* as the type of beings subject to change, because their functions refer respectively to the sphere of contemplation and the sphere of action. That is clear enough evidence of the questions of principle involved in all this, for they are of a kind that contain implications going far beyond the limits of the social sphere, in relation to which they have more particularly been considered here. Having shown how these principles are applied in the traditional organization of the Hindu civilization, we will not dwell any further upon the question of social institutions, which does not form the principal theme of the present book.

CHAPTER VII

Shivaism and Vishnuism

Should the Supreme Principle, total and universal, which the religious doctrines of the West call "God," be conceived of as impersonal or as personal? This question has given rise to interminable and moreover quite pointless discussions, because it originates from partial and incomplete conceptions which it would be useless to attempt to reconcile without going beyond the special domain, theological or philosophical, where they belong. Metaphysically, it must be said that the Principle is at once both impersonal and personal, according to the aspect under which It is viewed: impersonal, or, if preferred, "supra-personal" in Itself; personal in relation to universal manifestation, without however this "Divine Personality" partaking in the least degree of an anthropomorphic character, for "personality" must not be confused with "individuality." The fundamental distinction just formulated, by means of which the apparent contradictions between secondary and multiple points of view are resolved in the unity of a superior synthesis, is known in the language of Far Eastern metaphysic as the distinction between "Non-Being" and "Being"; it is no less clearly recognised in the Hindu doctrine, as follows necessarily from the essential identity of pure metaphysic beneath the diversity of the forms in which it may be clothed. The impersonal and therefore absolutely universal Principle is called *Brahma* ; the Divine Personality, which is a determination or a specification of this Supreme Principle, implying a lesser degree of universality, is generally known by the name of *Ishwara*. *Brahma* in Its Infinity cannot be characterized by any positive attribute, which is expressed by declaring It to be *nirguna* or " beyond all qualification," and again *nirvishesha* or "beyond all distinction" ; on the other hand *Ishwara* is called *saguna* or " qualified," and *savishesha* or " conceived distinctively," because He is capable of receiving such attributions, which are obtained by an analogical transference into the universal of the diverse qualities or properties of the beings of which He is the Principle. It is evident that an indefinite number of Divine Attributes may be conceived of in this manner, and indeed every quality enjoying a positive existence may thus be transposed by being envisaged in its principle ; each of these attributes, however, should be considered in reality only as a basis or support for meditation on a certain aspect of Universal Being.

It will be apparent from what we have said on the subject of symbolism how that same incomprehension which gives rise to anthropomorphism could have the result of turning the Divine Attributes into so many " gods," that is to say into entities conceived after the pattern of individual beings and endowed with an independent existence. This is one of the most obvious examples of idolatry, which takes the symbol for the thing symbolised, and which here assumes the form of polytheism ; but it is clear that no doctrine was ever polytheistic in itself and in essence, since it could only become so as the result of a profound corruption, which moreover happens on a large scale much more rarely than is commonly supposed ; in fact only one example of the generalization of this error is known for certain, in the Græco-Roman civilization, and even here there were at least some exceptions among its intellectual elect. In the East, where the tendency towards anthropomorphism is non-existent apart from individual aberrations that are always possible though rare and abnormal, nothing of the kind has ever succeeded in coming to light. This will no doubt surprise many Western people, who, being only acquainted with classical antiquity, are prone to look everywhere for "myths" and "paganism," but it is none the less true. So far as India is concerned, the symbolical image representing one or other of the Divine Attributes, and which is called *pratika*, is most certainly not an "idol,"[1] for it has never been taken for anything other than what it really is, namely a support for meditation and an auxiliary means of realization, each person moreover being free to attach himself according

[1] When trying to render *pratika* into English, a number of modern Hindus actually do employ the word "idol," though without the least consciousness of the opprobrious shade of meaning that it invariably bears in the Western languages; they have simply taken over the word uncritically from European writers whose intentions were far from friendly to Hinduism. Here we have a good instance of the sort of confusion that arises when mastery of a foreign language, though superficially complete, stops short of a real assimilation of the corresponding modes of thought; both Orientals and Westerners might take warning from this example.—*Translator.*

to preference to those symbols which are most in conformity with his personal tendencies.

Īshwara is conceived under a triplicity of principal aspects, together constituting the *Trimūrti* or "triple manifestation," from each of which are derived other aspects, more particular and secondary in relation to the three principal ones. *Brahmā* is *Īshwara* considered as the productive principle of manifested beings; He is so named because He is considered as the direct reflection in the realm of manifestation of *Brahma* the Supreme Principle. In order to avoid all confusion it should be observed that the word *Brahma*, without an accent, is neuter while the word *Brahmā* is masculine; the use, current among orientalists, of the single form *Brahman*, which is common to both genders, has the serious disadvantage of obscuring this essential distinction, which is sometimes further marked by expressions such as *Para-Brahma* or the "Supreme Brahma," and *Apara-Brahma* or the "non-supreme Brahma." The two other aspects constituting the *Trimūrti*, which are complementary to each other, are *Vishnu*, who is *Īshwara* considered as the animating and preserving principle of beings, and *Shiva*, who is *Īshwara* considered, not as the destructive principle, as He is commonly described, but as the transforming principle; these then, are truly universal functions, and not separate and more or less individualized entities. Each person, with a view to placing himself at the standpoint best adapted to his own possibilities, will naturally be able to give precedence to any one of these functions, and in particular, because of their apparent symmetry, to one or other of the two complementary functions represented by *Vishnu* and *Shiva* : hence the distinction between Vishnuism and Shivaism, which are not sects as Westerners suppose them to be, but simply different ways of realization, both equally legitimate and orthodox. It should however be added that Shivaism, which is less widely diffused than Vishnuism and attaches less importance to exterior rites, is at the same time more elevated in a certain sense and leads more directly to pure metaphysical realization : this may easily be inferred from the very nature of the principle to which it gives first place, for "transformation," which should be understood here in its strictly etymological sense, implies a passing "beyond form," which only appears as a destruction from the special and contingent point of view of manifestation ; it is a passing from the manifested to the unmanifested, representing the return of the being to the eternal immutability of the Supreme Principle, outside which nothing can exist save in an illusory manner.

The "Divine Aspects" are each regarded as being endowed with a power or energy of their own, called *Shakti*, which is represented symbolically under a feminine form : the *Shakti* of *Brahmā* is *Saraswatī*, that of *Vishnu* is *Lakshmī*, and that of *Shiva* is *Pārvatī*. Among both *Shaivas* and *Vaishnavas*, certain persons devote themselves more especially to the consideration of the *Shaktis*, and are for this reason called *Shāktas*. Furthermore, each of the principles we are discussing can be envisaged under a plurality of more particularized aspects, and from each of them also are derived other secondary aspects, this process of derivation being most often described as a symbolic filiation. We naturally cannot develop all these conceptions here, particularly as it is not our aim to expound the doctrines themselves but only to indicate the spirit in which they should be studied if they are to be really understood.

The *Shaivas* and *Vaishnavas* each possess their own special books, the *Purānas* and the *Tantras*, which form part of the body of traditional writings known collectively as *Smriti* and which correspond more particularly to their respective tendencies. These tendencies nowhere appear more clearly than in the way in which they respectively interpret the doctrine of *Avatāras* or "Divine manifestations"; this doctrine, which is closely bound up with the conception of cosmic cycles, deserves to be studied separately, but we cannot think of going into the subject at present. To conclude these remarks on the question of Shivaism and Vishnuism, we will simply add that, whatever the way each man may choose as being most in conformity with his own nature, the final end to which it leads, provided it be strictly orthodox, is always the same: the end in every case is effective realization of a metaphysical order, which will be more or less direct, and more or less complete, according to the circumstances in which it is undertaken and the extent of the intellectual possibilities of each human being.

CHAPTER VIII

Points of View within the Doctrine

The foregoing explanations show how a multiplicity of points of view can exist together within the essential unity of the same traditional doctrine without this unity being in any way affected thereby. Moreover, since each person brings with him a way of looking at things that is peculiarly his own, it may consequently be said that there are as many different ways of understanding as there are individuals ; but this is only true in so far as the point of departure is concerned, for once the individual domain has been left behind, all these differences, which are not in any way incompatible, necessarily disappear. Apart from the differences inherent in the particular natures of the various human beings, each one may also choose to place himself at any one of a variety of viewpoints in order to study the doctrine under some more or less well defined aspect, which will be the more closely defined the greater its degree of particularization, or in other words the further removed it is, in descending order of application, from the sphere of universal principles. The entire range of possible and legitimate points of view is always contained, synthetically and in principle, within the doctrine itself, and what we have already said on the subject of the plurality of meanings comprised within traditional texts will be a sufficient indication of the nature of this synthesis ; in every case, therefore, it is solely a matter of a strict interpretation of the basic doctrine developed in accordance with the point of view in question.

This is exactly what is expressed in India by the Sanskrit word *darshana*, which properly speaking denotes nothing more or less than "sight" or "point of view," for the principal meaning of the verbal root *drish*, from which it is derived, is to "see." The *darshanas* are really therefore "points of view" within the doctrine, and not, as most orientalists imagine, competing or conflicting philosophical systems[1]; in so far as these points of view are strictly orthodox, they naturally cannot enter either into conflict or into contradiction with one another. We have shown that every systematized conception, born of that intellectual individualism so dear to modern Westerners, implies the negation of metaphysic, which constitutes the very essence of the doctrine; we have also pointed out the profound distinction between metaphysical thought and philosophical thought, the latter being merely a special mode peculiar to the West which could not validly be applied to the knowledge of a traditional doctrine preserved in its integral purity. There is no such thing, then, as "Hindu philosophy," any more than there is a "Chinese philosophy," at all events not so long as it is intended to retain for philosophy the more or less well-defined meaning imposed upon it by the line of thought issuing from the Greeks; but it must be confessed, especially when one considers what

[1] Many present-day Hindu books published in English refer to the six *darshanas* as so many "philosophies," their writers being insufficiently aware of what the word "philosophy" actually implies; unnecessary confusion is thus produced in the minds both of Indian and European readers. It is time people opened their eyes to the dangers of these loose renderings.—*Translator.*

philosophy has become in modern times, that the absence of this mode of thought in a civilization is not particularly to be regretted. Nevertheless, orientalists are either unable or unwilling to see in the *darshanas* anything but philosophies and systems, to which they even pretend to attach Western labels: this they do simply because they are incapable of escaping from the "classical" framework, and because they ignore entirely the most characteristic differences between the Eastern and Western mentalities. Their attitude in this respect might be compared to that of a man who, knowing nothing of present-day European civilization and chancing to come across a syllabus of university lectures, jumped to the singular conclusion that the scholars of Europe are divided into several rival schools, each with its own particular philosophical system, the principal ones being those of the mathematicians, the physicists, the chemists, the biologists, the logicians and the psychologists; such a misunderstanding may sound quite ridiculous, but it is hardly more so than the present conception of the orientalists, who ought not even to have the excuse of ignorance, or rather it is their very ignorance which is inexcusable. Improbable as this may sound, it is only too certain that the questions of principle involved, which they seem deliberately to avoid, have never occupied their minds, which are in any event too narrowly specialized to be able to understand these principles and grasp their full significance; this is indeed a remarkable case of extreme "intellectual myopia" and one may be quite sure that, handicapped by such a disposition, they will never succeed in discerning the true meaning of the smallest fragment of any one of the Eastern doctrines which they have taken upon themselves to interpret after their own fashion, in conformity with their completely Western outlook.

Looking at things once again in their correct perspective, it may be said that the points of view from which the doctrine may be considered are evidently capable of being multiplied almost indefinitely ; on the other hand not all are equally irreducible, and there are some, more fundamental in certain respects, to which the others may be subordinated. It will therefore always be possible to group the secondary points of view around these principal ones, and only the latter need then be considered separately as so many branches of the study of the doctrine, the others representing nothing more than simple sub-divisions which in the majority of cases need not even be specified. It is the main divisions or principal branches which properly speaking constitute the *darshanas* in the accepted meaning of the word. Following the classification generally admitted in India, there are six of these main divisions, which should not be confused, owing to their number being the same, with what are called the six *Vedāngas*.

The word *Vedānga* literally means " limb of the *Veda*," and this name is applied to certain auxiliary sciences of the *Veda*, which are compared to the bodily limbs by means of which a being acts outwardly ; the fundamental treatises relating to these sciences, which we are about to enumerate, form part of *smriti*, in which indeed they occupy the first place by reason of their direct relationship with the *Veda*. *Shikshā* is the science of correct articulation and exact pronunciation, implying a knowledge of the symbolical value of letters, as also of the laws of euphony which are more important and more developed in Sanskrit than in any other language ; in a traditional language, in fact, the use of a phonetic method of writing is in no way inconsistent with the preservation of an ideographic meaning, as may also be observed in the case of both Hebrew and Arabic. *Chhandas* is the science of prosody, which determines the application of the various metres in correspondence with the vibrations of the cosmic order which they serve to express, thus setting them in quite a different category to that of " poetical " forms in the purely literary sense of the word : moreover the profound knowledge of rhythm and its cosmic correspondences, which leads to its use in certain preparatory methods of metaphysical realization, is common to all Oriental civilizations, totally strange though it is to Western peoples. *Vyākarana* is grammar, but instead of being presented simply as a body of rules that appear more or less arbitrary because the reasons for them are unknown, as commonly happens in Western languages, it is on the contrary based upon conceptions and classifications which are always in strict relationship with the logical meaning of language. *Nirukta* is the explanation of important or difficult terms which are found in the *Vedic* texts ; these explanations do not rest solely upon etymology, but also, and more often, upon the symbolic value of the letters and syllables of which the words are composed. This is a source of innumerable errors on the part of orientalists, who can neither understand nor even conceive of this last method of explanation, which is perfectly natural to the traditional languages and very similar to that found in the Hebrew *Kabbala* ; the result is that they are unwilling or unable to see anything but fanciful etymologies, or even a common play upon words, in what is obviously something very different. *Jyotisha* is astronomy, or more exactly it is both astronomy and astrology, which have never been separated in India, any more than they were by any of the ancient peoples, not even by the Greeks themselves, who employed these two words indifferently to describe one and the same thing. The distinction between astronomy and astrology is in fact quite modern, and it should also be added that the real traditional astrology, such as is still to be found in the East, has practically nothing in common with the divinatory speculations to which certain people wish to attach the same name in contemporary Europe. Lastly comes *kalpa*, a word which actually bears many different meanings, but which here stands for the whole body of precepts relating to the accomplishment of rites, knowledge of which is indispensable to give the latter their full efficacy ; in the *sūtras* where they are set forth, these precepts are condensed by means of a special symbolical notation into formulas which are in appearance not unlike those used in algebra.

In addition to the *Vedāngas*, mention must also be made of the *Upavedas*, a word designating branches of knowledge of an inferior kind, but which nevertheless rest upon a strictly traditional basis ; these branches of knowledge refer to the domain of practical applications. There are four *Upavedas*, which are attached to the four *Vedas* in which they find their respective principles : *Ayur-Veda* is the science of medicine, related thus to the *Rig-Veda* ; *Dhanur-Veda* is military science, related to the *Yajur-Veda* ; *Gāndharva-Veda* is music, related to the *Sāma-Veda* ; *Sthāpatya-Veda* includes mechanics and architecture, and is related to the *Atharva-Veda*. According to Western ideas these are arts rather than sciences properly so-called ; but the traditional principle given to them here confers a rather different character upon them. Naturally the foregoing enumeration of the *Vedāngas* and *Upavedas* in no way excludes other sciences not mentioned in this list, of which some at least have also been cultivated in India since ancient times ; it is known that mathematics in particular, comprising, under the general name of *ganita*, *pātī-ganita* or *vyakta-ganita*, arithmetic, *bīja-ganita*, algebra, and *rekhā-ganita*, geometry, received a remarkable development, especially as regards the first two of its three branches, from which Europe, through the mediation of the Arabs, was to benefit later on.

Having thus given a brief survey of the whole body of the traditional sciences of India, each of which moreover constitutes some secondary aspect of the doctrine, we will now return to the *darshanas*, which should also be regarded as forming an integral part of this body of knowledge, failing which one will never understand anything at all about them. It ought never to be forgotten that in India, as well as in China, one of the gravest insults one can offer to a thinker is to praise the novelty and originality of his ideas; in civilizations that are essentially traditional, this characteristic is sufficient to deprive such ideas of all real significance. No doubt, amongst those who attach themselves specially to the study of one or another of the *darshanas*, schools may sometimes be formed differing from each other on certain points of interpretation, but these divergencies have never been able to proceed very far without overstepping the bounds of orthodoxy; bearing usually only upon secondary points, they are in fact more apparent than real, amounting rather to differences of expression, and moreover having their uses through their being adapted to differing types of intelligence. Besides it is obvious that a " point of view " can never have been the exclusive property of any particular school, although to those who are content to regard things superficially it may sometimes appear to be identified with the conceptions of the school which has chiefly developed it; confusions of this kind seem to come naturally to Westerners, who are accustomed to attribute to particular individuals, as actual " inventions," all the conceptions they have ever heard of. This postulate is to a large extent implicit in their " historical method," and at the present time even the religious point of view does not escape the consequences of this special turn of mind, which directs against it all the resources of that anti-traditional exegesis to which we have already referred.

The six *darshanas* are *Nyāya* and *Vaisheshika*, *Sānkhya* and *Yoga*, *Mīmānsā* and *Vedānta*; they are usually enumerated in this order and in pairs in order to mark their affinities ; as for wishing to assign a chronological order of succession to their development, this is a vain question without any real interest for reasons already stated, since we are concerned with points of view which from the very beginning were implicitly contained in perfect simultaneity within the primordial doctrine. To characterize them briefly, it may be said that the first two points of view are analytical, while the four others are synthetic ; on the other hand the two last stand out from the others as being in a direct and immediate way interpretations of the *Veda* itself, from which the rest are derived more remotely ; also no heterodox opinions, be they even partially so, have ever been able to take root in these last two *darshanas*, while some have arisen in schools dedicated to the study of the four others. Since too abridged a definition of the *darshanas* would inevitably be incomplete, difficult to understand and consequently of little use, we have thought it preferable to allot a separate chapter to each one of them in turn, especially as the subject is sufficiently important in relation to the aims of the present work to merit being treated at some length.

CHAPTER IX

Nyāya

The meaning of *Nyāya* should properly be given as "logic" or even "method" : to maintain, as some people do, that this word began by denoting a school and subsequently became a synonym for logic, is to reverse the natural order of things ; clearly a school must be given a name bearing some previous meaning, and this view of the origin of *Nyāya*, by suggesting the exact opposite, contradicts this obvious fact ; besides it is not possible to admit that a *darshana* could become the monopoly of a particular school. In actual fact it is certainly logic which is and always has been the concern of the *darshana* in question, the development of which is ascribed to Gautama : this name however should not be taken as referring to any single individual ; it was in common use both as a personal and family name in ancient India and it is not accompanied in this case by any biographical details even of the vaguest kind. This is typical of what always occurs in the East in such a case, for individualities do not count where the doctrine is concerned. It is indeed quite possible there may have existed a man called Gautama at some remote and indeterminate date, who devoted himself to the study and teaching of the branch of knowledge that constitutes logic ; but this probable fact is not of any particular interest, and the name has only been handed on for a purely symbolical purpose, in order to denote what is really an "intellectual aggregate" made up of all those who, over a period the duration of which is no less indeterminate than its beginning, devoted themselves to one and the same study. Moreover this kind of "collective entity," an example of which we have already cited in the case of Vyāsa, does not constitute a school, in the usual sense of the word, but rather a genuine intellectual function ; and the same could be said of the proper names that we find associated in a similar way with each of the other *darshanas.* These remarks, made once for all, will relieve us of the necessity for again referring to this question.

We have said then that *Nyāya* is essentially logic ; but it must be added that the term should in this case be understood in a much less restricted sense than Westerners give to it, because what it deals with is looked upon, not as a mere branch of philosophy, but as a point of view pertaining to the whole doctrine. Hindu logic escapes that narrow specialisation which is unavoidable when logic is considered in its philosophic mode, nor can it be compressed within the limits of any system, so that it enjoys a much wider scope than Western logic. In order to appreciate this point, one need only recall what was previously said about the characteristics of metaphysic ; that which constitutes the proper object of a speculation is not so much the things themselves proposed for study, as the angle from which they are studied. Logic, as was pointed out before, is concerned with the conditions of human understanding : that which can be considered logically is therefore everything that is capable of being the object of human understanding, in so far as it is actually considered under this relationship. Consequently logic comprises within its point of view things treated as "objects of proof," that is to say as objects of reasoned or discursive knowledge : in *Nyāya* this is the sense of the term *padārtha*, and, in spite of certain differences, it is also, in the earlier logic of the West, the correct meaning of the "categories" or "predicaments." If the divisions and classifications established by logic possess at the same time a real ontological value, this arises from the fact that there must necessarily be a correspondence between the points of view of logic and ontology, provided that no radical and artificial opposition is set up between subject and object, such as occurs in modern philosophy. Furthermore, the logical point of view is analytical, because it is individual and rational: it is only as representing a simple application to the individual order that logical principles, even the most general ones, can claim to be derived from metaphysical or universal principles.

Nyāya recognises sixteen *padārthas*, the first of which is called *pramāna*. The ordinary meaning of this word is "proof," and it is also often translated as "evidence"; but the latter rendering is in many cases misleading, and there is the further drawback that it calls to mind the Cartesian conception of evidence, which is really only of value in the mathematical sphere. In order to fix the correct meaning of the word *pramāna* it must be pointed out that its primitive sense is that of "measure"; it denotes here the legitimate means of knowledge within the rational order, each of these means being in fact only applicable in a certain measure and under specified conditions, or, in other words, within a particular domain, the extent of which defines their scope; the enumeration of these means of knowledge or proof goes to make up the subdivisions of the first *padārtha*. The second is *prameya* or "that which is to be proved," namely that which can be known by one or other of the means just mentioned; it includes, as its subdivisions, a classification of everything that human understanding in its individual state can reach.

The remaining *padārthas* are less important and refer chiefly to the various modalities of reasoning or demonstration; we shall not try to give the complete list here, but we will content ourselves with mentioning in particular the one which is concerned with the terms of a regular argument.

The argument in question, which is also called *nyāya*, but in a secondary and more restricted use of the term, and which is in fact the type of a methodical demonstration, includes, in its fully developed form, five *avayavas* or constituent members or terms: *pratijnā*, the proposition or assertion requiring to be proved; *hetu*, the reason justifying this proposition; *udāharana*, the example cited in support of the reason, and serving, so to speak, as an illustration of it by recalling a well-known case; *upanaya*, the application to the particular case in question, namely to the first-mentioned proposition; lastly *nigamana*, the result or conclusion, which is a definite affirmation of that same proposition as proven. Such is the complete form of the demonstrative argument, but it is often set out in simplified or abridged forms, consisting either of the first three or the last three terms only: in the latter form especially, there is a marked likeness to the syllogism as established theoretically by Aristotle. Furthermore, the equivalents of the greater and the lesser term are to be found here, called respectively by the name of *vyāpaka* or container and *vyāpya* or content, which refer to the same point of view of logical extension; as for the intermediary term, its function is fulfilled by the reason, *hetu*, which is also called *linga* or the sign by which *vyāpti* can be recognised, that is to say the invariable connexion uniting the container to the content. Nevertheless, these undeniable points of likeness, which suggest as at least a probable hypothesis that Aristotle may have possessed some knowledge of *Nyāya*, must not cause us to forget that there are essential differences between the two viewpoints ; for whereas the Greek syllogism, when all is said and done, bears only on the concepts or notions of things, the Hindu argument has a more direct bearing on things in themselves.

This last remark calls for a few further comments ; in the first place, it evidently concerns the very core of what is implied in the reasoning, and not merely the outward form, which might be practically the same in both cases. We have said that the separation and opposition of subject and object is a special feature of modern philosophy ; but already, among the Greeks, the distinction between a thing and its notion had gone a little too far, in the sense that logic dealt exclusively with the relations between notions, as if it were only through notions that things could be known to us. Doubtless, rational knowledge is only indirect knowledge, and for that reason open to error ; yet, if it could not reach things themselves to a certain extent, it would be entirely illusory and could not be called knowledge in any sense of the word. If then it may be said that under the rational mode an object can only be known through the intermediary of its notion, this can only be because the notion possesses something of the object itself, and shares in its nature by expressing it in relation to ourselves. For this reason, Hindu logic considers not only the manner in which we conceive of things, but also the things themselves in so far as they are conceived by us, since our conception would have no reality if it were entirely separate and distinct from its object ; in this respect, the Scholastic definition of truth as *adæquatio rei et intellectus*, in all the degrees of knowledge, is that which comes nearest, in the West, to the point of view of the Eastern traditional doctrines, because it conforms most nearly to the purely metaphysical conception. Besides, the Scholastic doctrine, while carrying on the teaching of Aristotle in its main lines, corrected and completed it on many points ; unfortunately it did not quite succeed in breaking loose from the limitations which were its inheritance from the Hellenic mode of thought ; it is also to be regretted that the Schoolmen never quite seem to have grasped the profound consequences implied in the principle, already laid down by Aristotle, of identification through knowledge.

It is precisely in virtue of this principle that from the moment the subject knows an object, however fragmentary or superficial that knowledge may be, something of the object is present in the subject, and has become part of its being ; from whatever angle we consider things, it is always the things themselves that we reach, at least under a certain aspect, forming in every case one of their attributes, that is to say one of the elements that constitute their essence. Let it be admitted, if need be, that this is " realism " ; the truth is that such is the nature of things, and words make no difference ; but strictly speaking, the special viewpoints of " realism " and "idealism," with the systematic opposition implied in their correlation, are inapplicable here, since we have travelled far beyond the narrow province of philosophical thought. Nor must it be forgotten that the act of knowledge presents two inseparable facets ; if it is an identification of the subject with the object, it is also, for the self-same reason, an assimilation of the object by the subject : by reaching things in their essence, we "realize" them, in all the force of that word, as states or modalities of our own being ; and if the idea, in the measure in which it is true and adequate, shares in the nature of the thing, it is because, conversely, the thing itself shares also in the nature of the idea. Fundamentally there are not two separate and radically different worlds, as modern philosophy suggests when it qualifies them with the names of "subjective" and "objective," nor two superimposed worlds like the "intelligible world" and the "sensible world" of Plato ; but, as the Arabs say, "existence is unique" and all that it contains is but a manifestation, in multiple modes, of one and the same principle, which is Universal Being.

CHAPTER X

VAISHESHIKA

THE name *Vaisheshika* is derived from the word *vishesha,* which means "distinctive character" and consequently "individual thing" ; this *darshana* is therefore concerned with the knowledge of individual things as such, considered in distinctive mode, in their contingent existence. While *Nyāya* treats of things in their relationship with the human understanding, *Vaisheshika* considers them more directly for what they are in themselves ; it is easy to see the difference between these two points of view, though at the same time their connection also is apparent, since, in the last analysis, knowledge of a thing is one with the thing itself ; however, the difference between the two points of view only disappears when both have been transcended, so that their distinction is always maintained within the frontiers of the domain to which they can properly be applied. This domain is plainly that of manifested Nature, outside which the individual point of view, of which these two *darshanas* represent modalities, is devoid of meaning. But universal manifestation can be looked at in two different ways ; either synthetically, starting from the principles out of which it proceeds and which determine it in its every mode—this is the point of view of *Sānkhya*, as will be shown further on—or else analytically, in the distinguishing of its manifold constituent elements, and this is the line of approach of *Vaisheshika*. The latter point of view may even confine itself to the special consideration of a single mode of universal manifestation, such as that constituted by the sensible world ; and in fact, it is bound to limit itself to this world almost entirely, since the conditions of the other modes necessarily lie beyond the grasp of the individual faculties of the human being ; such modes can only be reached as it were, from above, namely through that element in man which transcends the limitations and relativities inherent in the individual. This clearly goes beyond the distinctive and analytical point of view that we now have to describe; but a particular point of view cannot be fully understood save by transcending it, given that it is not represented as being independent and as carrying its own justification wholly within itself but is recognized to be dependent on certain principles whence it is derived, being but an application, to a contingent order, of something belonging to a different and superior order.

We have seen that this reference to principles, which ensures the essential unity of the doctrine throughout its branches, is a feature common to every form of Indian traditional knowledge; it marks the profound difference that separates *Vaisheshika* from the scientific point of view as understood by Westerners, though it remains true to say that it is less remote from the latter than any of the other branches. In reality *Vaisheshika* approaches nearer to the point of view known among the Greeks as "physical philosophy"; though analytical, it is less so than modern science, and is therefore less subject to the narrow specialisation which causes the latter to lose its way in an endless maze of experimentation. The *Vaisheshika darshana* implies something which is fundamentally more rational and even, in a certain measure, more intellectual in the strict sense of the word than modern science: more rational, because, though it remains within the individual field, it is free from all empiricism; more intellectual, because it never loses sight of the fact that the entire individual order depends on universal principles, from which it derives all the reality it is capable of possessing. We have said that by the term "physics" the ancients meant the science of

Nature in the widest sense of the word; the same term would then be suitable here also, but as against this it must be borne in mind how narrow its meaning has become in modern usage, following on the general narrowing of the corresponding point of view. Wherefore, if a Western term is to be applied to a Hindu point of view, it seems preferable to speak of *Vaisheshika* as "cosmology"; and indeed, the cosmology of the Middle Ages, which was clearly regarded as an application of metaphysic to the contingencies of the sensible world, comes still closer to this *darshana* than the "physical philosophy" of the Greeks, which almost always finds its principles in the contingent order alone, or at best seeks them within the limits of the immediately superior but still particular point of view considered by the *Sānkhya*.

Nevertheless, owing to the nature of its subject matter, *Vaisheshika* finished by producing a somewhat "naturalistic" tendency in certain quarters among those who specially devoted themselves to its study; but this tendency, being generally foreign to the Oriental mind, never became as widely developed in India as it did in Greece through the influence of the "physical philosophers"; at least, only certain schools belonging to the most degenerate forms of Buddhism were destined to push it to its furthest logical conclusion, and this was only possible for them because they were openly outside the traditional unity of Hinduism. Nevertheless it is true to say that this tendency, which asserts itself plainly in the atomist conception, was already to be found in the ordinary teaching of *Vaisheshika*, since the origin of atomism, its heterodox character notwithstanding, is ascribed to Kanāda simultaneously with the development of *Vaisheshika* itself, though the two need not necessarily go together. The name of Kanāda seems moreover to contain some allusion to this theory, and if it belonged in the first instance to an individual, it can only have been as a mere surname; the fact that it alone has been handed down again shows the small importance attributed by the Hindus to individualities. In any case, in the implications at present carried by this name it is possible to detect something which, by reason of the deviation it indicates, is more akin to the "schools" of Western antiquity than anything analogous to be found in the other *darshanas*.

Like *Nyāya*, *Vaisheshika* distinguishes a certain number of *padārthas*, but naturally it determines them from a different point of view; these *padārthas* do not therefore coincide in any way with those of *Nyāya* and they might even be included among the subdivisions of the second one, the *prameya* or "object of proof." The first of these *padārthas*, which are six in number, is called *dravya*; this word is usually translated as "substance," quite an admissible rendering provided the term be taken, not in its metaphysical or universal sense, but in a relative sense only, in order to indicate the function of the logical subject; this is also the meaning that it bears according to Aristotle's conception of the categories. The second *padārtha* is "quality," called *guna*, a word we shall meet with again in *Sānkhya*, but differently applied; here the qualities in question are the attributes of manifested beings, or what the Scholastics called "accidents" when considering them in relation to the substance or subject serving as their support in the order of manifestation in individual mode. If these same qualities were to be transposed beyond this particular mode and considered in the very principle of their manifestation, they would have to be regarded as constituents of "essence," taken in the sense of a principle correlative and complementary to "substance," either in the universal order, or even, relatively and by analogy, in the individual order; but essence, even individual essence, the attributes of which reside in it "eminently" and not "formally," lies outside the point of view of *Vaisheshika*, which is concerned with existence taken in its strictest sense; that is why attributes are really nothing more for it than "accidents."

We have intentionally worded these last comments in a language which will make them readily comprehensible to those versed in the doctrine of Aristotle and the Scholastics; this language is moreover, in the present context, the least inadequate that Western usage has to offer. Substance, in both the senses that the word admits of, is the root of manifestation, but it is not itself manifested, becoming so only in and through its attributes, which are its modalities and which, conversely, enjoy no real existence in the contingent order of manifestation except in and through substance; it is in the latter that qualities reside and it is through the latter that action is produced. The third *padārtha* is in fact *karma* or action; and action, however it may differ in relation to quality, is included with the latter in the general notion of attributes, for it is nothing else but a "manner of being" of substance; this is indicated by the fact that in the constitution of language, both quality and action are expressed by the common form of attributive verbs. Action is taken as consisting essentially in movement, or rather in change, for this much more far-reaching notion, in which movement constitutes but one species, applies most aptly here, as well as to the analogous conception in Greek physics. It may be said in consequence that action is a passing and momentary mode of being, whereas quality is a relatively permanent and in some measure a stable mode; but if action were to be considered in the integrality of its temporal, and even non-temporal, consequences, this distinction also would disappear, as might indeed be foreseen when it is remembered that all attributes whatsoever issue alike from one and the same principle, and this may be said both under the heading of substance and of essence.

It is permissible to be more brief in speaking of the following three *padārthas*, which in short represent categories of relationships, that is to say certain other attributes of individual substances and of the relative principles which provide the conditions immediately determining their manifestation. The fourth *padārtha* is *sāmānya*, namely the association of qualities which, in all the various degrees that are possible, gives rise to the gradation of genera; the fifth is particularity or difference, more specially called *vishesha*, meaning whatever belongs exclusively to a given substance, that by which it is differentiated from all other substances; lastly, the sixth is *samāvāya*, or aggregation, that is to say the intimate relationship uniting a substance with the attributes inherent in it, and which is moreover itself an attribute of that substance. The association of these six *padārthas*, comprising in this way substances with all their attributes, makes up *bhāva* or existence; opposed to it correlatively is *abhāva* or non-existence, which is commonly counted as a seventh *padārtha*, though it is a purely negative conception: it is indeed the same thing as "privation" taken in its Aristotelian sense.

As for the subdivisions of these categories, time need not be spent on any except those of the first *padārtha*: these are the modalities and general conditions of individual substances. Here are to be found, in the first place, the five *bhūtas* or elements that go to make up corporeal things, namely *prithvī* or earth, *ap* or water, *tejas* or fire, *vāyu* or air and *ākāsha* or ether; they are numbered consecutively, beginning with the one that corresponds to the final term of this mode of manifestation, that is to say according to the order that correctly corresponds to the analytical point of view of *Vaisheshika*: *Sānkhya*, on the other hand, takes these elements in the contrary order, namely the order of their production or derivation. The five elements manifest themselves respectively through the five sensible qualities which correspond to them and are inherent in them, and which belong to the subdivisions of the second category. These qualities are substantial determinations, constitutive of all that belongs to the sensory world; it would be a great mistake to look on them as more or less analogous to the quite hypothetical "simple bodies" of modern chemistry, or even to assimilate them to "physical states," following a fairly common though inadequate interpretation of the cosmological theories of the Greeks. Besides the elements the *dravya* category comprises *kāla*, time, and *dish*, space : these are the fundamental conditions of corporeal existence, and it may be added in passing that they represent respectively, in the special mode of manifestation constituted by the sensory world, the activity of the two principles which are called *Shiva* and *Vishnu* in the realm of universal manifestation. These seven subdivisions concern corporeal existence exclusively ; but if an individual being (such as a human being) be considered as a whole, it includes, besides its bodily modality, constituent elements belonging to another order, and these elements are here represented by the two last subdivisions of the same category, *ātmā* and *manas*. *Manas*, or to translate this word by another derived from the selfsame root, "mind," comprises the whole of the psychic faculties belonging to the individual being as such, reason being the faculty among them that properly characterizes man. As for *ātmā*, a term which the word "soul" renders most imperfectly, it is properly the transcendent principle to which individuality is attached and which stands superior to it, a principle to which pure intellect must here be referred. It is distinguished from *manas*, or rather from the composite whole formed by *manas* and the bodily organism, in the same way that personality, in its metaphysical sense, is distinguished from individuality.

It is in the theory of the corporeal elements especially that the atomist conception makes its appearance: according to this theory an atom, or *anu*, partakes, potentially at least, of the nature of one or other of the elements, and it is from the grouping together of atoms of various kinds, under the action of a force said to be "non-perceptible" or *adrishta*, that all bodies are supposed to be formed. We have already said that this conception is formally opposed to the *Veda*, which asserts on the contrary the existence of the five elements with all that this implies: the two views therefore have really nothing in common. Besides it is quite easy to expose the contradiction inherent in atomism, the basic error of which lies in supposing that simple elements can exist in the corporeal order, whereas all that is bodily is necessarily composite, being always divisible from the very fact that it is extended, that is to say subject to the spatial condition; in order to find something simple or indivisible it is necessary to pass outside space, and therefore outside that special modality of manifestation which constitutes corporeal existence. If, as must be done in this instance, the word atom be taken in its true sense of "indivisible," a sense which modern physicists no longer give to it, it may be said that an atom, since it cannot have parts, must also be without area; now the sum of elements devoid of area can never form an area; if atoms fulfil their own definition, it is then impossible for them to make up bodies. To this well-known and moreover decisive chain of reasoning, another may also be added, employed by Shankarāchārya in order to refute atomism[1] : two things can come into contact with one another either by a part of themselves or by the whole ; for atoms, devoid as they are of parts, the first hypothesis is inadmissible ; thus only the second hypothesis remains, which amounts to saying that the aggregation of two atoms can only be realized by their coincidence purely and simply, whence it clearly follows that two atoms when joined occupy no more space than a single atom and so forth indefinitely; so, as before, atoms, whatever their number, will never form a body. Thus atomism represents nothing but sheer impossibility, as we pointed out when explaining the sense in which heterodoxy is to be understood ; but, atomism excepted, the point of view of *Vaisheshika*, reduced to essentials, is a perfectly legitimate one, and the foregoing exposition has sufficiently defined its range and meaning.

CHAPTER XI

SĀNKHYA

Sānkhya also is concerned with the domain of Nature, that is to say of Universal Manifestation, but, as we have already pointed out, this time Nature is considered synthetically, starting from the principles that govern its production and from which it draws all its reality. The expounding of this point of view, which is in a way intermediate between the cosmology of *Vaisheshika* and metaphysic, is ascribed to the ancient

[1] *Commentary on the Brahma-sūtras,* 2nd *Adhyāya,* 1st *Pāda, sūtra* 29.

sage Kapila; but, once again, this name does not stand for a person, and all references to it are of a purely symbolic character. As for the title *Sānkhya* it is variously interpreted; it derives from *sankhyā*, which means "enumeration" or "catalogue," also occasionally "reasoning"; it denotes especially a doctrine that devotes itself to the regular enumeration of the different degrees of manifested being, and this is indeed the character of *Sānkhya*, the whole teaching of which can be summed up in the distinction and consideration of the twenty-five *tattvas*, or true principles and elements, which correspond to those degrees revealed in their hierarchical order.

Having placed itself at the viewpoint of manifestation, *Sānkhya* takes as its starting-point *Prakriti* or *Pradhāna*, which is Universal Substance, undifferentiated and unmanifested in itself, but from which all things proceed by modification; this first *tattva* is the root or *mūla* of manifestation, and the *tattvas* that follow represent its modifications at different stages. At the first stage comes *Buddhi*, which is also called *Mahat* or the Great Principle. This is the pure intellect, transcendent relatively to the individual; here we are already situated in manifestation, but we still remain in the universal order. At the next stage, on the contrary, we find individual consciousness, *ahankāra*, which proceeds from the intellectual principle by a "particularising" determination, if one may so express it, and which produces in its turn the elements that follow. These include first of all the five *tanmātras*, elementary incorporeal and non-perceptible determinations, which will be the respective principles of the five *bhūtas* or corporeal elements; *Vaisheshika* had only to take the latter into account, and not the *tanmātras*, which need only be conceived when one's intention is to refer the notion of the elements or of the conditions governing the corporeal modality to the principles of universal existence. Next follow the individual faculties, produced by differentiation of the individual consciousness of which they may be said to represent so many functions, and these are reckoned to be eleven in number, ten external and one internal: the ten external faculties include five faculties of knowledge, which, in the bodily sphere, are faculties of sensation, and five faculties of action; the internal faculty is *manas*, which is a faculty both of knowledge and of action, and which is directly bound up with individual consciousness. Lastly, we come back to the five corporeal elements, numbered this time in the order of their production or manifestation: ether, air, fire, water and earth; and so we get the twenty-four *tattvas*, comprising *Prakriti* and all its modifications.

Up to this point *Sānkhya* considers things only in relation to substance, taken in its universal sense; but as was shown earlier, it is necessary to take into consideration, correlatively, as the other pole of manifestation, a complementary principle that can be called essence. This is the principle to which *Sānkhya* gives the name of *Purusha* or *Pumas*, and which it looks upon as a twenty-fifth *tattva*, entirely independent of the preceding ones; all manifested things are produced by *Prakriti*, yet, but for the presence of *Purusha* these productions could only enjoy a purely illusory existence. Contrary to some people's opinion, the consideration of these two principles does not imply the least suggestion of dualism: they are not derived from nor reducible to one another, but they both proceed from Universal Being, in which they constitute the first of all distinctions. However *Sānkhya* is not called upon to go beyond this particular distinction, and the consideration of pure Being does not enter into its point of view: but, not being systematic, it admits the possibility of all that transcends it, and this is the reason why it is in no wise dualistic. To connect this statement with our previous remarks on the subject of dualism, it must be added that the Western conception of spirit and matter only corresponds to the distinction of essence and substance under very special conditions and as a simple and particular application of that distinction, one among an indefinite number of other analogous distinctions all equally possible; it can thus be seen how far behind we have left the limitations of philosophic thought, even though we have not yet entered the realm of pure metaphysic.

It is necessary to return for a little to the conception of *Prakriti*: it is endowed with three *gunas* or constituent qualities, which in its primordial indifferentiation are in perfect equilibrium; every manifestation or modification of substance represents a rupture of this equilibrium, and all beings, in their various states of manifestation, participate in varying degrees in the three *gunas*, in indefinitely varying proportions. They are not therefore states, but conditions of universal existence to which all manifested beings are subjected, and it is important to distinguish them from the special conditions determining this or that state or mode of manifestation, such as space or time, which govern the corporeal state to the exclusion of others. The three *gunas* are *sattva*, conformity to the pure essence of Being or *Sat*, which is identified with intelligible light or knowledge and is represented as an ascending tendency ; *rajas*, the expansive impulse, in obedience to which a being develops in a certain state and, as it were, at a determined level of existence : lastly *tamas*, or obscurity, assimilated to ignorance, and described as a downward tendency. It is easy to see how inadequate and even false are the interpretations current among orientalists, especially in regard to the first two *gunas*, which they try to designate respectively by " goodness " and " passion," whereas quite clearly they do not imply anything of a moral or psychological nature. We cannot expound this most important conception in greater detail here nor go into the many different applications to which it gives rise, especially in so far as the theory of the elements is concerned : we must content ourselves with drawing attention to its existence.

Furthermore, as regards *Sānkhya* in general, we do not need to discuss it at such length as would have been necessary had we not already described many of its essential characteristics when comparing the point of view it adopts with that of *Vaisheshika* ; but there are still a few confusions to be dispelled. The orientalists, who mistake *Sānkhya* for a system of philosophy, readily represent it as a " materialistic " or " atheistical " doctrine : it goes without saying that it is the conception of *Prakriti* which they identify with their own notion of matter, an utterly false assimilation, while in addition they take no account of *Purusha* in their distorted interpretation. Universal substance is quite another thing from matter, which is at most but one restrictive and specialised determination of it ; and we have already had occasion to point out that the very notion of matter, as it exists among Westerners to-day, is no more known to the Hindus than it was to the Greeks themselves. It is not easy to imagine how there could be materialism without matter ; the atomism of the ancients, even in the West, cannot for that reason be reckoned materialistic, even if it was "mecanistic" ; modern philosophy can safely be left the monopoly of labels which were only invented for its own use, and cannot validly be employed elsewhere. Moreover, though it relates to Nature, *Sānkhya*, owing to its manner of approach, is never in danger of provoking a tendency towards naturalism, such as was noticeable in the atomist form of *Vaisheshika* ; all the more reason why it can in no wise be "evolutionary," as some have fancied, and this is true even if one takes evolutionism in its most general sense and without making it synonymous with a crude "transformism" ; such a confusing of points of view is too obviously absurd to merit further attention.

As for the reproach of atheism, this is what it amounts to : *Sānkhya* is "*nirīshwara*," that is to say it does not introduce the conception of *Īshwara* or the Divine Personality ; but, if this conception is absent from it, that is because it has no place there, given the point of view in question, any more than it has in *Nyāya* or *Vaisheshika*. The non-inclusion of something in a more or less specialised point of view only becomes denial when that point of view is declared to be exclusive, that is to say when it turns into a system, which is not the case here; the orientalists might well be asked whether European science, in its present form, should be labelled as essentially atheistic because it does not introduce the idea of God into its particular province (which indeed it is no more qualified to do than *Sānkhya*), since that is something which lies outside its purview. Moreover, side by side with *Sānkhya* as we have just described it, there exists another *darshana* which is sometimes looked upon as a second branch of *Sānkhya*, complementary to the first, and which is then qualified, in order to distinguish it, as *Seshwara*, because on the contrary it does introduce the conception of *Īshwara*; this *darshana*, which must now be examined, is the one usually called *Yoga*, thus identifying the doctrine with the goal that it expressly sets before itself.

CHAPTER XII

Yoga

The word *yoga* properly means "union"[1]; it should be mentioned in passing, though it is really a matter of small importance, that we do not know why numerous European authors make this a feminine word, whereas in Sanskrit it is masculine. The principal meaning

[1] The same root, in almost identical form, appears in the English word "yoke."—*Translator.*

of the term is the effective union of the human being with the Universal; applied to a *darshana*, of which the formulation in *sūtras* is attributed to *Patānjali*, it signifies that the *darshana* in question has as its goal the realization of this union and provides the means of attaining it. While the *Sānkhya* viewpoint remains a theoretical one, we are here essentially concerned with realization, in the metaphysical sense that we have already explained, notwithstanding the opinions of the professional orientalists, who imagine that they are concerned with a "philosophy," or of the would-be "esotericists" who, attempting to make up for their own lack of doctrine by fanciful inventions, look upon *Yoga* as a "method for developing the latent powers of the human organism." The point of view in question refers to a totally different order of things, incomparably superior to anything that is implied in such interpretations, and it escapes the comprehension of both orientalists and occultists alike; this is natural enough however, since nothing of the kind is to be met with in the West.

On the theoretical side *Yoga* completes *Sānkhya* by introducing the conception of *Īshwara* or Universal Being; this conception permits of the unification, first of *Purusha*, a multiple principle only so long as it is considered in relation to separate existences, and next of *Purusha* and *Prakriti*, since Universal Being, as their common principle, is beyond the distinction between them. *Yoga* again admits the development of Nature or manifestation as described in *Sānkhya*; but since it is here taken as the basis of a realization which is destined to lead beyond its own contingent sphere, it is considered, so to speak, in an order inverse to that of its development, namely, from the standpoint of return to its final end, which is identical with its initial principle. In relation to manifestation, the first principle is *Īshwara* or Universal Being ; that is not to say that this principle is absolutely first in the universal order, since we have explained the fundamental distinction to be made between *Īshwara*, who is Being, and *Brahma*, which is beyond Being ; but for the manifested being, union with Universal Being may be looked upon as constituting a necessary stage on the way towards ultimate union with the supreme *Brahma*. Besides, the possibility of going beyond Being, either theoretically or from the point of view of realization, implies a complete metaphysical doctrine, which the *Yoga-shāstra* of Patānjali does not claim to represent by itself alone.

Since metaphysical realization essentially consists in identification through knowledge, whatever is not itself knowledge has value only as an accessory means ; accordingly *Yoga* takes as its starting-point and fundamental means what is called *ekāgrya*, that is to say "concentration." This concentration, as Max Müller admitted,[1] is something quite foreign to the Western mind, accustomed as it is to direct all its attention upon externals and to disperse itself amidst their indefinitely changing multiplicity ; it has indeed become almost an impossibility for this type of mind, and yet it is the first and most important of all the conditions of effective realization. Concentration, especially at the outset, can take for its support either a thought or

[1] *Preface to the Sacred Books of the East*, pages xxiii-xxiv.

else a symbol such as a word or an image; subsequently, however, these auxiliary means become needless, as well as the rites and other "aids" that may be employed concurrently in view of the same end. It is evident, moreover, that this end could not be attained solely by use of the accessory means we have just mentioned, which are extraneous to knowledge; but it is none the less true that these means, though in no wise essential, are not to be despised, for they can possess a large measure of efficacy in assisting realization, and in leading, if not to its final goal, at least to its earlier stages. Such is the real utility of everything that is covered by the term *hatha-yoga*, which is designed, on the one hand, to destroy, or rather to "transform" those elements in the human being which form an obstacle to union with the Universal, and, on the other hand, to prepare for that union by the assimilation of certain rhythms, connected chiefly with the control of the breath; but for reasons previously given, we do not intend to dwell here on questions affecting realization. In any case, it must always be borne in mind that, of all preliminary means, theoretical knowledge alone is really indispensable, and that later, when one passes to actual realization, it is concentration that matters most and that leads to it in the most immediate way, for it is directly bound up with knowledge. An action is always separated from its results, but meditation or intellectual contemplation, called in Sanskrit *dhyāna*, bears its fruit within itself; moreover action cannot bring about deliverance from the realm of action, a result which is implicit in the final aim of metaphysical realization. However, this realization may not always be complete and, it is possible for it to stop short at the attainment of states which are of a higher order but not final ; it is to these lesser degrees of realization that the special observances prescribed by the *Yoga-Shāstra* refer ; but instead of traversing them in succession, it is also possible, though doubtless more difficult, to pass them over in one leap in order to arrive directly at the final goal, and it is this last way which is often referred to by the term *rāja-yoga*.[1] Actually, this last expression should be taken to refer also, in a stricter sense, to the goal of realization itself, whatever may be the means or particular modes employed, which should naturally be those best adapted to the mental and even to the physiological conditions of each person ; in this case the chief purpose of *hathayoga*, at all its stages, will be to lead up to *rāja-yoga*.

The *Yogī*, in the strict sense of the word, is he who has realised perfect and final union ; the name cannot therefore be applied without abuse to the man who simply gives himself up to the study of *Yoga* as a *darshana*, nor even to one who in fact follows the path of realization indicated in it but without having yet reached the supreme goal towards which it leads. The state of a true *Yogī* is that of a being who has attained and possesses the highest possibilities in their fullest development ; all the secondary states we have mentioned belong to him as well, automatically so, but as it were by superaddition, and without

[1] In Tibet this way is known as the "direct path" (literally "the short-cut").—*Translator.*

being given greater importance than is their due, each according to its rank, in the complete hierarchy of existence of which they form so many constituent elements. The same can be said of the possession of certain special and more or less extraordinary powers, such as those called *siddhis* or *vibhūtis* : far from being worth pursuing for their own sake, these powers amount to no more than simple accidents, derived from the realm of the "great illusion," as does all that belongs to the phenomenal order, and the *Yogī* only exercises them in quite exceptional circumstances ; regarded otherwise, they can only form obstacles to complete realization. It can be seen how unfounded is the popular opinion that would make of the *Yogī* a sort of magician, not to say a sorcerer ; in truth, those who make a display of certain peculiar faculties, corresponding to the development of possibilities that do not however belong exclusively to the "organic" or physiological order, are not *Yogīs* at all, but they are men who, for one reason or another, and most often through intellectual insufficiency, have stopped short at a partial and inferior realization which does not extend beyond the limits of human individuality, and one can rest assured that they will never travel any further. On the other hand, through true metaphysical realization, detached from all contingencies and therefore essentially of a supra-individual order, the *Yogī* has become identical with "Universal Man," to use an expression borrowed from Moslem esoterism to which we have already referred ; but in order to draw the conclusions that this implies, we should have to go beyond the limits we wish to set ourselves in the present work. Furthermore, it is especially to *hatha-yoga*, that is to say to the preparatory tasks, that the present *darshana* refers, and our remarks were chiefly intended to strike at the root of the commonest errors on the subject ; what remains to be said, namely whatever concerns the final goal of realization, should be reserved rather for the purely metaphysical side of the doctrine, which is represented by the *Vedānta*.

CHAPTER XIII

Mīmānsā

The word *mīmānsā* literally means "inward reflection"; it is applied in a general way to the reflective study of the *Veda*, its purpose being to determine the precise meaning of *shruti* and to draw out the consequences implied in it, whether these belong to the practical or to the intellectual order. Thus interpreted, *Mīmānsā* includes the two last of the six *darshanas*, and these are then entitled *Pūrva-Mīmānsā* and *Uttara-Mīmānsā*, that is to say the first and second *Mīmānsā*, referring respectively to the two orders mentioned above. The first *Mīmānsā* is also entitled *Karma-Mīmānsā*, since it concerns the realm of action, while the second is called *Brahma-Mīmānsā*, as consisting essentially of the knowledge of *Brahma* ; it should be noted that here it is the supreme *Brahma* and no longer *Īshwara* that is envisaged, the point of view being that of pure metaphysic. This second *Mīmānsā* properly constitutes the *Vedānta* ; and when *Mīmānsā* without epithet is mentioned, as is the case in the present chapter, it is always the first *Mīmānsā* only that is intended.

The exposition of this *darshana* is attributed to Jaimini and the method that it adopts is as follows : mistaken opinions about a question are first put forward, and then refuted, and finally the correct solution of the question is given as a conclusion of the whole discussion ; this method of exposition offers a remarkable analogy with that adopted by the Scholastic doctrine of the Middle Ages in the West. As to the nature of the subjects treated, this is described, at the very beginning of the *sūtras* of Jaimini, as a study that aims at establishing the proofs and justifications of *dharma* in its connexion with *kārya* or " that which must be accomplished." We have already dwelt sufficiently on the notion of *dharma* and on what is meant by conformity of action with *dharma*, which is precisely in point here ; it should be recalled that the word *karma* bears a twofold meaning ; in a general sense, it embraces action in all its forms, which is often opposed to *jnāna* or knowledge, a contrast which also answers to the distinction between the last two *darshanas* ; in a more special and technical sense, *karma* means ritual action as enjoined by the *Veda*, and this latter acceptation naturally occurs frequently in *Mīmānsā*, which sets itself the task of supplying the reasons for these ritual ordinances and of defining their scope.

Mīmānsā starts by considering the various *pramānas* or means of proof which are given by the logicians, with the addition of certain other sources of knowledge that lie outside their particular province ; it would moreover be easy to reconcile the different classifications of these *pramāṇas*, by looking on them simply as more or less developed and complete as the case may be, for they do not contradict one another in any way. Subsequently a distinction is drawn between various classes of rules and injunctions, the most general line of division being between direct and indirect injunctions ; the portion of the *Veda* which contains precepts is called *brāhmana*, in contradistinction to the portion called *mantra* or ritual formula, all that is contained in the Vedic texts being either *mantra* or *brāhmana*. However the *brāhmanas* do not merely consist of precepts, since the *Upanishads* themselves, which are purely doctrinal and which form the foundation of *Vedānta*, enter into this category ; but there is a practical class of *brāhmana* with which *Mīmānsā* is specially concerned and which sets out the manner of accomplishing rites, the conditions governing their performance and their application to different circumstances ; it also explains the significance of the symbolical elements that enter into these rites and indicates the *mantras* which can be suitably employed in each special case. Concerning the nature and efficacy of *mantra*, as also, in a more general way, concerning the traditional authority and non-human origin of the *Veda*, *Mīmānsā* unfolds the theory of the perpetuity of sound which we alluded to before, with particular reference to the theory of the original and perpetual association of articulated sound with the sense of hearing, which makes of language something far deeper than a more or less arbitrary convention.

In addition *Mīmānsā* expounds the theory of the infallibility of the traditional doctrine, an infallibility which must be conceived of as inherent in the doctrine itself and which consequently in no wise belongs to human individuals ; they only participate in it in so far as they possess an effective knowledge of the doctrine and interpret it faithfully, and, even then, this infallibility must never be ascribed to individuals as such, but always to the doctrine expressing itself through them. That is why only those who know the integral *Veda* are qualified to compose authentic traditional scriptures, the authority of which is a participation in the authority of the primordial tradition whence it is derived and on which alone it is founded, without the individuality of the author playing the smallest part ; this distinction in the traditional sphere between fundamental authority and derived authority is expressed by the terms *shruti* and *smriti*, which have already been mentioned in connection with the " law of *Manu*." The conception of infallibility as inherent in the doctrine alone is moreover common to both Hindus and Moslems; fundamentally, it is also the same conception that is applied by the Catholic Church from its specifically religious point of view, since the pontifical authority, if regarded in its principle, appears as essentially bound up with a function, namely the authorised interpretation of the doctrine, and not with an individuality, for the latter is never infallible apart from the exercise of that function, under conditions strictly laid down.

Owing to the nature of *Mīmānsā*, it is to this

darshana that the ancillary sciences of the *Veda* known as the *Vedāngas* are most directly attached ; we have previously described these sciences and it is enough to refer to their descriptions in order to realize the close link between them and the present subject. Thus *Mīmānsā* dwells with insistence on the importance, for the understanding of texts, of correct spelling and true pronunciation as taught by *shikshā* ; it also distinguishes various classes of *mantras*, in accordance with the rhythm proper to each one, following the principles laid down by *chhandas*. Furthermore we find considerations relating to *vyākarana*, that is to say questions of grammar, such as the difference between the normal meaning of words and their dialectic or barbarous uses, as well as observations on certain special forms employed in the *Veda*, and on the terms which are applied there in an unusual sense ; to this must be added, in many places, etymological and symbolical interpretations which fall within the province of *nirukta*. Lastly, a knowledge of *jyotisha* is required in order to decide the times when rites are to be accomplished, and as for *kalpa*, we have seen that it sums up the rules that govern their actual performance.

Over and above all this *Mīmānsā* treats of a large number of questions of jurisprudence, and this should not be a cause for surprise, since in the Hindu civilization all legislation is essentially traditional ; a certain similarity is in fact noticeable in the manner in which debates at law and discussions of *Mīmānsā* are conducted, and there is even identity in the terms used to describe the successive phases in either case. This resemblance is certainly no accident, but it would be a mistake to see in it anything more than what it really is, namely a sign that one and the same spirit has been applied in two connected, though distinct, spheres of activity. This fact moreover reduces certain pretensions of the sociologists to their true value: impelled by the perverse habit, common among experts, of referring everything to their own special subject, they take advantage of every point of likeness in vocabulary that they can discover, particularly in the field of logic, in order to infer borrowings from social institutions, as if ideas and modes of reasoning could not exist independently of these institutions, which, truth to tell, only represent one application of necessarily pre-existing ideas. Some have tried to evade this issue, and to maintain the priority of the social point of view by inventing what they have called the "pre-logical mentality"; but this strange theory, as well as their generally accepted conception of "primitive peoples," does not rest on any serious basis; it is even contradicted by all that is known for certain about antiquity and it would be best to relegate it to the realms of pure phantasy, together with all the "myths" that its inventors gratuitously ascribe to peoples whose real mentality they have failed to understand. There are quite enough real and profound differences between the modes of thought peculiar to every race and period, without inventing non-existent varieties, which complicate things much more than they explain them. Nor is it necessary to go and seek for the so-called primitive human type among the members of some degenerate tribe, which is no longer very certain about what it does think, but which at any rate has never possessed the thoughts that are attributed to it ; but the real modes of human thought, excepting those of the modern West, lie just as much outside the understanding of sociologists as of orientalists.

To return from this digression to *Mīmānsā*, mention should be made of another idea that plays an important part in it : this notion, which goes by the name of *apūrva*, is one of those which are difficult to translate into the terms of a Western language ; nevertheless we shall try to give some idea of its meaning and implications. In the last chapter it was said that action, which is radically different from knowledge in this as in all else, does not carry its consequences within itself ; in this respect, the opposition is, fundamentally, that between succession and simultaneity, for the very conditions governing every action make it impossible for it to produce its effects otherwise than in successive mode. However, for anything to be a cause, it must actually exist, for which reason the real causal relationship can only be conceived as a relationship of simultaneity ; were it to be conceived as a relationship of succession, there would have to have been a moment when something that no longer existed produced something that had not yet come into existence, obviously an absurd suggestion. It follows then that if an action, which is itself but a momentary modification, is to have future and more or less remote results, it must have, at the moment of its accomplishment, an effect not immediately perceptible, yet which, subsisting at least in a relatively permanent fashion, is destined eventually to produce in its turn the perceptible result. It is this non-perceptible effect, potential in some measure, that is termed *apūrva*, because it is superimposed on and not anterior to the action ; it may be looked on either as a posterior state of the action itself, or as an antecedent state of the result, since an effect must always be virtually contained in its cause, from which it could not otherwise proceed. Besides, even in the case where a given result seems to follow directly on the action without a pause, the intermediate existence of an *apūrva* is none the less necessary, given that there is still succession and not perfect simultaneity, and that the action, in itself, must always be separate from its result. In this fashion, the action escapes momentariness, and even, to some extent, the limitations of the temporal condition ; in fact the *apūrva*, germ of all its future consequences, since it does not belong to the realm of corporeal and sensible manifestation, is outside ordinary time, but not outside all duration, for it still belongs to the contingent order.

The *apūrva* can be regarded, on the one hand, as remaining attached to the being which has performed the action, since it is henceforth a constituent element of its individuality considered in its non-corporeal aspect, and will continue to exist as long as the individuality itself ; on the other hand, it may also be regarded as quitting the limits of that individuality in order to enter the realm of potential energies of the cosmic order ; in this second case, if one pictures it, to use an admittedly imperfect image, as a vibration sent out at a certain point, then this same vibration, having travelled to the furthest confines of the realm to which it has access, will return in a contrary direction to its point of departure, and this it will do, as causality demands, in the form of a reaction of like nature to the original action. This is in perfect agreement with the Taoist theory of "concordant actions and reactions": inasmuch as every action, and also, in a more general sense, every manifestation marks a rupture of equilibrium, as was pointed out when treating of the three *gunas*, a corresponding reaction is demanded in order to restore that equilibrium, since the sum of all differentiations must in the last instance be equivalent to the total indifferentiation. This theory, in which the human and cosmic orders meet, completes the idea that can be formed of the relationship between *karma* and *dharma*; and it must forthwith be added that a reaction, being a perfectly natural consequence of an action, is in no wise a "sanction" in a moral sense: there is nothing in all this which provides any warrant for the moral point of view to assert itself, and indeed that point of view may well have been born of a failure to understand these things, resulting in a sentimental distortion. However that may be, the reaction, in its influence by rebound on the being which put forth the initial action, takes on again the individual and even temporal character which the intermediate *apūrva* had not retained; if that being is then no longer to be found in the state where it was originally situated, and which was but a passing mode of its manifestation, the same reaction, divested henceforth of the conditions characterising the original individuality, can still reach the being in another state of manifestation, through the intermediary of those elements that ensure the continuity of this new state with the earlier state ; it is here that the causal connexion between the various cycles of existence becomes apparent, and whatever is true for a given being is also true, following the closest analogy, for the whole of universal manifestation.

If we have gone into these explanations at considerable length, it is not simply because we have here an interesting example of a certain type of Oriental theory, nor even because we shall later have occasion to refer to a false interpretation of this theory which has been put forward in the West ; we have done so chiefly because this is a question which has a vast range of application, even in the practical field, though in respect of the latter an attitude of reserve is often advisable ; it is preferable to be content with giving a few quite general indications, as we have done here, leaving to each individual the task of drawing from the theory those developments and conclusions that fall in best with his own aptitudes and personal tendencies.

CHAPTER XIV

VEDĀNTA

WITH *Vedānta* we find ourselves in the realm of pure metaphysic, as we have already explained, and it is needless therefore to repeat that it is neither a philosophy nor a religion, although the orientalists seem determined to see one or the other in it, or even both at the same time, as Schopenhauer has done. The name of this final *darshana* etymologically means "end of the *Veda*," and the word "end" should here be taken in the double sense, which it also possesses in English, of conclusion and goal; in fact, the *Upanishads*, on which it is essentially based, form the last portion of the Vedic texts and what they teach, in so far as it can be taught, is the final and supreme goal of the whole of traditional knowledge, detached from all the more or less specialised and contingent applications to which it may give rise in various spheres. Their very title of *Upanishads* shows that they are destined to destroy ignorance, the root of the illusion that keeps beings fettered by the bonds of conditioned existence, and it also shows that they achieve their purpose by furnishing the means of approaching to the knowledge of *Brahma*; if it is only a question of approaching this knowledge, that is because it is entirely uncommunicable in its essence and can be effectively reached only by a strictly personal effort, which cannot be made up for by any external teaching, however exalted or profound. The interpretation just given is the one accepted by all competent Hindus; it would hardly be reasonable to prefer the unauthorised conjecture of various European writers who would have it that *Upanishad* means knowledge obtained by sitting at the feet of a teacher; moreover Max Müller,[1] even while accepting the latter interpretation, felt bound to admit that it indicated nothing really characteristic and could be just as well applied to any of the other parts of the *Veda*, since oral teaching is their usual method of regular transmission.

[1] *Introduction to the Upanishads*, pages lxxix-lxxxi.

Complete and final knowledge owes its incommunicable character to the fact that the metaphysical order contains ideas that are not susceptible of outward expression, and also to the fact that if it is to be all that it should be, it cannot stop short at mere theory but must imply a corresponding realization ; that is why we say that it can only be taught up to a point, and it is evident that this restriction applies in a double sense to both theory and realization, though it is in respect of the latter that the obstacle is most unquestionably insurmountable. In actual practice, so far as theory is concerned, recourse can always be had to some symbolism or other in order at least to suggest possibilities of conception, even if they cannot be wholly expressed, and besides this there are certain methods of transmission which are effected outside and beyond any kind of formal representation, though the mere suggestion of them would appear so improbable to a Westerner that there is no point in attempting to describe them here, which indeed would hardly be possible. It remains true, on the other hand, that all understanding, even theoretical understanding in its most elementary stages, presupposes an indispensable personal effort and is conditioned by the individual aptitude for receiving knowledge shown by the person to whom the teaching is being imparted : it is quite obvious that a master, however remarkable he may be, cannot understand on behalf of his pupil, and that it is for the latter alone to assimilate whatever is brought within his reach. The reason for this is that all true knowledge, provided it is genuinely assimilated, already constitutes in its own right, if not an effective realization, at least a virtual realization—if it is permissible thus to correlate these two words, which contradict one another only in appearance ; otherwise one could not say with Aristotle that a being "is all that it knows." As for the purely personal character of all realization, it can be quite simply explained by the following remark, which may appear strange but which is none the less axiomatic, namely that a being cannot be other than itself, and that what it is it alone can be ; if it is necessary to formulate such primary truths, this is because they are just the truths that are most commonly forgotten, and because they imply much more far-reaching consequences than people of a superficial or analytical turn of mind can ever be led to suspect. What alone can be taught, and incompletely at that, is the more or less indirect and mediate means of metaphysical realization, as we pointed out when speaking of *Yoga* ; and the first, the most indispensable and indeed the only indispensable means is theoretical knowledge itself. However it should also be added that in a metaphysically complete doctrine, theory and realization are never entirely separated ; this can be perceived at every turn in the *Upanishads*, where it is often hard to distinguish what refers respectively to the one and to the other, and where, truth to tell, the same things may refer to both, according to the way they are considered. In such a doctrine, the point of view of realization reacts even on the formulation of the theory, which presupposes it at least implicitly and ean never be independent of it, since theory, possessing value only as a preparation, must be subordinated to realization in the same way as a means is kept subordinate to the end in view of which it has been instituted.

All these considerations must be taken into account if one wishes to understand the point of view of *Vedānta*, or rather its spirit, since the metaphysical point of view, not being any single point of view in particular, can only be referred to as such purely by analogy; moreover these remarks could be applied with equal force to any of the diverse forms assumed by traditional metaphysic in other civilizations, since metaphysic, for the reasons already given, is one in its essence and cannot be otherwise than one. Too much stress can never be laid on the fact that it is the *Upanishads* which, forming an integral part of the *Veda*, represent the primordial and fundamental tradition; *Vedānta*, in the form in which it has been deliberately extracted from them, has been synthetically co-ordinated (which does not mean systematized) in the *Brahma-sūtras*, the composition of which is ascribed to Bādarāyana; he, morever, is identified with Vyāsa, which is particularly suggestive for those who bear in mind the intellectual function indicated by that name. The *Brahma-sūtras*, the text of which is extremely concise, have been the subject of many commentaries, among which those of Shankarāchārya and Rāmānuja are by far the most important; both these commentaries are strictly orthodox, in spite of certain apparent divergencies, which amount really to nothing but differences of adaptation: that of Shankarāchārya more particularly represents the *Shaiva* tendency and that of Rāmānuja the *Vaishnava*; the general explanation we have already given on the subject makes it needless to discuss this distinction here, which only has reference to different ways leading towards a single goal.

The *Vedānta*, being a purely metaphysical doctrine, appears essentially as *advaita-vāda* or the "doctrine of non-duality"; we have explained the meaning of this expression when differentiating between metaphysical and philosophic thought. In order to indicate its scope as far as such a thing is possible, it may now be said that whereas Being is "one," the Supreme Principle, known as *Brahma*, can only be described as "without duality," because, being beyond every determination, even beyond Being which is the first of all determinations, It cannot be characterised by any positive attribute; such is the consequence of Its infinity, which is necessarily absolute totality, containing in Itself all possibilities. Thus there can be nothing really outside *Brahma*, since such a supposition would be tantamount to limiting It; it follows immediately that the world, taking the word in the widest possible sense, that is as universal manifestation in its entirety, is not distinct from *Brahma*, or at least is distinguished from It in illusory fashion only. On the other hand, *Brahma* is absolutely distinct from the world, since none of the determinative attributes that belong to the world can be applied to It, the whole of universal manifestation being strictly nil in relation to Its infinity; and it will be noticed that this irreciprocity of relationship implies a formal condemnation of "pantheism," as well as of all "immanentism." Moreover, pantheism, if one wishes to preserve for the term a sufficiently exact and reasonable meaning, is inseparable from "naturalism," which amounts to saying that it is plainly anti-metaphysical ; it is therefore idle to look for pantheism in *Vedānta*, and yet this opinion, ridiculous though it be, is the one commonly put forward by Westerners, even by specialists ; here indeed is something likely to give the Orientals, who are well aware of what pantheism really implies, a high idea of the value of European science and of the intelligence of its representatives.

It is clearly impossible to give even a brief account of the doctrine as a whole ; but some of the questions with which it deals, such as, for instance, the constitution of the human being considered metaphysically,[1] can later be made the object of special studies. We will pause here over one point only, concerning the supreme goal, which is called *moksha* or *mukti*, that is to say "Deliverance," because the being who reaches it, whatever state he may belong to and whatever his rank within that state, is freed from the bonds of conditioned existence by perfect identification with the Universal : this is the realization of what Moslem esoterism calls the "Supreme Identity" and it is through this realization, and through it alone, that a man becomes a *Yogī* in the true sense of the word. The state of *Yogī* is not then analogous with any particular state whatsoever, but it embraces all possible states as the principle embraces all its consequences ; he who has reached it is also called *jīvan-mukta*, that is to say "delivered during life," by

[1] *See* the companion volume "Man and his Becoming according to the Vedānta." (Translator.)

contrast with *videha-mukta* or "delivered when out of the bodily form," an expression describing a being for whom realization is only reached (or rather for whom realization, from having been virtual, only becomes effective) after death and the dissolution of the human compound. Nevertheless, in either case, the being is definitely freed from individual conditions, or from all that is comprised by *nāma* and *rūpa*, "name" and "form," and even from the conditions of all manifestation whatsoever; he escapes the indefinite causal chain of actions and reactions, which is not the case when simply passing to another individual state, even one that occupies a rank superior to the human state in the hierarchy of the degrees of existence. Moreover it is evident that action can produce no effects except within the realm of action and that its efficacy stops short at the exact point where its own influence ceases; action cannot therefore have the effect of freeing from action nor of leading to the obtaining of Deliverance; indeed an action, whatever its nature, can only lead to partial realizations, corresponding to certain higher, but still determined and conditioned states.

Shankarāchārya expressly declares that "there is no other means of obtaining complete and final Deliverance except knowledge; action, not being opposed to ignorance, cannot overcome it, whereas knowledge dispels ignorance as light dispels darkness"[1]; and since ignorance is the root-cause of every limitation, when once this has disappeared, individuality, which is characterised by its limitations, disappears automatically. Moreover this "transformation," in the

[1] *Ātmā-Bodha.*

etymological sense of "passage beyond form," changes nothing in the appearance of things; in the case of the *jīvan-mukta*, individual appearance naturally continues without exterior change, but it can no longer affect the being whom it clothes, once the latter is effectively aware that it is illusory; but it must be added that to be effectively aware of this truth goes far beyond the mere theoretical conception of it. In the passage following the words quoted above, Shankarāchārya describes the state of the *Yogī* in the very restricted measure in which it can be put into words or rather suggested through them; his observations form the real conclusion of the study of the nature of the human being which we alluded to before, by showing the highest possibilities to which that being is capable of attaining, as the supreme and final goal of metaphysical wisdom.

CHAPTER XV

Some Supplementary Remarks on the Doctrine as a Whole

In this survey, which has intentionally been made as synthetic as possible, we have tried to show in the case of each *darshana* not only its distinctive features but also its relationship to metaphysic, which is the common centre of all branches of the doctrine and the starting-point of their several developments; we have also taken the opportunity of emphasising a certain number of important points bearing on the doctrine conceived as a whole. In this connexion it should be clearly understood that *Vedānta*, though it is reckoned to be the last of the *darshanas* in that it represents the final summing up of all knowledge, is none the less, in its essence, the principle whence all the remainder are derived, as so many specifications or applications. If any branch of knowledge were not dependent in this way on metaphysic, it would literally be lacking in principle, and therefore bereft of any traditional character ; this shows the radical difference between scientific knowledge, in the sense given to the word in the West, and that which corresponds to it least inadequately in India. It is evident for example, that the point of view of cosmology is not equivalent to that of modern physics, and that even the point of view of traditional logic is not equivalent to that of philosophical logic, conceived, for example, after the manner of Stuart Mill ; we have already drawn attention to these differences. Cosmology, even within the limits of the *Vaisheshika*, is not an experimental science like the present-day physics ; through its attachment to principles, it is much more a deductive than an inductive science, like all the other branches of the doctrine. It is true that Cartesian physics was also deductive, but it suffered from the serious defect of resting, in so far as it acknowledged principles at all, on a simple philosophical hypothesis, and this accounts for its failure.

The difference of method which we have just pointed out, and which reveals a profound difference of conception, applies with equal force to sciences that may properly be called experimental, but which are nevertheless much more deductive than those of the West, and so avoid all empiricism ; it is only on this condition that such sciences have a claim to be looked upon as traditional sciences, even though of secondary importance and belonging to an inferior order. In this connexion we specially have in mind medicine, considered as an *Upaveda* ; and our remarks would apply equally well to the traditional medicine of the Far East. Without in any way losing its practical character, medicine in this instance represents something far more comprehensive than the science usually referred to under that name ; besides pathology and therapeutics, it includes many elements which in the West would be considered as belonging to physiology, for instance, or even to psychology, but here they are dealt with in quite a different way. The results obtainable in the application of such a science might in many cases appear extraordinary in the eyes of those who have formed but a hazy idea of its real nature ; moreover we believe that it would be very difficult for a Westerner to arrive at sufficient proficiency in this kind of study, as very different methods of investigation are employed in it from those to which he is accustomed.

We have just said that applied sciences, even when affiliated to tradition as their common source, cannot be considered as anything but inferior branches of knowledge ; the fact of their derivation proves them to be subordinate, as is only logical, and moreover the Orientals, who both by temperament and deepest conviction trouble their minds very little about immediate applications, have never dreamed of adulterating the order of pure knowledge with anything of a material or sentimental nature, which is the only factor that could upset the natural and normal hierarchy of the various kinds of knowledge. It is this same cause of intellectual disorder which, on becoming generalised in the mentality of a race or of a period, more than anything else leads people to forget pure metaphysic and unwarrantably to substitute for it more or less specialised points of view, besides giving birth to sciences which cannot claim to be linked up with any traditional principle. Such sciences are no doubt legitimate enough so long as they abide within their proper limits, but they must not be taken for anything greater than they really are, namely an analytical, fragmentary and relative kind of knowledge; and thus, by separating itself radically from metaphysic, with which its particular point of view in fact forbids any relationship, Western science was bound to lose in range whatever it gained in independence, and its uncontrolled development in the direction of practical applications was inevitably paid for by a decrease in speculative power.

These few remarks complete our previous discussion of the wide differences in the respective points of view of East and West; in the East tradition is in a real sense the entire civilization, since it embraces, as its derivatives, all the branches of true knowledge, whatever order they may belong to, as well as the whole fabric of social institutions: tradition contains everything in embryo from the start, by the very fact that it lays down the universal principles whence all things are derived together with their laws and conditions, and the adaptation called for at any given time can only amount to an elaboration of the doctrine, carried out in a strictly deductive and analogical spirit, in conformity with the needs of the period in question. It is easy to see that under these circumstances the influence of tradition wields a power from which it would scarcely be possible to detach oneself, and that any schism, if it does arise, is forced at once to constitute itself as a pseudo-tradition ; as to breaking every traditional bond openly and finally, no person could dream of such a thing, even were it feasible. This should also make it possible to understand the nature and characteristics of traditional teaching, which serves to transmit not only the principles but also the practical means of assimilating and integrating every element into the intellectuality of a civilization.

CHAPTER XVI

The Traditional Teaching

We have said that the primary function of the highest caste, the *Brāhmanas*, is the preservation and transmission of the traditional doctrine ; the discharging of this office provides the real reason for the existence of such a caste, since the whole social order rests on the basis of the doctrine, outside of which it cannot hope to find those principles that alone confer stability and the power to endure. Where tradition means everything, those who act as its custodians must logically stand supreme; in other words, if the diversity of the functions necessary to the subsistence of the social organism entails a certain incompatibility between those functions, so that they require to be exercised by different individuals, all these individuals always remain essentially dependent on the custodians of the tradition, for it is only by an effective participation in the tradition that anyone is enabled to play a correspondingly effective part in the life of the community: this is the real and complete explanation of the spiritual and intellectual authority belonging to the *Brāhmanas*. At the same time, this also explains the deep and indissoluble bond which unites the disciple to his master, not only in India but throughout the East, a relationship that has no parallel in the modern West; the function of a teacher is in fact a true "spiritual fatherhood," and that is why the ritual and symbolic act by which it is inaugurated constitutes a "second birth" for the man who is to receive the teaching through a regular transmission. This idea of "spiritual fatherhood" is accurately expressed by the word *guru*, which is the name given to a teacher by the Hindus and which also bears the secondary meaning of "ancestor"; among the Arabs the same idea is conveyed by the word *sheikh*, which literally means "elder," and serves an identical purpose. In China, the prevailing conception of "racial solidarity" lends a slightly different flavour to the corresponding idea, so that the office of teacher becomes assimilated to that of "elder brother," the guide and natural guardian of those who come after him in the traditional path, though he will not become an "ancestor" until after his death; but in China, as everywhere else, the phrase "to be born into knowledge" is in daily use.

The traditional teaching is handed down under conditions which are strictly determined by its nature : to produce its full effect, it must always be adapted to the intellectual possibilities of each man to whom it is offered, and should be graduated according to the degree of understanding reached at any given moment, and this demands, on the part of a recipient who aspires to advance still further, an unremitting personal effort to assimilate effectively the teaching imparted to him. This is a natural consequence of the way in which the doctrine is treated as a connected whole, and it is this fact which makes necessary the oral and direct teaching which nothing else can replace ; indeed, in its absence, the chain of a regular and unbroken "spiritual filiation" is bound to be broken, except in certain quite unusual cases, where continuity can be preserved by other means which it would however be too difficult to describe in a Western language for us to undertake to do so here. In any case Orientals are free from the all too common illusion of the West, which consists in believing that everything can be learned from books, with the result that memory is set up in the place of intelligence; for the Easterner, texts count as no more than "supports," in the sense that we have so often given to that word, and their study merely furnishes the basis for an intellectual development, without ever being mistaken for that development itself ; in this way, erudition is given its proper value and is placed on the lower level which normally belongs to it, as a means subordinate and accessory to true knowledge.

The Oriental way is in complete antithesis to

Western methods in yet another respect : the modes of the traditional teaching, which confer on it a character not precisely "esoteric" but rather "initiatic," are obviously opposed to any sort of thoughtless diffusion, which is more harmful than helpful in the eyes of anyone who is not in some way or other the dupe of appearances. First of all, one may be forgiven for having doubts about the value and scope of any teaching that is distributed indiscriminately and in an identical form among the most variously endowed individuals differing widely in their aptitudes and temperament, as happens at present among all the European peoples. This system of education, surely the most imperfect of any, has been called into being through the mania for equality which has destroyed not only the true notion of hierarchy, but almost every trace of feeling for it as well ; and yet, but for the utter blindness induced by the indulgence of sentimental prejudices, it would seem impossible to present people who regard "facts" as the only standard of criticism, in accordance with the spirit of modern experimental science, with any fact more obvious than that of natural inequalities, both in the intellectual and the physical orders.

Furthermore, there is yet another reason why Orientals, who are free from the spirit of propaganda and feel no urge to spread their own conceptions at any price, are resolutely opposed to all "popularisation" : the reason is that by attempting to bring down the doctrine to the level of the common mentality under the pretext of making it accessible to all, it must inevitably be distorted and denatured in the process ;

it is not for the doctrine to abase itself or to conform to the limited powers of understanding of the many ; it is for individuals to rise, if they can, to an appreciation of the doctrine in its integral purity. This is an indispensable condition for the formation of an intellectual elect, which will take place by a natural process of selection, since each man must necessarily stop short at the degree of knowledge corresponding to his own "mental horizon" ; it also furnishes a protection against the manifold disorders brought about by the diffusion of a semi-education which is far more deadly than ignorance pure and simple ; the Orientals will always be far more conscious of the drawbacks of "compulsory education" than of its supposed benefits and, as it would seem, with ample justification.

There is much more that might be said about the nature of traditional teaching, which can be considered under aspects that are still more profound ; but as we do not profess to have made an exhaustive survey, we will confine ourselves to these few remarks, which refer more directly to the point of view we are considering at present. The foregoing observations, it must be repeated, are valid not only for India but for the whole of the East ; it might be thought that they would have found a better place in the second part of this volume, but we preferred to keep them back until this moment, thinking that they would be rendered more readily understandable by coming after what we had to say in particular about the Hindu doctrines, which offer a representative example of traditional doctrines generally. All that remains to be done now is to indicate, as briefly as possible, how the Western interpretations of these same Hindu doctrines should be assessed ; in the case of some of them, we have indeed already done so in almost sufficient detail, profiting by such opportunities as have arisen during the course of our exposition.

PART IV

WESTERN INTERPRETATIONS

CHAPTER I

Official Orientalism

It is not necessary to say a great deal here about official orientalism, for we have already on many occasions pointed out both the inadequacy of its methods and the falsity of its conclusions: if we have kept it fairly constantly in sight, whereas we have hardly concerned ourselves with other Western attempts to interpret the East, this is because it presents at least a semblance of seriousness which the others lack, so that we were forced to make a distinction in its favour. We do not wish to contest the good faith of the orientalists, for that is usually beyond doubt, nor would we dispute the reality of their special kind of scholarship; what we do contest is their competence in respect of anything that lies outside the field of pure erudition. It is moreover only fair to pay some tribute to the commendable modesty which some of them show in declining to touch the work of interpreting doctrines, being only too well aware of their own limitations; but unfortunately these people are in the minority, and the majority, as we have said from the beginning, is made up of those who take erudition for an end in itself and who sincerely believe that their linguistic and historical researches give them the right to pronounce on every conceivable subject. On these people we think it would hardly be possible to pass too severe strictures, either concerning the methods they follow or the results they obtain, although we are always prepared to pay whatever respect is due to them personally, since they cannot altogether be held accountable for their prejudices or their illusions. An exclusive attitude is the natural result of a narrow outlook, or of what we have called "intellectual myopia," and this mental defect seems quite as incurable as physical short-sightedness: like the latter, mental short-sightedness also is a distortion induced by certain habits that bring it on gradually and imperceptibly, although there must doubtless be some predisposition towards it as well. This being the case, the ill-will shown by the majority of orientalists towards those who will not submit to their methods or accept their conclusions should not be a cause of surprise; it is only one more example of the results that normally follow on the abuse of specialisation, and one of the countless manifestations of that pseudo-scientific attitude of mind which is so easily mistaken for the true scientific spirit.

Nevertheless, in spite of all the excuses that can be made for the standpoint of the orientalists, it is none the less certain that the few positive results which their researches have yielded in the special field of erudition are far from compensating for the damage they have done to intellectuality in general, by blocking all the other paths along which those possessed of the requisite aptitudes might have been led, and led much further; if the intention be to scare away from these paths nearly all those who might be minded to enter upon them, it is enough, given the prejudices of the modern West, to declare solemnly that such and such an approach "is unscientific," simply because it does not conform to the methods and theories accepted and officially taught in the universities. When it is a case of defence against some danger or other, it is not usual to spend time over questions of personal responsibility; therefore if certain opinions are intellectually dangerous—and we think this is the case in the present instance—one must strive to expose their untruth irrespective of the feelings of those who advance or support them, the question of their personal good faith not being in any way in dispute. Suchlike considerations, which are quite unimportant in the face of ideas, cannot be allowed to intervene when combatting theories which stand in the way of the realization of certain possibilities: and since the bringing to pass of these possibilities, to which we will return in the concluding chapter, is not immediately practicable, and since any consideration of propaganda is for us out of the question, the most effective way of opposing these theories is not to engage in endless discussion of them on their own ground, but to cause their falseness to stand out by the simple act of re-establishing the truth, which alone matters to anyone who is capable of understanding it.

Herein lies the chief point of difference, upon which no agreement is possible with the specialists of erudition: when we speak of truth, we do not merely refer to a truth of fact, which of course has its importance, secondary and contingent though it may be; what interests us in a doctrine is the truth of that which it expresses, in the absolute sense of the word. On the contrary, those who adopt the point of view of erudition are in no wise concerned with the truth of ideas ; in reality they are almost totally unaware of what this implies, or even of whether such a thing exists, and they do not trouble to inquire ; truth means nothing to them, the special case of historical exactitude apart. The same tendency is also noticeable among historians of philosophy ; what interests them is not whether a certain idea is true or false, or in what measure it is so ; their only concern is to find out who first propounded the idea, in what terms he formulated it, and at what date and under what accessory circumstances he did so ; and this history of philosophy, which busies itself exclusively with the scrutiny of texts and biographical details, claims to take the place of philosophy itself, thus bringing about its final divorce from any small intellectually valuable residue that it might have retained in modern times. It is indeed obvious that such an attitude is as unfavourable as possible to the understanding of any doctrine whatsoever : by clinging to the letter only, it is unable to enter into the spirit, and so the very goal it aims at is certain to be missed ; absence of true understanding can only give birth to wild and arbitrary interpretations, that is to say to real falsehoods, even when it is only a question of historical exactitude.

This occurs in orientalism more frequently, perhaps, than in any other similar field of activity, because an attempt is made to deal with conceptions that are entirely foreign to the mentality of those who profess to study them ; it spells the bankruptcy of the so-called "historical method" even under the heading of that plain historical truth which is its chief justification, as is shown by the name that has been given to it. Those who follow it commit a double error : for on the one hand they are unaware of the more or less dubious theories behind it all, which can for the most part be traced back to the "evolutionary" hypothesis, while on the other hand they labour under serious delusions as to its scope, since they think their method can be applied wholesale ; we have already explained why it is totally inapplicable to the metaphysical realm, from which the merest notion of evolution is excluded. In the eyes of the partisans of this method the first condition required for the studying of metaphysical doctrines is evidently not to be a metaphysician ; similarly those who apply the same method to the "science of religions" more or less openly contend that a man is disqualified from this line of study by the very fact of belonging to a religion : it amounts to saying that in any branch of study only those may be considered competent who possess a purely external and superficial knowledge of it, such as may be gained through book-learning only, and this is doubtless the reason why in respect of the Eastern doctrines, the opinion of the Orientals themselves is treated as null and void. In this we see above all an instinctive fear of everything that transcends ordinary scholarship and threatens to show it up for the insignificant pursuit that it really is ; but this fear derives added strength from the fact that it agrees with the much more conscious interest of preserving the monopoly that the representatives of official science have in practice established in their own favour, the orientalists perhaps more than most. The fixed resolve not to tolerate anything that might prove dangerous to accepted opinions, and the attempt to discredit it by every means, alike find their justification moreover in the very prejudices that blind these narrow-minded people, and which lead them to deny the value of anything that is not a product of their own school: here again, we do not impugn their good faith, but we simply observe the effect of a very human tendency, whereby men find it all the easier to persuade themselves of a thing, the more directly their personal interests are engaged.

CHAPTER II

The Science of Religions

At this point a few remarks may suitably be made concerning what is called "the science of religions," since it owes its origin precisely to the researches of the "indianists"; this fact shows from the outset that the word "religion" is not used in the exact sense which we have given to it. In fact Burnouf, who seems to have been the first scholar to attach its title to this science, or so-called science, omits to count morals among the elements constituting religion, which are therefore reduced to two, namely doctrine and ritual; and this enables him to include things which in no wise pertain to the religious point of view, for even he admits with justice that the moral outlook is absent from the *Veda*. Such is the fundamental confusion of thought that is to be found at the starting-point of the "science of religions," which claims to group under the same name all traditional doctrines, whatever their real nature may be ; but many further confusions have been added to the first one, especially since the most up-to-date scholarship began to apply to this field of study its formidable apparatus of exegesis, of "textual criticism" and "hypercriticism," more calculated to impress simple minds than to lead to serious results.

The whole of this pretended "science of religions" rests on a few postulates which are nothing but sheer preconceptions ; thus its exponents lay it down that every doctrine must have taken its start in "naturalism" (whereas on the contrary we, for our part, see nothing in naturalism but a deviation which, at its every appearance, has always been opposed to the primordial and regular tradition) ; and by continually twisting round texts the real point of which they have missed, they always end by reading into them some interpretation or other that agrees with the "naturalistic" spirit. In this way a whole theory of "myths" has been elaborated, of which the best known example is the famous "solar myth" ; one of its chief propagators was Max Müller, whom we have had occasion to mention several times as a typical representative of the orientalist turn of mind. As for the theory of the "solar myth" itself, it is merely a revival of the astromythological theory that was put forward and upheld towards the end of the Eighteenth Century by Dupuis and Volney.[1] It is well known that this conception was applied to Christianity as well as to every other doctrine, and we have already pointed

[1] Dupuis, *Origine de tous les cultes* ; Volney, *Les Ruines*.

out the confusion that it necessarily implies ; as soon as a symbolism is seen to correspond with certain natural phenomena, the "scientists" fly to the conclusion that its only concern is to represent these phenomena, whereas in reality the phenomena themselves merely serve as symbols of something else belonging to quite a different order, while the correspondence that is observable is but an application of the analogies which harmoniously interconnect all the degrees of the being. Under such conditions it is not very difficult to discover "naturalism" everywhere, and it would indeed be surprising if it were not so to be found when symbols, which must of necessity belong to the natural order, are once mistaken for what they represent ; fundamentally, the error is the same as that of the "nominalists," who confound the idea with the word that serves to express it ; and it is thus that modern scholars, through their misunderstanding of symbols, and under the influence of the prejudice that encourages them to believe that all civilizations are constructed on the Græco-Roman model, themselves become the inventors of "myths", this being the only way in which such myths could take birth.

It should by now be apparent why we have described a study of this kind as a "so-called science" and why we find it quite impossible to take it seriously ; and it must be added that this "science of religions," while affecting an air of disinterested impartiality and even advertising its ridiculous and indeed positively outrageous claim to "stand above all the doctrines,"[1]

[1] E. Burnouf, *La Science des Religions*, page 6.

serves most of the time simply as a weapon of polemic in the hands of people whose real purpose is to employ it against religion, understood this time in its correct and customary sense. Such a use of scholarship in a negative and subversive spirit is natural to the fanatics of the "historical method"; it is indeed of the very essence of that method, which is by its nature anti-traditional, or at least becomes so as soon as it is allowed to overstep its legitimate bounds; and that is why all those who attach a real importance to religion for its own sake are considered to be disqualified from the service of this science. However, among the specialists of the "science of religions" there are some who, in appearance at least, do not go so far as that; chief among them are the adherents of the "liberal Protestant" school of thought, but these people, even though in theory they keep to the ordinary standpoint of religion, seek to reduce it to a simple "moralism," which amounts to destroying it by the double suppression of dogma and ritual in the name of a rationalism which is nothing but disguised sentimentality. Thus the final result is the same as in the case of avowed unbelievers, supporters of an "independent morality," although in the former case the real intention is perhaps better concealed; and this, when all is said and done, is but the logical outcome of the tendencies that the Protestant spirit carried within it from the outset. We have even witnessed an attempt, happily frustrated, to introduce this spirit, under the name of "modernism," into the Catholic Church itself. This movement aimed at replacing religion by a shadowy "religiosity," that is to say by a sentimental aspiration which the "moral life" would be sufficient to satisfy, and in order to achieve this purpose, it had first to try and discredit the dogmas by applying "criticism" to them, and by bringing out a theory of their "evolution," that is to say by resorting to the use of that same weapon, the "science of religions," which perhaps never had any other real purpose.

We have already stated that the "evolutionist" attitude is inherent in the "historical method"; to choose one of many examples, an application of it is to be seen in the strange theory according to which religious, or supposedly religious conceptions must necessarily have passed through a series of successive phases, the chief of which are commonly known as fetishism, polytheism and monotheism. This hypothesis is comparable to another that has appeared in the linguistic field, according to which languages, in the course of their development, are supposed to have passed through the successive stages of the monosyllabic, agglutinative and inflected forms: this is a quite gratuitous supposition, borne out by no facts, and indeed flatly contradicted by the facts, since it has never been possible to discover the least evidence of an actual passage from one of these forms to another; what have been taken for three successive phases, on the strength of a preconceived idea, are simply three differing types to which the various linguistic groups are attached, each always remaining true to the type to which it already belongs. The same may be said of another more general hypothesis, which Auguste Comte formulated under the title of the "law of the three states" and in which he turns into successive states the different provinces of thought; though these can always coexist simultaneously, he insists on discovering an incompatibility between them, because he imagines that every possible kind of knowledge always took natural phenomena as its object, whereas this really applies to scientific knowledge alone. It can be seen that this fanciful conception of Comte's, without being directly "evolutionary," was partly affected by the same spirit, and is akin to the hypothesis of a primitive "naturalism," according to which religions can only be premature and provisional experiments, though at the same time an indispensable prelude to what will later on become a scientific explanation; and in the development of the religious phase itself, Comte believed he could distinguish, as so many subdivisions, the same three degrees of fetishism, polytheism and monotheism. We will not discuss this theory further, as it is in any case widely known, but it seemed advisable to point out the correlation, too often overlooked, between various points of view, all springing from the same tendencies of the modern Western outlook.

In order to clear up the question of these three supposed phases in the "evolution" of religious conceptions, we will begin by recalling our previous statement that there never has existed any essentially polytheistic doctrine, because polytheism, like the "myths" that are closely bound up with it, is but a gross distortion arising out of a complete lack of understanding; besides, polytheism and anthropomorphism really never became general except among the Greeks and Romans ; everywhere else they remained within the province of individual error. Every genuinely traditional doctrine is then in reality monotheistic, or, to be more accurate, it is a "doctrine of unity" or rather of "non-duality," becoming monotheistic when it has to be translated into the religious mode ; as for the religions properly so-called, Judaism, Christianity and Islam, it is quite obvious that they are purely monotheistic. Now as regards fetishism, this word, which is of Portuguese origin, literally means "sorcery" ; what it designates is therefore neither religion nor anything more or less analogous to it, but definitely magic and even magic of the lowest kind. Magic is in no wise a form of religion, either of a primitive or of a degenerate kind, neither is it something radically opposed to religion as some have maintained, a species of "counter-religion," if one may use such an expression ; nor lastly is it something from which both religion and science are descended, in accordance with a third opinion which is as unfounded as the two foregoing ones ; all these confusions show that people who so glibly talk about magic are none too sure of their ground.

In reality magic belongs to the sphere of science and, to be more precise, of experimental science : it has to do with the wielding of certain forces which, in the Far East, are called "wandering influences," and the effects of which, however strange this may seem, are none the less natural phenomena governed by laws like other phenomena. This science is certainly capable of being given a traditional basis, but even then it never possesses value beyond that of a contingent and secondary application : in order to be perfectly clear about its degree of importance, it should be added that it is usually despised by the real representatives of the tradition, who, except in a few special cases, abandon it to the itinerant jugglers who turn it to profit by amusing the public. These magicians, such as are often to be met with in India where they are usually given the Arabic name of *faqirs*, that is to say of " poor men " or " mendicants," are usually people who, through intellectual incapacity, have stopped short on the path of metaphysical realization ; they chiefly arouse the interest of foreigners, and they deserve no greater consideration than that accorded to them by their own countrymen. We have no wish to deny the reality of the phenomena produced in this way, although in some cases they are merely copied or simulated in circumstances which none the less presuppose remarkable powers of suggestion, compared to which any results obtained by Westerners who have tried to experiment on similar lines appear quite insignificant ; what we do deny is the interest of these phenomena, which are quite unconnected with the pure doctrine or the metaphysical realization that is inseparable from it. We here take the opportunity of recalling that nothing that pertains to the experimental field can ever prove anything except in a negative sense, all it can do being to serve as an illustration of a theory ; an example constitutes neither an argument nor an explanation, and nothing is more illogical than to make a principle, even a relative one, depend on its own particular applications.

If we have been at pains to explain the true nature of magic, this is because it is made to play an important part in one theory of the "science of religions," the theory put forward by what is called the "sociological school"; after trying for a long time to provide a psychological interpretation for "religious phenomena," there is now an attempt to give them a sociological explanation. We have already mentioned this in connection with the definition of religion; in our opinion, both points of view are equally erroneous and alike incapable of giving a true account of religion and still less of tradition in general. Auguste Comte wished to compare the mentality of the ancients to that of children, which is ridiculous enough; but the theories of the present-day sociologists are hardly less absurd, when they compare it to the mentality of savages, whom they call "primitives," but whom in many cases one would rather be inclined to regard as degenerate. If the savages had always been found in the state where we now see them, there would be no possible explanation for the fact that they follow a large number of customs which they themselves do not understand, and which cannot be looked on as foreign importations, because they differ too markedly from anything to be met with elsewhere; such customs can only be considered as the traces of lost civilizations, which in the long distant past, even in prehistoric times, must have belonged to peoples of whom the present-day savages are the descendants and last vestiges; we mention this in order to confine ourselves to the province of facts, but without prejudice to other and deeper reasons that seem to us still more decisive, but which are inaccessible to the sociologists and other analytical "observers." We will only add that by a judicious application of analogy, and bearing in mind the diversity of adaptations necessitated by the diversity of human mentalities, it is often possible, owing to the essential and basic unity of all traditions, to discover the conceptions to which the customs mentioned above were originally attached before they were reduced to the level of "superstitions"; in a similar way, this basic unity permits of a large measure of understanding of those civilizations that are only known to us through the inscriptions and symbolic figures engraved on their surviving monuments. This, moreover, is what we had in mind at the outset when speaking of the services that a real knowledge of the East could render to all those who wish to make a serious study of antiquity in the hope of deriving valuable knowledge from it, unlike those others who are content with the quite exterior and superficial point of view of ordinary scholarship.

CHAPTER III

Theosophism

Although one may feel obliged to respect at least the good faith of the official orientalists even while deploring their lack of vision, the same no longer applies when dealing with the authors and propagators of certain theories which must now come up for discussion. These theories can only result in bringing discredit on Oriental studies and in turning away serious-minded though ill-informed people, by offering them a tissue of incoherent absurdities, quite unworthy of attention, as an authentic expression of Hindu doctrines. The spreading of such idle imaginings not only has the disadvantage just mentioned, which is bad enough in itself, but, like the dissemination of many other similar notions, it is also eminently suited to upset the balance of those feebler minds and unsteady intellects who take such things seriously; in this respect it constitutes a real danger for the average intelligence, a danger which has already revealed itself by only too many sad examples.

These activities are all the less innocuous because the Westerners of to-day show a marked tendency to let themselves be taken in by everything which savours of the extraordinary or the marvellous; the development of their civilization in an exclusively practical direction, by depriving them of all effective intellectual guidance, opens the door to every kind of pseudo-scientific and pseudo-metaphysical extravagance, unlikely though it is that such things could ever be sufficient to satisfy the sentimentalism that plays such an important part in their lives, as a secondary consequence of that same absence of true intellectuality. Furthermore, the habit of giving precedence to experimentation in the scientific field, of clinging almost exclusively to facts and of attributing greater value to them than to ideas, helps to strengthen the hands of all those investigators who, in order to substantiate the most unlikely theories, claim to base their hypotheses on phenomena of some kind or other, whether real or imaginary, often insufficiently verified and in any case wrongly interpreted ; such people stand a much better chance of success with the general public than persons who, being desirous of teaching serious and well-founded doctrines only, address themselves exclusively to pure intelligence. This also makes it possible to explain quite naturally a fact which is noticeable in England and still more so in America, and which at first sight might appear rather surprising, namely the association of an exaggerated development of the practical outlook with the almost unlimited dissemination of all sorts of follies of a would-be religious nature, in which both the experimentalism and the false mysticism of the Anglo-Saxons are simultaneously pandered to ; this goes to prove that, despite appearances, the most "practical" mentality is not always the best balanced. Even in France, the danger we are describing is not negligible though it may be less obvious ; indeed quite the contrary is the case, since a propensity to imitate anything foreign, coupled with the influence of fashion and the intellectual snobbery of society, all work together to favour the expansion of such theories in certain quarters and to supply the material means for their still wider dissemination, through propaganda assuming many different forms in the hopes of reaching the most diverse sections of the public.

The nature of the danger and its gravity do not permit of any circumspection in our attitude towards those who are responsible ; here we are in the realm of charlatanism and phantasmagoria, and though one may sincerely pity the simple-minded people who go to form the great majority of those taking pleasure in such things, the same cannot be said of certain others who consciously set out to mislead their followers for their own ends, of whatever nature these may be ; such people are only fit to inspire contempt. Moreover, in matters of this kind there are several different ways of becoming a dupe, and adherence to the theories in question is far from being the only way ; even those who for various reasons set out to combat these theories are for the most part insufficiently forearmed, so that they commit the involuntary but nevertheless cardinal error of mistaking what is only the product of a purely Western aberration for genuinely Oriental ideas ; their attacks, often inspired by the most laudable intentions, are deprived on that account of all effective power. On the other hand, certain of the official orientalists take these theories seriously ; we do not mean to say that they regard them as true in themselves for, given the special point of view they have adopted, the question of their truth or falseness does not even enter their minds ; they wrongly consider them, however, to be representative of a certain part or aspect of the Eastern mentality, and it is through their own lack of knowledge of this mentality that they are deceived, the more so because they do not feel themselves threatened by any serious competition from that quarter. Sometimes strange alliances take place, notably in the field of the "science of religions" where the case of Burnouf is an example ; perhaps this fact can be explained quite simply by the anti-religious and anti-traditional tendency of this so-called science, which naturally places it in a relationship of sympathy and even of affinity with all the subversive elements which by different means carry on a parallel and corresponding activity. Anyone not content to rely solely on appearances could make some very curious and instructive observations in this as in other fields, showing how disorder and incoherence, or what appear as such, can sometimes be turned to account with a view to the execution of a well-defined plan, unperceived by those who act as its more or less unconscious instruments: these are in a sense political devices, though of a somewhat special kind; moreover, contrary to what might be supposed, politics, even taken in the narrower sense usually given to the word, are not altogether divorced from the matters which we are considering at the moment.

Among the pretended doctrines which exercise a nefarious influence over fairly extensive sections of the Western public, and which, being of quite recent origin, can in most cases be classified under the common denomination of "neo-spiritualism," there are some, like Occultism and Spiritualism,[1] of which we need say nothing here, because they have no point of contact with Oriental studies; the one with which we are more particularly concerned, though it has nothing Eastern about it except the exterior form under which it is presented, is what is known as "Theosophism." The use of this word, though people are not quite agreed about it, is sufficiently justified as a precaution against confusion; it is certainly not advisable in this case to employ the word "Theosophy," which

[1] The author has treated this subject in detail in his book, *L'Erreur spirite*, 1923.—(*Translator.*)

has long served to describe something belonging to the field of Western speculation which is quite different and far more worthy of respect, its origins being traceable as far back as the Middle Ages ; here we are only concerned with conceptions that belong exclusively to the contemporary organisation styling itself the "Theosophical Society," the members of which are known as "Theosophists"—an expression in common use in English—and not "Theosophers." We are not able, neither do we wish, to give here, even briefly, a historical account, however interesting it might be in some respects, of this "Theosophical Society," the founder of which, thanks to the extraordinary influence she exercised on her surroundings, was able to turn to account the distinctly varied knowledge she possessed, which is however completely lacking in her successors[1] ; her so-called doctrine, made up of elements borrowed from the most diverse sources, often of doubtful value and assembled together in a confused and barely coherent syncretism, was first presented as an "esoteric Buddhism" which, as we have mentioned earlier on, is purely imaginary ; it has recently led to the formulation of a so-called "esoteric Christianity," which is no less fanciful. This organisation of American origin, while posing as international, has become purely Anglo-Saxon in its leadership, with the exception of a few dissident branches of little importance ; in spite of all its efforts, supplemented by a protection that it owes to certain political considerations which we

[1] The author did actually publish a full history of the movement in his book *Le Théosophisme : Histoire d'une pseudo-religion*. Paris, 1921.—*Translator*.

will not examine here, it has never succeeded in recruiting more than a small number of misguided Hindus, profoundly despised by their compatriots, but whose names help to take in ignorant Europeans ; besides, it is fairly widely believed in India to be nothing more than a Protestant sect of a rather special kind, an assimilation which its personnel, its methods of publicity and its " moralistic " tendencies alike seem to justify—not to mention its hostility, now disguised and now violent, towards all traditional institutions. Under the heading of intellectual productions, we have witnessed the appearance, after the earlier indigestible compilations, of quantities of fantastic narratives, the results of the special " clairvoyance " which, so they say, is acquired through the " development of the latent powers of the human organism." There have also been some rather ridiculous translations of Sanskrit texts accompanied by still more ridiculous commentaries and interpretations, which their authors dare not exhibit too publicly in India, preferring rather to retail other works in that country which distort the Christian doctrine under the pretext of revealing its hidden meaning ; if Christianity contained no greater mysteries than these, secrecy would be inexplicable and moreover objectless, for it goes without saying that it would be a sheer waste of effort to look for profound revelations in all these " Theosophical " effusions.

What appears at first sight to be characteristic of Theosophism is the use of a rather complicated Sanskrit terminology, the words of which are often given a meaning quite different from the ones they really bear ; this is not surprising, seeing that they serve merely to cloak essentially Western conceptions, as far removed as possible from Hindu ideas. Thus, to quote an example, the word *karma*, which, as already stated, means "action," is regularly used in the sense of "causality," which is worse than an inaccuracy ; but what is more serious still, this causality is conceived in an entirely special way, by a false interpretation of the theory of the *apūrva* which we set forth in our chapter on *Mīmānsā*, whereby people manage to distort it into a moral sanction. We have already given sufficient explanations on this subject to enable the reader to gauge the confusion of points of view which this travesty presupposes, even stripped of all the incidental nonsense with which it is surrounded. Howbeit, the chief point is that it shows to what extent Theosophism has been permeated by the sentimentality peculiar to Westerners. Moreover, in order to realise how far it has pushed moralism and pseudo-mysticism, it is only necessary to refer to any one of the works where these conceptions have been set forth ; and indeed, when one examines publications of more recent date it is noticeable that these tendencies become even more accentuated, perhaps as a result of the ever increasing intellectual mediocrity of the heads of the organisation and perhaps also because this orientation is really the one that corresponds best with the goal they have set themselves. The only real use of the Sanskrit terminology in Theosophism is to endow that which occupies the place of doctrine in it—for we cannot consent to call it a doctrine—with an appearance calculated to create an illusion in the minds of Westerners and to win over a certain number of those people who hanker after whatever is exotic in form but who, as far as the substance is concerned, are only too glad to discover conceptions and aspirations agreeing with their own ideas, since they are incapable of understanding the least part of the authentically Oriental doctrines ; this state of mind, which is typical of the so-called "intelligentsia," is comparable to that of the philosophers who feel the need of having recourse to unusual and high-sounding words in order to express ideas which, fundamentally, do not differ greatly from those of the common herd.

Theosophism attaches considerable importance to the characteristically Western and modern notion of "evolution," and like most of the branches of Spiritualism, with which it is fairly closely connected through its origins, it associates this idea with that of "reincarnation." The latter conception seems to have first made its appearance among some of the socialist dreamers of the first half of the nineteenth century, who saw in it a way of accounting for the inequality of social conditions, which in their eyes was particularly shocking though in reality it is quite a natural thing ; to anyone who understands the principle of the institution of caste, founded on the differences of individual natures, the problem does not even arise. Besides, theories of this kind, like those of "evolutionism," really explain nothing ; while putting the difficulty back into the past, one might even say indefinitely, they finally allow it to remain in its entirety —given that a difficulty really does exist ; and if it does not, why then this theorising ? With regard to the assertion that the origin of the "reincarnationist" conception goes back to antiquity, this claim is founded on nothing but the misunderstanding of certain symbolical expressions such as has lent support to a crude interpretation of the Pythagorean "metempsychosis," in the sense of a sort of psychic "transformism"; similarly, it has been found possible to take for a succession of terrestrial lives what is really, not only in the Hindu doctrines but also in Buddhism, an indefinite series of different states of existence, each state having its own characteristic conditions, differing from those of other states and constituting for the being a cycle of existence which it can only pass through once—earthly existence, or still more generally, corporeal existence thus representing only one particular state among an indefinite series of others. The real theory of the being's multiple states is of supreme importance from the metaphysical point of view[1]; we cannot develop it here, but we have been obliged to allude to it, notably in connection with the *apūrva* and the "concordant actions and reactions." As for "reincarnationism," which is but an inept caricature of this theory, all Orientals, with the possible exception of a few ignorant and more or less Westernised persons whose opinion is of no value whatsoever, are unanimously opposed to it; moreover its metaphysical absurdity is easily demonstrable, because to admit that a being can pass more than once through the same state is tantamount to admitting a limitation

[1] This most fundamental doctrine has been treated by M. Guénon in two works: *Le Symbolisme de la Croix*. Paris, 1931. and *Les États multiples de l'Être*, 1932: translations of both are due to appear in this series.—*Translator.*

of Universal Possibility, that is to say, to denying the Infinite, and this denial is in itself contradictory in the highest degree. There are good reasons for making a special effort to combat the notion of "reincarnation," firstly, because it is flatly opposed to the truth, as we have shown in a few brief words and secondly from another more contingent motive, since this idea, made popular by Spiritualism, which is the most unintelligent as well as the most widespread of all the "neo-spiritualist" schools, is one of the principal agents of that mental aberration which we spoke of at the beginning of this chapter, and to which far greater numbers of people fall a victim than might be thought likely by those who are not well acquainted with the facts. We cannot, of course, afford to spend much time over this question here; but it may be added that whereas Spiritualists try to prove their theory of "reincarnation," as well as the immortality of the soul, "scientifically," that is to say by the experimental method—though this method is quite incapable of yielding the smallest result in this direction—the majority of Theosophists seem to see in the idea a kind of dogma or article of faith, which must be accepted from sentimental motives, but without seeking to establish it by means of any rational or sensible proof. This clearly shows that we are dealing with an attempt to constitute a pseudo-religion, in competition with the real religions of the West, and more especially with the Catholic Church, for, as far as Protestantism is concerned, it finds no difficulty in accommodating itself to a multiplicity of sects, to which it seems to give birth spontaneously because of its want of doctrinal principles. This Theosophical pseudo-religion is at present trying to assume a definite form by taking for its central theme the forthcoming appearance of a "great teacher," who is represented by his prophets as the future Messiah and as a "re-incarnation" of Christ: among the various transformations of Theosophism, this one, which sheds a remarkably clear light on its conception of an "esoteric Christianity," is the latest in date, anyway up till now, but it is not the least significant of its many changes.

CHAPTER IV

Vedānta Westernised

Mention must now be made of certain "movements" belonging to an order of ideas more or less akin to Theosophism; in these movements, the inspiration of which was entirely Western even though they arose in India itself, an important part was played by the political influences alluded to in the preceding chapter. Their origin goes back to the first half of the nineteenth century, when Rām Mohun Roy founded the *Brahma-Samāj* or "Hindu Reformed Church," the idea of which had been suggested to him by Anglican missionaries, and in which a "religious office" was organised, closely modelled on the pattern of Protestant services. Up to that time there had never existed anything meriting the denomination of "Hindu Church" or "Brahmanic Church," for the essential point of view of the Hindu tradition and the nature of the organisation corresponding to it were incompatible with such an assimilation; it marked in fact a first attempt to convert Brahmanism into a religion in the Western sense, and at the same time it showed that its promoters wished to make of their venture a religion animated by the self-same tendencies that characterise Protestantism. As was to be expected, this "reforming" movement was warmly encouraged and supported by the British Government and by British missionary societies in India; but it was too openly anti-traditional and too flatly opposed to the Hindu spirit to succeed, and people plainly took it for what it really was, an instrument of foreign domination. Furthermore, as an inevitable consequence of the introduction of "free private judgment," the *Brahma-Samāj* soon split up into numerous "churches," like Protestantism, which it came to resemble more and more, to the point of earning the designation of "pietism"; and after many vicissitudes that it would be pointless to recount, it ended by dying out almost completely. However, the spirit that had presided over the birth of this organisation did not confine itself to this one appearance, for other similar attempts were set on foot as opportunity offered, though generally with no better success; we will mention one only, the *Ārya-Samāj*, an association founded about half a century ago by Dayānanda Saraswatī, who has sometimes been spoken of as the "Luther of India," and who was in touch with the founders of the Theosophical Society. It is noticeable that here, as in the *Brahma-Samāj*, the anti-traditional tendency took as its pretext a return to primitive simplicity and to the pure Vedic doctrine;

in order to judge the value of this claim it is enough to note how foreign to the *Veda* is the "moralism" that forms the chief concern of all these organisations; but Protestantism also claims to restore primitive Christianity in all its purity, and this point of likeness is anything but a simple coincidence. A certain cleverness in getting innovations accepted is not lacking in such an attitude, especially in a society that is strongly attached to tradition, with which it would be imprudent to make too open a break; but if the basic principles of that tradition were truly and sincerely accepted, it would follow that all developments that are logically and regularly derived from them would also be admitted; but the so-called "reformers" do not accept this, and thus those who possess a sense of tradition can easily see that the real deviation is in no wise to be laid to the charge of those against whom the "reformers" level the accusation.

Rām Mohun Roy, in particular, aspired to interpret *Vedānta* according to his own ideas. Though he rightly stressed the conception of "Divine unity," which however no competent person had ever thought of contesting, he expressed it in terms that were much more theological than metaphysical, and in order to accommodate the doctrine to Western ways of thinking, which had also become his own, he distorted it to such an extent that he ended by reducing it to something like a mere philosophy tinged with religiosity, a kind of "Deism" decked out in Oriental phraseology. Such an interpretation is in its spirit as far removed as possible from tradition and pure metaphysic; it represents nothing but a private theory devoid of the least authority, and it entirely ignores realization, which is the sole object of the whole doctrine. This movement became the prototype of various distortions of the *Vedānta*, for others were destined to arise in due course and on the invariable plea of drawing closer to the West ; in every case, however, it was the East that was to bear the cost of this accommodation, to the marked detriment of doctrinal purity. It was indeed a foolish enterprise and one diametrically opposed to the intellectual interests of both civilizations ; but on the whole it has produced little effect on the Oriental mind, which looks on such attempts as quite insignificant. Truly, it is not for the East to approach the West through copying its mental deviations or by yielding to the insidious but vain persuasions of the propagandists of every hue that Europe sends out to it ; but it is on the contrary for the West to return, when it is able and willing, to the pure sources of intellectuality which the East, for its part, has never deserted ; on that day agreement on all secondary and contingent matters will come of itself almost unsought.

To return to deformations of the *Vedānta* ; although no one of consequence in India pays much attention to them, as we said before, some exceptions must be made in the case of persons who have a special interest in so doing, but one in which intellectuality plays not the slightest part ; in fact some of these deformations have arisen from purely political motives. We shall not try to describe here under what circumstances a certain usurping *Mahārāja* of the *Shūdra* caste, actuated by the desire to receive the semblance of an otherwise unobtainable traditional investiture, was led to dispossess the authentic school of Shankarāchārya and to install in its place another school, falsely displaying Shankarāchārya's name and authority and giving to its head the title of *Jagad-guru* or "world instructor," which only belongs legitimately to the true spiritual successor of the founder. The new school, as was to be expected, only teaches a defective and partly heterodox doctrine; in order to adapt its expounding of *Vedānta* to present-day conditions, it pretends to base it on the conceptions of modern Western science, which have nothing to contribute in this field; and in fact it chiefly addresses its teachings to Westerners, even going so far as to confer on several of them the honorific title of *Vedānta-Bhūshana* or "ornament of the *Vedānta*," a fact which is not without its own irony.

Another still more completely aberrant branch, better known in the West, is that founded by Vivekānanda, the disciple of the illustrious Rāmakrishna though unfaithful to his teaching; it has recruited its adherents mostly in America and Australia, where it runs "missions" and "temples." There *Vedānta* has become, like Schopenhauer's conception of it, a sentimental and "consoling" religion, with a strong dose of Protestant "moralism"; in this degenerate form, it approaches very close to Theosophism, towards which it stands in the position of a natural ally rather than a rival or competitor. The "evangelical" attitude assumed by this pseudo-religion has earned it a certain success, chiefly in Anglo-Saxon countries; while its inherently sentimental character is well attested by the ardour for propaganda animating its votaries; for, as might be expected, an altogether Western propensity for proselytism rages intensely in these organisations, which are Eastern in nothing but the name, apart from a few merely outward signs, calculated to interest the curious and to attract dilettantes by playing on their taste for an exoticism of the feeblest type. This so-called *Vedānta*, which is a product of that queer American and characteristically Protestant creation called the "Parliament of Religions," and which pleases the West all the better the more completely it is distorted, has practically nothing left in common with the metaphysical doctrine the name of which it bears. No more time need be wasted on it; but it seemed best at least to mention its existence, in order to put people who have heard of it on their guard against possible false assimilations; as for those who have not come across these movements, it is best that they should be made aware of them, since they are not nearly so harmless as might appear at first sight.

CHAPTER V

Additional Remarks

When discussing Western interpretations, we have purposely confined ourselves to general questions as far as possible in order to avoid raising personal matters which are often irritating and moreover without purpose if one is adopting a strictly doctrinal point of view, as in the present case. It is strange what difficulty most Westerners find in understanding that considerations of this nature prove nothing whatsoever either for or against a conception ; this clearly shows how far intellectual individualism, as well as the sentimentality that is inseparable from it, has been carried. In practice, one knows the importance attributed to the most insignificant biographical details in what purports to be a history of ideas, in keeping with the common illusion which makes people believe that they possess real knowledge by the mere fact of having ascertained a name or a date : how could it be otherwise in a society where facts are valued above ideas ? It is after all only natural that the appraising of ideas should be affected by a person's knowledge of the characters and actions of the men to whom they are ascribed, when once those ideas are no longer valued for their own sake, but have come to be looked upon merely as the invention and property of this or that individual, and when, in addition, people let themselves be influenced and even dominated by all sorts of moral or sentimental irrelevancies ; in other words, sympathies or antipathies felt for the men who conceived them are carried over to the ideas themselves, as if their truth or falseness could be dependent on such contingencies.

Under these circumstances people are perhaps still prepared to admit, though with reluctance, that a perfectly honourable individual may have formulated and defended more or less foolish ideas ; but there is one thing they positively refuse to agree to, namely that some other individual, who is considered unworthy, may nevertheless have possessed intellectual or even artistic qualities amounting either to genius or to talent of some sort; and yet such cases are by no means unusual. If there is one quite unfounded prejudice especially dear to the upholders of "compulsory education," it is the notion that real knowledge is inseparable from what is usually called "moral worth"; there is no logical reason for supposing that a criminal is necessarily an idiot or an ignoramus, or that a man cannot make use of his intelligence and his science for the injuring of his neighbours, as on the contrary quite often happens; nor can we see why the truth of a conception should depend on whether it was put forward by such and such a person; but nothing is less reasonable than sentiment, although some psychologists have gone so far as to speak of a "logic of the feelings." So-called arguments influenced by personal considerations are entirely valueless: that they should be employed in the field of politics, where sentiment plays a major part, is understandable up to a point, when one comes to think of it, although it is hardly a compliment to address one's appeals to a person's sentimentality alone; but to introduce similar methods of discussion into the intellectual field is totally inadmissible. We have thought fit to underline the point, not only because this tendency is so general in the West, but also because, had we not made our position clear, certain critics might be tempted to blame us for an attitude which seemed to them too vague and lacking in precise "references," even though we have adopted such an attitude of set purpose and quite deliberately.

We hope, however that we have now replied adequately and in advance to most of the likely objections and criticisms ; even so, this will quite probably not prevent their being raised, but in that case it will be purely and simply from lack of understanding. For example, we shall perhaps be accused of failing to submit to certain methods reputed to be "scientific," but such a suggestion would be quite beside the mark, since the methods in question, which are really purely "literary" in character, are the very ones the inadequacy of which we have tried to demonstrate ; for reasons of principle already given, we consider it both impossible and inadmissible to apply those methods to the subject of our present study. But the mania for texts, "origins" and bibliography is so widespread to-day, because it answers to the general craving for systematization, that many people, especially among the "specialists," will suffer a real sense of discomfort at not meeting with anything of the sort here, as always happens with those who have fallen under the tyranny of a set habit ; and at the same time, they will find it very hard to understand—if indeed they ever manage to do so, even supposing they give themselves the trouble—how it is possible to adopt, as we have done, a standpoint which is not that of erudition, since that is the only attitude they have ever conceived of. It is not to these "specialists," however, that our remarks are chiefly addressed, but to people of a less narrow-minded outlook, more free from prejudice, and unaffected by the mental distortion that inevitably accompanies the practice of certain methods, a distortion which gives birth to the disease which we have called "intellectual myopia." It would be a mistake to see in these remarks an appeal "to the public," for we put no trust in its competence to judge, and have moreover a horror of anything that savours of "popularisation" for reasons we have already given; but neither do we commit the error of confusing the true intellectual elect with the professional men of learning. A power of wide understanding is worth incomparably more in our eyes than mere scholarship, which is nothing but an obstacle to understanding as soon as it is turned into a "speciality," instead of remaining, as it normally should remain, simply an instrument in the service of that understanding, that is to say an adjunct of pure knowledge and genuine intellectuality.

While we are still occupied with explaining our attitude towards possible criticisms, there is yet another detail, in itself of small interest, which might however arouse some comment: in regard to the use of Sanskrit terms, we have not thought it necesary to avail ourselves of the strange and complicated method of transcription used to-day by orientalists. Since the Sanskrit alphabet contains many more letters than the European alphabets, one is naturally compelled to represent several distinct characters by one and the same letter, choosing the one that is most closely akin in sound to the Sanskrit letter in question; it must not be concluded that the differences thus slurred over are not appreciable, but they simply cannot be rendered exactly in the European tongues with their scantier resources. Therefore no transcription can be really faithful, and it would be far the best thing not to resort to any ; but apart from the fact that it is extremely difficult to obtain Sanskrit characters of correct form for use in a work to be printed in Europe, the reading of these characters would present quite an unnecessary difficulty to those readers who are unacquainted with Sanskrit, but yet who are not for that reason less qualified than others for the understanding of the Hindu doctrines ; besides, unlikely as it may appear, there even exist some " specialists " who are hardly able to read Sanskrit texts except in " romanised " transcriptions, and editions are to be had published under that form expressly for their use. It is doubtless possible, by means of a few artifices, to make up to a certain extent for the orthographic ambiguity resulting from the fact that the Latin alphabet is short of letters ; this has been precisely the intention of the orientalists, but the method of transcription they have hit upon is far from being the best possible one, since it makes use of too many rather arbitrary conventions ; had it been a matter of any importance for our present purposes, it would not have been difficult to devise a different and preferable method which would not disfigure the words so much and which would approximate more closely to their real pronunciation. However, those who possess some knowledge of Sanskrit will have no trouble in recovering the exact spelling, while others will not need to do so in order to understand the ideas, which alone are of fundamental importance. Accordingly we decided that there could be no serious objection to doing away with all artifices of spelling and typographical complications, and we have adopted the transcription which seemed to us both the easiest and the nearest in pronunciation ; those who are specially interested in the details of the subject can refer to the technical books.

Howbeit, we owed at least this amount of explanation to the analytically-minded inquirers, always eager for discussion—it is one of the rare concessions to their mental habits that we are prepared to make, as is demanded by that courtesy that should always be shown towards people of good faith ; it is likewise prompted by a wish to forestall misunderstandings which bear only on points of secondary importance and on accessory questions, and which do not immediately arise from the irreducible difference between the traditional and metaphysical point of view here expounded and that of its possible critics ; for the latter we can do nothing, since there is unfortunately no means of supplying to them those powers of discernment that they lack. After saying this, we can now go on to draw from our study certain conclusions in which questions of erudition obviously play no part at all ; in so doing we shall point out, though without abandoning a certain indispensable reserve, the essential and effective benefit which must result from a real and deep knowledge of the Eastern doctrines.

CONCLUSION

If a few people in the West, through reading the preceding pages, could become conscious of all that is lacking to them intellectually, if they could, we do not say understand, but only just catch a glimpse and a suspicion of it, then this work would not have been written in vain. We do not mean to refer only to the priceless personal gain that would accrue to those who were thus led to study the Eastern doctrines, wherein, if they were endowed with the smallest aptitude of the necessary kind, they would discover knowledge the like of which exists nowhere in the West, and compared to which philosophies that there are looked upon as the sublime creations of genius are but as child's play : there is no common measure between truth comprehended in its fulness, by means of a conception opening out upon limitless possibilities and accompanied by a correspondingly effective realization, and any hypothesis whatsoever that has been propounded by the essentially limited imagination of an individual. Other results can also follow more general in scope, and related to the former as its more or less distant consequences ; here we are alluding to the doubtless long drawn out but none the less effective preparation for an intellectual understanding between East and West.

When speaking of the divergence of the West in relation to the East, which has become increasingly marked in modern times, we said that we did not think this divergence could go on developing indefinitely, in spite of all appearances. In other words, it seems difficult to believe that the West, both in respect of its mentality and all its characteristic tendencies, can continue to draw further and further away from the East, as it is now doing, without sooner or later calling forth a reaction which might, under certain circumstances, have the happiest results; indeed such an uninterrupted divergence seems to us all the more unlikely since the realm within which modern Western civilization is developing is, by its very nature, the most restricted of any. Furthermore, the changeful and unstable character peculiar to the West permits us to entertain the hope that a considerable and even a radical change of direction may occur one day, in which case the remedy would emerge from that very thing which seems to us the chief sign of inferiority; but we must repeat that such a change would only provide a remedy under certain circumstances, in default of which the condition of the world could not fail to become still worse than it is at present. This may appear a somewhat vague statement, and we fully recognise that it is not easy to make it as explicit as one might wish, even by adopting the standpoint of the West and trying to speak to it in its own language; nevertheless it is worth attempting, but with the warning that the explanations we are about to offer do not cover the whole of our thoughts on the subject.

First of all, what we know of the mental characteristics of certain Westerners compels us to say plainly that we have no intention of uttering a single word that could possibly be described as a "prophecy"; it would perhaps not be difficult to create such an impression by publishing the results of a process of deduction couched in suitable terms, but this proceeding would savour of charlatanism, unless one happened to have a predisposition towards a kind of auto-suggestion : of these two choices, the first inspires disgust while the second condition is fortunately not our own. We shall therefore under all circumstances avoid statements that cannot be substantiated, and which are as dangerous as they are useless ; we are not one of those who believe that a detailed knowledge of the future would be advantageous to mankind, and in our opinion the discredit attaching in the East to the practice of the arts of divination is fully justified. This, in itself, is a sufficient reason for condemning occultism and other similar speculations that attach importance to this kind of thing, quite apart from additional and far more serious and decisive reasons of a doctrinal nature, which impose a downright rejection of conceptions which are both chimerical and dangerous.

We admit that it is not at present possible to foresee the circumstances that could determine a change of direction in the development of the West ; but the possibility of such a change can only be denied by those who believe that development on the present lines constitutes "progress" in an absolute sense. This notion of progress in the absolute is really meaningless, and we have already pointed out the mutual incompatibility of certain lines of development, resulting on the one hand in relative progress in a given field and inevitably on the other hand in a corresponding retrogression in other fields ; we said "corresponding," not equivalent, since one cannot use the latter term when referring to things that are neither similar in nature nor of the same order. This is what has occurred in Western civilization : researches carried out solely with a view to practical applications and material advancement have necessarily been accompanied by retrogression in the purely speculative and intellectual order ; and since there is no common measure between these two realms, the loss on the one side has been incomparably greater than any supposed gain on the other ; a man must be suffering from all the mental distortion that afflicts the vast majority of modern Westerners to be able to regard things in any other light. But however that may be, if one only considers the fact that a one-track development is necessarily subject to certain limiting conditions, which are all the narrower when that development takes place in the material sphere, it will be realized that a change of direction such as we have been discissing is almost sure to take place sometime or other.

As for the nature of the events that will lead up to this re-orientation, it is possible that people will one day begin to notice that things which now appear all-important are unable to yield the results expected of them ; but this in itself would presuppose a certain change in the general mental trend, even though the disillusion were chiefly sentimental in character, arising for instance from having come to realize the non-existence of a "moral progress" running parallel with the progress called scientific. Indeed, if they are not to be supplied from an outside source, the means of change will necessarily be as mediocre in quality as the mentality which they are called upon to influence ; but this mediocrity would not augur very well for the results to follow. It is also possible to suppose that mechanical inventions, developed ever further and further, may reach a point where they will seem so dangerous that men will feel impelled to renounce them, either from the terror gradually aroused by some of their consequences, or else following on a cataclysm which everyone is at liberty to picture as he pleases. Even in the latter case, the motive force of the change would be of a sentimental nature, but derived from that side of feeling which relates most closely to the physiological order ; and it might be added, but without over-stressing the point, that symptoms connected with both the above-mentioned possibilities have already appeared, though on a very small scale, as a result of the recent events that have shaken Europe ; however, these events have not yet assumed sufficiently large proportions, whatever people may think, to bring about deep and lasting effects in the direction we are discussing. Furthermore, changes such as we have in mind could either come about slowly and gradually, requiring several centuries in which to mature, or on the other hand they might occur rapidly after sudden and unforeseen upheavals ; however, even in the first case, it is probable that a moment will come when a more or less violent rupture will take place, amounting to a real severing of continuity with the pre-existing state. In any case, we fully admit that it is impossible to calculate the date of such a change beforehand, even approximately ; however, truth compels us to add that those who possess some knowledge of the cyclic laws and their application to historical epochs might allow themselves at least a few forecasts in order to determine periods comprised within certain limits ; but here we shall abstain entirely from entering into questions of this kind, the more so since a knowledge of the laws we have just alluded to has sometimes been falsely claimed by persons who found it all the easier to speak of such things the less they understood them : this last observation must not be taken for a paradox, for it expresses something that is literally a fact.

The next question to be asked is this : supposing certain events bring about a reaction in the West at some date as yet unspecified, causing those things to be given up that form the substance of present-day European civilization, what results must be expected to follow ? Several eventualities are possible, and it is well worth pausing to consider the various hypotheses corresponding to them : the most unfavourable result would occur if nothing were introduced to take the place of the civilization in question, so that, as it disappeared, the West, abandoned to its own fate, would sink into the lowest forms of barbarism. To understand this possibility, it is enough to call to mind several examples of civilizations that have been entirely obliterated, even without having to go back beyond what are called historical times. Some of these civilizations belonged to peoples who disappeared along with them, but this fate could hardly apply except to fairly localised cultures ; in the case of civilizations enjoying a widespread extension it is more likely that the survivors would find themselves reduced to a degenerate state more or less comparable with that which, as we remarked earlier, is represented by certain of the present-day savages ; it is hardly necessary to spend a long time pointing out the disquieting nature of the picture called up by this first hypothesis.

The second eventuality is the one in which representatives of other civilizations, namely Eastern peoples, in rescuing the Western world from this incurable decay, would assimilate it by consent or by force, either as a whole or in respect of some of its component parts—that is assuming that the thing were possible and that the East were willing to do this. It is to be hoped that no one is so blinded by Western prejudice as not to recognise how much this hypothesis is to be preferred to the first one : under such circumstances there would doubtless be a transitional period of extremely painful ethnical revolutions, which are difficult to picture but which in their final result would be of a nature to compensate for the damage certain to be sustained during a catastrophe of this kind ; but in that case the West would have had to forego its own character and would find itself absorbed purely and simply.

For these reasons a third possibility may be regarded as being far more favourable from the Western point of view, though merely equivalent, truth to tell, from the general point of view of humanity, since, were it to be fulfilled, its effect would be to have brought about the disappearance of the Western anomaly, not by suppression as in the first case, but, as in the second, by a return to true and normal intellectuality ; but this return, instead of being imposed under duress, or at most accepted and experienced through external influence, would in this case be effected voluntarily and as it were spontaneously. It is easy to see what this last possibility implies, if it is to be realizable: it would mean that the West, at the very moment when its development in the present direction was nearing its end, had succeeded in discovering within itself the principles of a development in a different direction, which it would thenceforth carry out in quite a natural manner; and this fresh development, by turning its civilization into something comparable with those of the East, would allow of its occupying in the world, not a position of preponderance to which it is not entitled and which it owes at present only to its employment of brute force, but at least the position that it would lawfully occupy as one civilization among others, a civilization moreover which, under these conditions, would cease to be an element of maladjustment and of oppression for the rest of mankind.

It must not indeed be supposed that the Western domination can be otherwise looked upon by the peoples of different civilizations at present subject to it; we are not referring, of course, to certain degenerate tribes, though even in the latter case Western influence is probably more harmful than useful, since they tend to copy only the worst traits of their conquerors. As for the Orientals, we have already explained on several occasions how justifiable their contempt for the West appears in our eyes, all the more justifiable the oftener the European race insists on repeating its odious and absurd claims to a quite non-existent mental superiority, and the greater its efforts to force all men into an assimilation which its own unstable and ill-defined characteristics fortunately prevent it from consummating. Only a delusion and a blindness begotten of the most ridiculous prejudice could allow a man to believe that the Western mentality can win over the East, or that men who acknowledge no real superiority save that of the intellect will allow themselves to be seduced by mechanical inventions, which inspire them with a strong disgust and with not the slightest admiration. It may well happen that the Orientals will accept or rather submit to certain unavoidable effects of the present age, but they will look on them as purely temporary, and much more inconvenient than advantageous, and at heart they will only be waiting for an opportunity to get rid of all this material "progress," which can never be of any real interest to them. There are, it is true, a good many individual exceptions to be found among those who have undergone an entirely Western education; otherwise, generally speaking, defections in this sense remain far more superficial than outside observers, judging only by appearances, might be led to believe, and this is true despite the most ardent and untimely efforts expended by Western proselytism.[1] Intellectually, it is in every way in the interest of the Orientals not to change to-day any more than they have changed in the course

[1] It is almost needless to say that the author is not referring solely, or even chiefly, to religious missions, narrow and subversive though their aims usually are; he has in mind the entire movement to impose the values of modern Western "civilization" upon the East, under any of its various disguises, whether religious, "educational," "humanitarian," or frankly commercial.—*Translator.*

of preceding centuries ; all we have said here goes to prove it, and this is one of the reasons why a real and deep understanding can only arise, as is logical and normal, out of a change taking place on the Western side.

We must now return once more to the three hypotheses we have outlined, in order to lay down more explicitly the conditions that would determine the realization of any one of them ; everything clearly depends on the mental state of the Western world at the moment when it reaches the furthest term of its present civilization. If that mental state were then the same as it is now, the first hypothesis must perforce be realized, since nothing would be found to replace those things that were about to be given up, and because, on the other hand, no assimilation by other civilizations would be possible, the differences of mentality amounting to direct opposition. The assimilation which corresponds to our second hypothesis would require, as a minimum condition, the existence in the West of an intellectual kernel, even if it were only constituted by a numerically small elect, but one strong enough to provide the indispensable intermediaries for guiding back the mentality of the people towards the sources of true intellectuality, by imparting to it a direction which would however in no wise need to be consciously felt by the masses. From the moment that it is admitted that a term to the present Western civilization is a possibility, the preliminary establishment of this elect necessarily appears as alone capable of saving the West from chaos and dissolution at the appointed moment ; and besides, in order to enlist the interest of the accredited representatives of the Oriental traditions in the fate of the West, it would be essential to prove to them that although their severest strictures on Western intellectuality as a whole were not undeserved, yet there might be at least a few honourable exceptions to be found, as evidence that the degradation of that intellectuality was not entirely beyond remedy.

We have said that the realization of the second hypothesis would not be free from certain unpleasant features, at any rate temporarily, and in this case the function of the elect would be confined to supplying the pivot of an action in which the West would not take the initiative ; but that function would be quite a different story if events allowed the elect time to exercise such an activity directly and on its own responsibility, an eventuality which would then correspond to the realization of the third hypothesis. One can in fact imagine how the intellectual elect, once constituted, might act rather after the fashion of a "leaven" in the Western world, with the purpose of preparing the way for a transformation which, once effected, would allow the West to treat with the authorised representatives of the Eastern civilizations if not as one equal with another, then at least as an autonomous power. In that case the transformation would have an appearance of spontaneity, all the more so since it could then operate without shock, provided the elect had really gained sufficient influence to be in a position to direct the general outlook ; besides, the support of the Orientals would not be denied it in this task, for they will always be favourable, as is only natural, to an understanding brought about on such a basis, all the more so since they too would have an interest in it which, though quite of another order from that animating the Westerners, would be by no means negligible ; but it would perhaps be rather difficult, and moreover useless, to try to define the nature of this interest here. Howbeit, the point we wish to stress is that in order to prepare the way for the changes in question it is in no wise necessary for the mass of Westerners, or for the generality of so-called intellectuals even, to take part in the work at the outset ; even were this not quite impossible, it would in certain respects do more harm than good ; it is enough, therefore, as a start, for a few individuals to understand the need for such a change, but of course on condition that they understand it truly and thoroughly.

We have shown the essentially traditional character of all the Eastern civilizations ; the absence of an effective attachment to a tradition is the fundamental cause of the Western deviation. A return to a traditional civilization, both in principle and in respect of the whole body of institutions, is evidently the basic condition for the transformation we have been speaking about, or rather it is identical with that transformation itself, which will have been achieved from the moment that this return to tradition is fully effective ; under such conditions it would be possible to preserve whatever really valuable elements the present Western civilization may contain under any heading, always provided that before that time things had not reached a pass where there was no other alternative left but a complete renunciation. This return to tradition appears then as the most essential of the objects to which the intellectual elect ought to devote its activities; the difficulty would be to give effect to all that this implies in the various orders of activity, and also to determine the precise means which would have to be employed to that end. We can only say that the Middle Ages afford us an example of a traditional development that was truly Western; ultimately it would be a case not purely and simply of copying or reconstructing what existed then, but of drawing inspiration from it in order to bring about an adaptation to suit the actual circumstances. If there exists a "Western tradition" that is where it must be looked for, and not in the fantasies of occultists and pseudo-esotericists; this tradition was formerly conceived after the religious mode, and we do not see that the West is suited to conceive it otherwise, now less so than ever; it would be enough if a few minds became conscious of the essential unity of principle of all the traditional doctrines, as must formerly have been the case, judging by many suggestive signs and notwithstanding the absence of tangible or written proofs; the absence of such documents is quite natural under the circumstances and objections based on the "historical method" are quite irrelevant.

During the course of the present work we have already had occasion to point out the principal characteristics of the Mediæval civilization, in so far as it offers quite real though incomplete analogies with the Eastern civilizations, and we will not repeat ourselves now; all that need be said is that the West, once it had entered into possession of the tradition most suited to its own particular conditions and best able to provide for the wants of the great majority of individuals, would be freed from the necessity of adapting itself by more or less painful means to other traditional forms that were never made for this section of humanity ; it is easy to see how considerable an advantage this would be.

The work to be undertaken would have to be confined at the start purely to the intellectual order, which comprises all that is really essential, since it is concerned with the principles on which all else depends ; it is obvious that its consequences would spread later on, more or less quickly, into every other sphere, by a perfectly natural repercussion. Modifying the mental outlook of a people is the one and only means of bringing about any deep or lasting change, even in the social sphere ; to think of starting out from consequences is a pre-eminently illogical method, only worthy of the impatient and sterile agitation of present-day Westerners. Besides, the intellectual point of view is the only one that is immediately accessible, since the universal character of the principles makes them able to be assimilated by every man, whatever race he may belong to, on the sole condition of his possessing sufficient powers of understanding ; it may seem strange that it is precisely the highest element in a tradition that is most easily grasped, but the reason is really not so very far to seek, since this element alone is independent of all contingencies. This explains why the secondary traditional sciences, which are only contingent applications, are not, under their Oriental form, entirely assimilable by Westerners; as for building up or restoring equivalent sciences in a mode that suits the Western mind, that is a task the realization of which cannot but appear as a rather remote possibility ; its importance however, although great, must be looked upon only as accessory to the principal need.

If we have confined our attention to the intellectual point of view, that is because it is in all respects the first thing to be attended to ; but we will remind the reader that he must not narrow his conception of it in any way whatsoever,[1] since it comprises possibilities that are literally unlimited, as we explained when treating of metaphysical thought. We are here essentially concerned with metaphysic, because it is the only thing that can be called truly and purely intellectual ; and this leads us to explain further that for the elect about whom we have been speaking, tradition, in its innermost essence, is not to be conceived according to the specifically religious mode, which is, after all, but a case of adaptation to the conditions of the general and average mentality. Moreover this elect, even before it had effected any appreciable change of direction in the common outlook, could already, through its own influence, be in enjoyment of some quite tangible advantages in the contingent order, such for example as the removal of the difficulties and misunderstandings that are otherwise unavoidable during intercourse with Eastern peoples ; but we must repeat that these are but secondary results of that purely inward realization which alone is

[1] E.g., by confusing it partly or wholly with the rational point of view as many, in spite of warnings, may be minded to do from mere habit.—*Translator.*

indispensable in the first place ; for this realization necessarily governs all else, being itself governed by no other thing. Therefore what must come first is an understanding in the sphere of principles, the real nature of which we have tried to explain here, and this understanding implies, fundamentally, an assimilation of the essential modes of Eastern thought ; moreover so long as different lines of thought are being followed, and above all so long as one side is not conscious of these differences, no agreement is evidently possible, any more than when two different languages are being spoken and one of the parties to the conversation is totally ignorant of the language of the other.

That is why the works of the orientalists are of no service to our present purpose, if indeed they are not a hindrance for reasons we have already given ; it also explains our motives, now that we have judged it advisable to write of these things, for proposing to define and develop certain additional points in a series of metaphysical studies, either by directly expounding certain aspects of the Eastern doctrines and more especially the doctrines of India, or by adapting those same doctrines in the manner that may seem to us most likely to be understood, whenever we consider such an adaptation preferable to a direct exposition. In any case, what we shall present thus will always remain, in spirit if not in the letter, as scrupulously exact and faithful an interpretation of the traditional doctrine as we can possibly make it ; if it contains anything of our own, that must be put down chiefly to unavoidable imperfections of expression,

In trying to show the need for an understanding with the East, apart from the question of intellectual benefit that would be its direct result, we have kept to a point of view which is, in spite of everything, a contingent one, or at least which seems to be so when it is not linked up with certain other considerations that we have not found it possible to enter into and which depend especially on the deeper implications of those cyclic laws the existence of which we have merely alluded to ; but this does not prevent us from thinking that such a point of view, even as expounded, is worthy of occupying the attention of serious minds and of providing them with food for thought, on the sole condition that they are not wholly blinded by the prejudices usually found among modern Westerners.

The achieving of the purpose we have outlined consists therefore of two main phases, namely the constituting of the intellectual elect and its action on the Western environment ; as for the means for accomplishing this twofold task, nothing definite can at present be said, for to do so would in every way be premature ; we must repeat that we have been considering possibilities that are doubtless remote, but which are none the less possibilities, which is a sufficient reason for considering them. Among all these things there are some that we would perhaps have hesitated to write about before the occurrence of recent events, which seem to have brought such possibilities a step nearer, or at least to have made them easier to apprehend : without attaching too much importance to historical contingencies, which in no wise affect the truth, we must not forget that there are questions of opportunity that must often intervene in its external formulation.

Many things are still lacking from this concluding chapter before it can be considered complete, and these are the things that concern the deepest, and therefore the most truly essential characteristics of the Eastern doctrines and of the results that may be obtained from their study by those who are capable of carrying it far enough. The nature of these results can be sensed, in some measure, from the few words we have said on the subject of metaphysical realization; we have explained our reasons for not dwelling on things of this nature at greater length, especially in an introductory treatise like the present one; perhaps we shall come back to this question on another occasion, but it is above all in a case like this that one must bear in mind the Far Eastern saying that "he who knows ten should only teach nine." However that may be, such things as can be expounded without reservation, that is to say whatever ideas can be expressed on the purely theoretical side of metaphysic, are more than enough to enable those who can understand them, even if they go no further, to see through the analytical and fragmentary speculations of the West; these will then appear to them in their true colours, namely as a vain and illusory research without principle and without ultimate goal, a pursuit yielding mediocre results that are worth neither the time nor the effort of any man whose intellectual horizon is wide enough to preserve him from such a cramping of his activities.